SINGING THROUGH STRUGGLE

SINGING THROUGH STRUGGLE

Music, Worship, and Identity in Postemancipation Black Churches

Carolynne Hitter Brown

University Press of Mississippi / Jackson

The University Press of Mississippi is the scholarly publishing agency of the Mississippi Institutions of Higher Learning: Alcorn State University, Delta State University, Jackson State University, Mississippi State University, Mississippi University for Women, Mississippi Valley State University, University of Mississippi, and University of Southern Mississippi.

www.upress.state.ms.us

The University Press of Mississippi is a member of the Association of University Presses.

Any discriminatory or derogatory language or hate speech regarding race, ethnicity, religion, sex, gender, class, national origin, age, or disability that has been retained or appears in elided form is in no way an endorsement of the use of such language outside a scholarly context.

An earlier version of chapter 3 was originally published as "African American Identity and the Sunday School at Zoar ME Church" in *Annals of Eastern Pennsylvania, Journal of the Historical Society and the Commission on Archives and History of the Eastern Pennsylvania Conference of the United Methodist Church*, no. 8 (2011): 50–61.

Copyright © 2025 by University Press of Mississippi
All rights reserved
Manufactured in the United States of America

∞

Publisher: University Press of Mississippi, Jackson, USA
Authorised GPSR Safety Representative: Easy Access System Europe - Mustamäe tee 50, 10621 Tallinn, Estonia, gpsr.requests@easproject.com

Library of Congress Control Number: 2025932624
ISBN 9781496856340 (hardback)
ISBN 9781496856333 (trade paperback)
ISBN 9781496856357 (EPUB single)
ISBN 9781496856364 (EPUB institutional)
ISBN 9781496856371 (PDF single)
ISBN 9781496856388 (PDF institutional)

British Library Cataloging-in-Publication Data available

For my children,
Grant, Adelaide, and Henderson

First in loving art with all their might,
They steadily strove in the unequal fight,
Till Prejudice, convinced at last,
Retired, ashamed of the cruel past.
Now *all* who prize fair Music's ways
Pursue their journey with far brighter days.
The laurel crown, then, give the *pioneer*,
Whom ever in our memories hold we dear.

—James M. Trotter (1878)

CONTENTS

Introduction 3

Chapter One
Remembering, Remaking, Retelling:
Black Religious Music and Reconstruction 15

Chapter Two
Stabilizing Structures and Spontaneous Song: The Case of Bethel African Methodist Episcopal Church, Baltimore. 50

Chapter Three
Education, Empowerment, and Essential Music in the First Freedom Schools: The Case of Zoar Methodist Episcopal Church, Philadelphia. 78

Chapter Four
Finding Freedom and Performing Power: The Case of St. Luke's Protestant Episcopal Church, Washington, DC. 105

Afterword. 135

Acknowledgments 139
Notes 145
Bibliography 173
Index 191

SINGING THROUGH STRUGGLE

INTRODUCTION

When Booker T. Washington sat down as a guest to dinner in the rough single-room home of some formerly enslaved neighbors, he noticed only one fork on the table. Most days if these folks had meat, they wrapped it in bread and ate it on the way to work or play. Mama ate out of the pan. Sitting down to a meal was for Washington's benefit, and his visit presented an embarrassing situation.

The organ in the corner of the room is what intrigued Washington most. To him it was ironic they owned only one fork but managed to make payments on a sixty-dollar parlor organ no one could play. Experiencing firsthand this family's rugged homelife and their seemingly out of place shiny instrument was curious to Washington, who admitted that they in turn found his conventional ways and formal manner bewildering.[1]

Today it might be Versace, Bulgari, or an Escalade, but in 1875, it was an organ. The family in that cabin home took on a mantle of freedom and a mindset of democracy significantly different from Washington's ideas of assimilation and refinement. Washington questioned why they, and others like them, purchased luxury items when they were far from economic security—you can't eat an organ, after all. The recently emancipated family wondered what difference a fork made without hope, which was just what the organ and its music represented. It was an emblem of their status as free people.

Washington's anecdote gets at the essence of what previously free and newly emancipated Black people faced in border city churches during Reconstruction when southern migrants joined established congregations. They came from various class and cultural backgrounds, yet they were thrust together by the realities of racism and the need for survival. Not only that, but they had very real differences of opinion about what mattered in daily life. In church they teased out what it meant to be a community of shared sufferers discovering a clear Black consciousness while expressing full humanity in the context of a hostile society and amid dire social conditions. Religious music was perhaps the most accessible and evocative mode of exchange African Americans had for contemplating and ameliorating Black existence in this developing social space and in a period of such fluidity and rapid change.

This is the story of some of the ways African Americans sang their way through struggle during the postemancipation era. No snapshot captures the realities of this historical moment; rather, the picture is a messy, deeply complex, multilayered story of rich intricacies; varying agendas and motives; and personalities. In essence, it is a story of beautiful humanity. Because it is a story of humanity, music as a tool for exploration and discovery offers much. Music, like all art, conveys emotion, and emotion provides a powerful way of knowing. Marc Brackett, Yale's director for the Center for Emotional Intelligence, puts it clearly: "Emotions are information. . . . They determine what you care about in the moment."[2] In using music as a historical lens, we forage out some of the deepest feelings and knowledge of past people. Not only can we examine what they said and did, we can take their experiences in our hands and turn them over and around to get a sense of the things they felt but did not say.

Music is active. Unlike visual art, it exists in a single moment and changes each time it is performed. A song can be reimagined every time it is sung or played and by every group or person who renders it. Music taps life realities, present moment thoughts, nondiscursive ideas, group dynamics, individual expression, and the full range of human emotion. Music is representational art; yet as James Cone put it so clearly, there is an "inseparable bond that exists between Black life and Black art."[3] Nowhere is this more evident than in African American religious music. Prince Rivers was enslaved in the 1860s when he described the music-making process Black people used to integrate visceral feelings about faith and life saying, "My master call me up, and order me a short peck of corn and a hundred lash. My friends see it, and is sorry for me. When dey come to de praise-meeting dat night dey sing about it. Some's very good singers and know how; and dey work it in—work it in, you know, till they get it right; and dat's de way."[4]

Though it is impossible to hear the music discussed in this book, we can observe the conflicts it inspired, the ways it supported social alignment, and the values and emotions it held for subgroups and individuals in the nineteenth-century Black church. Exploring how church people infused their songs and musical choices with authentic meaning and then ritualized them in community lends valuable insight into how people connected, especially through times of anxiety and when needing to feel solidarity.[5] Scholars have established that the religious music of the enslaved and twentieth-century

"Colored Emigrants Seeking Homes in the North," *Harper's Weekly*, August 3, 1867. Schomburg Center for Research in Black Culture, Photographs and Prints Division, New York Public Library, https://digitalcollections.nypl.org/items/510d47df-79c1-a3d9-e040-e00a18064a99.

gospel music held transformative power for their creators because of their unsanitized expressions of suffering, or as Cornel West would say, its "voices—keeping track of the catastrophic."[6] This is no less true for the Black church at the time of emancipation. Here music was multifunctional; it expressed an authentic response to great sorrows and oppressive realities, it was encoded with meanings in service to Black democracy, and it welcomed prophetic vision for a people constantly devalued and bombarded by injustice.

Singing through Struggle is primarily a work of history, diving deeply into fresh archival material from the border cities of Baltimore, Philadelphia, and Washington, DC.[7] It seeks to employ insights and conceptual frameworks from other disciplines, including anthropology, ritual studies, African American studies, aesthetic theory, and musicology. The aim is to bring to life musical traditions and social interactions in African American communities during the postemancipation era using a broad range of approaches rather than strict adherence to a particular theoretical or methodological construct. In that sense, this is a work predominantly of historical reconstruction in the tradition of scholarship some have called "lived religion." From this vantage point, it is possible to grow our understanding of the meaningful

Table 1. African American Population Increase in Baltimore, Philadelphia, and Washington, DC, 1860–1890

	African American Population in 1860	African American Population in 1890	Percentage Increase from 1860 to 1890
Baltimore	27,898	67,104	140.53%
Philadelphia	22,185	39,371	77.46%
Washington, DC	14,316	75,572	427.88%

ways church music functioned in the lives of regular people after the various emancipations and into Reconstruction.

After emancipation, Baltimore, Philadelphia, and Washington, DC, were flooded with African American migrants. In only three decades, each of these cities increased by 75 percent or more, yet all have unique tales to tell. From 1860 to 1890, Philadelphia's Black population increased 78 percent, Baltimore's 141 percent, and Washington's 428 percent—Baltimore's more than doubled and Washington's quintupled.[8]

Fluctuations before and after emancipation show a traveling free Black population in addition to southern migrants moving to these cities. In the period from 1850 to 1860—the decade of the Fugitive Slave Law—the Black population of Philadelphia increased almost 107 percent. Washington, DC's increased by 39 percent, while Baltimore, a difficult city to live and work in for free Black people before emancipation, experienced a decrease of 1.73 percent in its Black population.[9]

After emancipation, Philadelphia experienced a temporary drop as African Americans like African Methodist Episcopal (AME) pastor Thomas Henry, an accused associate of abolitionist John Brown, returned to their home cities. Henry recounted, "In 1865 I received my transfer back to the Maryland District. As liberty was proclaimed throughout our country, I made no hesitation in returning to my native home."[10] Still, between 1870 and 1880 Philadelphia grew by 43 percent. Of the three cities, Washington, DC, began with the smallest African American population but by 1890 had the largest; many traveled there in response to promises of protection and assistance that never materialized. Elizabeth Keckley, an African American businesswoman, observed the massive numbers of migrants arriving in the capital "with a great hope

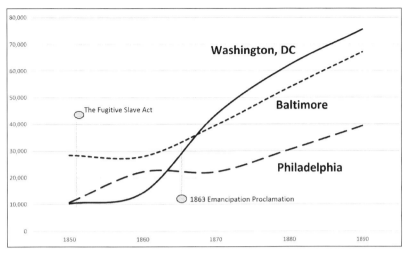

African American populations in Baltimore, Philadelphia, and Washington, DC, 1850–1990. Data compiled by author and illustrated by Michael Hanken.

in their hearts, and with all their worldly goods on their backs." Yet too often "the bright joyous dreams of freedom to the slave faded—were sadly altered, in the presence of that stern, practical mother, reality . . . the mute appeals for help too often were answered by cold neglect."[11]

Getting at the ways music expressed Black consciousness, aspirations, and cultural identity in the postemancipation Black church means digging into the historical realities and mindsets of the newly free southerners who joined established Black communities and the previously free who received them. When they arrived, migrants merged with a welcoming, yet stressed, Black population facing bold discrimination, government failure, meager employment opportunities, fears for life and freedom, disproportionate ratios of males to females, inadequate housing, high mortality rates, and countless social restrictions. External factors, but also internal ambiguities, affected the evolving identities of Black people in mid-Atlantic cities as migrants arrived. Free Black women, for example, dared not complain of their burdens, considering the afflictions their recently enslaved sisters faced. Hallie Q. Brown spoke of this push–pull reality, saying, "From the South have come many women who literally fought the stars in their courses, to step out of the darkness of bondage into the light of personal liberty. Throughout the North and other sections our thoughtful women have lived clouded lives, made dim by the tales of the indescribable sufferings endured by their sisters by blood and lineage."[12] Struggling free Black people in mid-Atlantic cities nevertheless made room in their congested communities for the newly freed.

This book explores the convergence of cultural identities Black people encountered as they gathered in solidarity at church. Church was where African Americans could gather under one roof away from the prejudices, injunctions, and the arrogance of whites. They could speak and act freely, pool their resources, negotiate ideas, and develop leadership and a public voice. Black churches offered a reprieve from the hardships and grief prevalent in Black lives; they expressed religious beliefs that gave meaning and validation to Black existence. The choice to participate in such communities, despite differences, was a form of strong Black resistance to the noise and entanglements of white society. As historian Steven Hahn has shown, coming to church was part of a grassroots endeavor to build "socially meaningful power" through religious communalism.[13]

Serving as the superstructure of Black society, the Black church enfolded multiple organizations designed to promote mutual aid, the rights of Black workers, home and foreign missions, education, and community. Shiloh Baptist Church of Washington, DC, for example, organized volunteers who "provided carfare, clothing and adult escort service to needy families in church attendance."[14] They managed schools, libraries, homes for the elderly and for orphans, burial grounds, mission churches, and rental properties. Members could belong to a choir, attend lectures, borrow books, or just get away from it all. Ora Fisher, a seamstress and domestic worker recalled, "You'd get there early for church meetings. For us children it was just a place to play and play. Nobody wanted you to do no chores, like at home. And I know it was the only place you could go and not feel somebody was going to make you do something other than sit down and sit still. That was a relief for sure."[15]

One of the most creatively useful social functions of the Black church was its ability to foster the public exchange of ideas by providing an arena for free speech and utilizing the power of religion in what Jürgen Habermas has called the "public sphere."[16] Nineteenth-century church records frequently make note of members' lengthy discussions at meetings even when the particulars of the discussion are not spelled out. The secretary for the Official Board of Bethel Baltimore AME, for example, described group exchanges with more detail than he did other business. Comments like "various arguments were addressed. The motion after much discussion was Laid upon the Table, . . . the brethren freely discussed the cause pro or con," and "The Brethren Bros. Russ and Gilbert wandered into a very Irregular harangue of doctrines" are telling in that their record is evidence of the value African Americans placed on the process of negotiation and exchange in a safe community.[17]

In the early Reconstruction era, optimism prevailed, as Black Americans believed they were awarded all the privileges, access, and rights of American citizens. Because industrialization and a changing economic landscape were widening America's middle class and creating imprecise class boundaries, the ability to move up in social standing was a reality as never before. Black people asserted a positive Black identity and tested the limits of these new options and aspects of American culture they were entitled to, much in the same way all Americans did. Why wouldn't the family Washington dined with buy a parlor organ if they could? It was possible, pretty, and a placard for freedom.

Access to musical performances was, for nineteenth-century middle-class Americans, a new commodity. Now average people could attend public venues and acquire instruments to hear and play music previously reserved for the gentry. Music of the European cultivated tradition found preeminence in family parlors and church concerts as well as theaters. Women were especially influenced by the expectations of this phenomenon. As men of growing means could support servants and free their daughters from domestic duty, the display of musical skill became a prominent occupation for young ladies, particularly as a means for distinguishing oneself and signaling the family's social standing. Beauty and grace were associated with female musicians, and their musical performance was tied to moral improvement as well as cultural and social capital; as a result, women were both useful to the middle-class pursuit and casualties of it.[18]

For African American women, this was both a road to remaking oneself and one that added weight to Black women's burden. Pre-Victorian ideals of domesticity combined with the pressure to act as angel and idol through musical performance could be oppressive. Yet as Evelyn Higginbotham explains, "By claiming respectability through their manners and morals, poor Black women boldly asserted the will and agency to define themselves outside the parameters of prevailing racist discourses."[19] Negotiated opportunities, like the commemorative service at Zoar Methodist Episcopal (ME) Church in Philadelphia featured in this book, illustrate how the Black church could make room for women's duties as well as aspirations. The service took place one week after Easter instead of on Easter as white denominational materials promoted, mostly likely to accommodate domestic workers' requirements with white families on Easter Sunday. Constancy of adaptation was the rule for these female musicians as they toggled between grueling realities and self-expression through art and achievement.

Singing through Struggle makes clear how strong a priority education was for nearly all nineteenth-century African Americans, whatever their reasons. As they increased educational capital, musical choice and preference became an elegant indicator of their success and a reflection of their taste. As Phyllis Weliver stresses in her work on women musicians, "Being able to decipher meaning in a work of art, occurs by a lengthy process of accumulation and education—educational institutions impart a sense of value and appreciation."[20] For nineteenth-century African Americans the educational process she describes was heavily burdened with the reality of internalized racism and an acceptance of the dominant culture's preferences in art; however, Pierre Bourdieu's argument for "the choice of the necessary" may lend more dimension to the story. He explains, "The awakening of political consciousness is often bound up with a whole process of rehabilitating and rebuilding self-esteem, which, because it involves a reaffirmation of cultural dignity that is experienced as (and indeed always is) liberatory, implies a submission to the dominant values and to some of the principles on which the dominant class bases its domination."[21] African Americans treasured their access to privileged forms once denied. In relying on their intuition and imaginative skills to listen for abstract ideas and information in historical music, they accessed their humanity and resisted racist beliefs about their capabilities. Josephine Henderson Heard, an educated free Black woman who was born to enslaved parents, expressed this feeling in her poem "Music":

> O, wondrous depth to which my soul is stirr'd,
> By some low tone, some softly breathed word—
> Some thrill or cadence sweet which fills my heart,
> My inmost powers wake, and thrill and start.
> My bosom seems too narrow a confine,
> For such a power, dear music as thine.
>
> E'en when my heart is wrapt in sorrow's night,
> Mine eyes of clay are clos'd, but heavenly light
> Doth shine into the desert of my soul,
> And billows of sweet music o'er me roll.[22]

In this way, music both affirmed cultural dignity and played an important role in what has been called "respectability politics."[23] As Black Americans built narratives of respectability and cultural refinement through musical accomplishment and taste, they banked equity in a strategy to demand social, cultural, and political change based on equality.

Additionally, democracy entitled African Americans to whatever cultural forms appealed to them. Music critic Alex Ross gives the bottom line when he says, "They were taking possession of the European inheritance and pulling it into their own sphere. More elementally, they loved the music, and had no need to justify their taste."[24] The importance of music as a marker of class, its association with moral reform, its role in building respectability narratives and supporting cultural dignity, and freedom of preference were important factors at play in the nineteenth-century Black church.

This study regularly refers to, and at times takes for granted, the uplift ideologies influencing some of the Black church leaders featured in these case studies. Many, if not most, African American ministers assumed responsibility for the betterment and "uplift" of Black people, linking moral, cultural, and educational improvement to "respectability" and the end of racism. A typical assertion by the Black Methodist Episcopal Church (MEC) Delaware Annual Conference in 1882 affirms this: "Notwithstanding the various institutions for the spread of civilization, we recognize the church of our Lord Jesus Christ as the only efficient and sufficient instrumentality and organization for the ultimate reformation and salvation of the world."[25] Much scholarship on the Black church, Black ministers and teachers in particular, has emphasized the internalized racism church leaders manifested as they talked about the "civilization" or the "elevation" of the masses of struggling African Americans they considered ignorant spiritually and intellectually. I simply wish to point out there may be more to it than that.

During Reconstruction, African Americans wrestled with the race-conscious desire to establish cultural equality, *and* what the blurring of American class identities due to accessibility meant for them, *and* how cultural and economic freedom would play out in their lives. This is not said to dismiss the powerful construct uplift ideology provides for understanding Black religious activity and cultural expression in the nineteenth century. Rather, this ternary view peels back another layer of the deeply complex lives African Americans lived during Reconstruction. The dialectical argument suggesting elite or middle-class Black people used musical taste and accomplishment to vindicate themselves culturally to the point of ignoring the folk and Africanized tastes of the formerly enslaved is overly simplistic.[26] It does not allow for the individual choices various congregations and people made as they sought to redefine who they were in the context of American society or the belief that church life set them up to access all the benefits of an American democracy. It does not account for the sounds that reverberated from soul to soul, singing Black connectivity into place.

Class boundaries were not cut-and-dried; there was ambiguity between the internalized racism of uplift ideology and straightforward self-identification with an upwardly mobile and burgeoning American middle class. At the time of emancipation, African Americans imagined themselves free to enjoy the cultural and class markers most Americans were rowing toward. Musical choice, as a primary indicator of cultural refinement, made them feel they were climbing the social ladder and accessing previously inaccessible luxuries.

Like hitting a moving target, pinpointing Black authenticity is hard to do.[27] Various ideas and opinions float about staking claims in what "Blackness" is. *Singing through Struggle* endeavors to bring forth as many stories of Black people, Black churches, Black creativity, Black struggle, and Black success as possible to enrich the conversation and allow historical reality to inform current thought. Unearthing ways Black people claimed certain cultural forms as their own, over and against white definitions or uses, allows a bolder, broader picture of African American agency in determining identity and an empowered personhood. For instance, hymnal use in Black churches was often supportive of authentic Black expression. This book highlights stories like that of "Silas," as told by "Uncle John," who explained how a hymn learned in white church became one of Black identification embedded with meanings no white person can grasp. Silas, a slave, ran away and

> was caught by the dogs one morning . . . and Silas give one dog a blow and almost killed him. The hound was one of the best ones his marster had. Madam, Silas's marster got off of his horse right there where they caught him and beat Silas with his pistol all over for nothing because he would not let the dog bite him. He made the dogs bite Silas all over his body. The dogs bit him under the throat. When he got Silas home he put him in irons, but Silas could not walk. Silas was almost dead when his marster put the irons on him.

Incredibly, Silas "crawled way off from his plantation and died under a shadetree." Uncle John recalled his friendship with Silas and the faith they shared, saying, "We used to go to church on Sundays together. O, how he used to love that hymn, 'How firm a foundation!' He knowed every word of it by heart."[28] Uncle John and Silas "used to hear the white people sing":

> How firm a foundation, ye saints of the Lord,
> Is laid for your faith in his excellent word!
> What more can he say, than to you he hath said,
> To you, who for refuge to Jesus have fled?
>
> Fear not, I am with thee, O be not dismayed,
> For I am thy God, I will still give thee aid;

> I'll strengthen thee, help thee, and cause thee to stand,
> Upheld by my gracious, omnipotent hand.
>
> When through the deep waters I call thee to go,
> The rivers of sorrow shall not overflow;
> For I will be with thee thy trials to bless,
> And sanctify to thee thy deepest distress.

African Americans sang new meaning into hymns—hymns that reinforced a liberating mindset and morphed again as they were imported with new significance during different freedom struggles after emancipation. Numerous stories recount how a Black preacher or singer would "hol' his han' out an' mek lak he was readin' when no book was available."[29] Possessing and holding a hymnal was a privilege to be claimed whether you could read or not; on this African Americans in border city churches agreed.

At the same time, many African Americans continued treasured forms of religious worship and song creation, as the case study on Bethel AME in Baltimore will show; the Holiness tradition, women's home groups, bush meetings, mission churches, and other gatherings outside of Sunday service were sites of Black resistance to both Black and white confinements. These fought-for opportunities nurtured authentic musical and religious expression even as freedom and cultural blending stimulated new questions of identity for the Black church. Historical record shows the expanding palette of choices nineteenth-century Black church members chose from when it came to musical expression in worship.

Drawing from fresh archival work and a deep case study approach, *Singing through Struggle* strives to demonstrate that no one monolith suited African American congregations in the last half of the nineteenth century. In some cases, such as Bethel AME, it is obvious the pastors of the church endeavored to lead their congregations in the values of the dominant culture, prioritizing cultural and religious expression that demonstrated refinement and the cultural preferences of mainstream society; however, as is highlighted in the St. Luke's Protestant Episcopal (PE) case study, it was the people, against the will of the pastor, who used the church as an arena for social standing and musical performance. In fact, it was the pastor who advocated for the marginalized and lower classes and fought against "showy" music that set up the Black church as a house for class stratification. The story of Zoar ME characterizes yet a third scenario, where musical taste and uplift ideologies were less sharp and congregational homogeneity and happiness were obtained through worship and mutually agreed upon songs of their tradition. Echoing Lawrence Levine's conviction that all Americans shared a public culture "less fragmented into relatively rigid adjectival boxes than their descendants were to experience a century later,"[30] I hope to help broaden the conversation around African American expressive culture and suggest ways nineteenth-century Black churches handled polarities and held space for Black resistance of varying forms.

Implicit to this study are several tensions—tensions between mainstream and African culture, urban versus rural backgrounds, moral and cultural capital, assertions of uplift ideology and hostility toward it, the power of leaders versus that of the laity, and yearnings for old ways versus hunger for new ones. Rather than drawing hard and fast conclusions about African American thought after emancipation, this book seeks to emphasize the active, dialectic, organic, and imaginative character of Black thinking that was cultivated in a period of immense instability and uncertainty. This work emphasizes how blurred identities and imprecise racial objectives stimulated African Americans to discuss, confer, bargain, collaborate, and fight. It seeks to explore the ways women, "middle management" leaders, and ministers rejected domineering attitudes, financial control, and decisions they believed would repress their authentic expression and purpose. It shows Black democracy in the making.

In *Singing through Struggle,* I hope to demonstrate the importance public worship holds in creating and supporting a collective identity and, conversely, how divisive it can be if its attached meanings are not fully understood or valued. Through processes of ritualization and conferred symbolic meaning, songs and musical expression can be understood to play essential roles in supporting unity, expressing feelings, clarifying values, channeling resistance, and more. As future leaders and scholars consider the Black church's role in what some call the Third Reconstruction,[31] I hope these real stories of creative resistance during the first Reconstruction will offer hope and insight.

Chapter One

REMEMBERING, REMAKING, RETELLING
Black Religious Music and Reconstruction

Black congregations always had their own unique sound, one that bloomed from Black bodies, effervescent and original. Though service structure or songs were sometimes borrowed from white church traditions, voices were not. Historical record conveys arguments over institutionalization, but not intonation. Sociologist Perry Hall asserts that northern Black churches were "culturally divorced from the rural folk sensibilities of the vast majority of Black people of that time" and "employed a worship style more like the white denominations from which they emerged than like the heavily Africanized worship style of the enslaved brothers and sisters on whose behalf they campaigned."[1] Harriet Beecher Stowe once complained African American religious music was "closely imitated from the white people, which is solemn, dull and nasal," but how many Black churches did she visit?[2] Black congregations resisted white spectatorship and at times modified performance in the presence of white visitors. Claims like Hall's and Stowe's do not resonate with the real worship conflicts and reports nineteenth-century pastors and lay leaders passed on or the racist, yet telling reports of most white journalists and observers. Like so many nineteenth-century Black musicians who sang in front of whites, the well-known and tremendously popular Jubilee Singers were at first criticized when they performed. On January 3, 1872, the New York *Musical Gazette* blasted: "Their performance is a burlesque on music, and almost on religion . . . as for calling their effort a concert, it is ridiculously absurd. We regret to see that . . . the appreciation of music is at such a low ebb that [New Yorkers] can enjoy the 'singing' of these well-meaning but unmusical people."[3] In both delivery and character, the Jubilee Singers were unique. The quality of their sound reflected what African American musicologist Olly Wilson referred to as a "heterogeneous sound ideal" in which "the desirable musical sound texture is one that contains a combination of diverse timbres [sounds]" and displays a "fundamental bias for contrast of color."[4] Nineteenth-century Black music manifested an African and African American aesthetic that increasingly captivated mainstream hearers craving authentic musical experiences as the century pressed on. Black church choirs, as well as instrumental groups like Professor Johnson's Monumental Band in Baltimore,[5] were criticized less and pursued more and more. The Black churches of Washington, DC, were especially known for their unique choral sound, and white travelers visited these churches when they were in town to hear their music. Charles E. Jackson, a member of Asbury ME Church, recorded, "Soon after the close of the Civil War excursion parties from all parts of the country coming to [Washington, DC] would inquire for the Asbury Church for the purpose of hearing the choir sing. The writer has known gentlemen to give five and ten dollars to have the choir repeat a selection."[6] However urban Black music sounded in the nineteenth century, it didn't sound white.

SELF-DEFINING SOUND

African American churches in border cities experienced a flurry of musical activity during the second half of the nineteenth century, and this activity was directly connected to their goals of religious and democratic freedom. They claimed musical preferences, applauded achievement, upheld originality and expression, talked to God, and enjoyed worship and music in community while establishing a new narrative. As neuroscience shows, music can "enhance the production of self-defining memories, that is, memories that contribute to self-discovery, self-understanding, and identity."[7] Intuitively Black Americans utilized music in this evolutionary era to literally work out who they were as free people and nurture a positive self-perception. Music of the past and present was crucial, as African Americans insisted on new memories and a counternarrative to white supremacy. Singing at church services, commemorative services, and other Black community events was a way to practice leadership and self-expression in public life, as performers envisioned their role in the republic.[8] The creation of religious music in sacred community was an ongoing process of recording, reminding, reflecting, renouncing, and reworking what Black life was and what it wasn't.

When the African ME Zion Church in New York City celebrated its centennial, it featured an organ prelude, "Praise God, from whom all blessings flow," sung by the Grand Chorus and a hymn by Reverend E. George Biddle titled "Hail the Church That Varick Started."[9] James Varick is credited with founding the African Methodist Episcopal Zion (AMEZ) Church when he and others walked out of John Street Methodist Church in New York City and began worshipping separately from whites. Biddle's hymn was sung to the tune "Hold the Fort," which alone would have aroused significant feeling in the singers. "Hold the Fort" was composed by Philip Bliss, who like many hymnists of his day, captured the public's elevated emotions surrounding the Civil War and recast them as a heavenly battle between the "great Commander" and "Satan leading on." Bliss based his lyrics on a real account of Union soldiers holding the fort at Altoona Pass until Sherman arrived, then forcing the Confederates to retreat. The chorus zealously proclaimed:

> "Hold the fort, I am coming!"
> Jesus signals still,
> Wave the answer back to Heaven
> "By Thy grace, we will!"[10]

Bliss's hymn, written in 1870, was later rewritten as a political statement and circulated by the Knights of Labor, a Philadelphia labor group that welcomed Black people to its membership. It declared:

> We meet today in Freedom's cause
> And raise our voices high.
> We'll join our hands in union strong
> to battle or to die.
>
> Hold the fort, for we are coming
> Union men be strong!
> Side by side we battle onward,
> Victory will come.[11]

Biddle's choice of the familiar and rousing tune "Hold the Fort" for his hymn about Varick is striking. The tune, attached to ideas like victory, freedom, unity, economic equality, and divine favor, conjured memories as it stimulated new ones:

> Hail the church that Varick started
> An hundred years ago:
> "Mother Zion" filled with gladness
> And centennial glow.
>
> CHORUS.
> Shout, O shout in "Mother Zion,"
> Here your offerings bring;
> Wave, O wave our Zion banner,
> Make the welkin ring.
>
> Varick's faith pierced gloom and darkness
> An hundred years ago;
> Toiling on 'mid joy and sadness,
> Gospel seed to sow.[12]

When Biddle relied on what Courtney Brown calls "associational political music" to evoke fierce determination and civil rights fervor, he ensured that the marriage of sacred and political feeling was core to Zion's identity.[13]

While America sought to discount Black existence, the Black church called up the sacred tradition of storytelling and relied on music to safeguard the stories they wanted told. As Samuel A. Floyd Jr. put it, "Black-music making [is] the translation of the memory into sound and the sound into memory."[14] Nineteenth-century African American liturgy, which used music as the foremost means for safeguarding African American experience for future generations, can be recovered through Black newspapers, printed commemorative and celebration services, Black hymnals with their expressive commentary on purpose, as well as exhortations for use, memoirs, journals, and church records. In border city Black churches, music was history—music was story.

Music is often understood as "a language of the heart," able to express human feeling, but this catchphrase falls short of Black music's ability to facilitate imaginative thinking and actively process collective experience. Susanne Langer contends that music conveys the singer's "imagination of feelings rather than his own emotional state, and expresses what *he knows about* the so-called 'inner life'; and this may exceed his personal case, because music is a symbolic form to him through which he may learn as well as utter ideas of human sensibility."[15] After emancipation African Americans used song to understand their lives as free people, to exchange information about experience, and to work through ideas about God and existence. The very structure of music lends it the ability to communicate complexities. Langer explains:

> The tonal structures we call "music" bear a close logical similarity to the forms of human feeling—forms of growth and of attenuation, flowing and stowing, conflict and resolution, speed, arrest, terrific excitement, calm or subtle activation and dreamy lapses—not joy or sorrow perhaps, but the poignancy of either and both—the greatness and brevity and eternal passing of everything vitally felt. Music is a tonal analogue of emotive life.[16]

Congregational singing in the nineteenth-century Black church possessed all these musical possibilities as well as what Samuel Floyd has called "ring tropes," a continuation of Africanized singing techniques like the conversational call-and-response. This trait in particular enabled worshippers to speak both to God and to each other about their condition.[17] Floyd points out that even in hymn singing "power relations were significantly reversed, turning white texts into Black" through subtle variations in timbre, harmonic contrast, and layered rhythmic patterns. Black congregations affirmed one another's humanity and value through songs like "Come Sinners to the Gospel Feast" by Charles Wesley, which despite its sexist language, was egalitarian and especially reassuring to congregations comprising all classes of people. The 1872 AME hymnal opens with:

> Come, sinners, to the gospel feast,
> Let every soul be Jesus' guest;
> Ye need not one be left behind,
> For God hath bidden all mankind.[18]

In singing, African American churchgoers grappled with circumstances, proclaimed their God-given worth, and dreamed about their lives as fully free citizens.

Consistent with an African heritage, urban Black people used religious music to define themselves as a unified community. They sang at every church gathering: trustees' meetings, stewards' meetings, society meetings, "entertainments," Sunday school, baptisms, class meetings, and Sunday morning and evening services. For such occasions they sang hymns like

> Help us to help each other, Lord,
> Each other's cross to bear;

> Let each his friendly aid afford,
> And feel his brother's care.
>
> Help us to build each other up;
> Our little stock improve;
> Increase our faith, confirm our hope
> And perfect us in love.
>
> Up into thee, our living Head,
> Let us in all things grow;
> Till thou hast made us free indeed,
> And spotless here below.[19]

The emotional, cathartic, creative process of singing meaningful words about belief and unity intensified the bond between African Americans of various backgrounds and experience. They viewed their ancestors, the living dead, as part of their religious communities too, and remembering them in song was part of how they transmuted experience and memory into a new Black identity. When together as a body, they sang hymns that lyricized an eschatology of connectedness between the dead in Christ and those still on earth. For example:

> The Lord of Sabbath let us praise,
> In concert with the blest,
> Who, joyful in harmonious lays,
> Employ an endless rest.
>
> Thus, Lord, while we remember thee
> We bless'd and pious grow
> By hymns of praise we learn to be
> Triumphant here below.[20]

When African Americans drew on their Protestant evangelical heritage for musical resources, they invested songs of their tradition with meaning relevant to their own spiritual views and experiences. This manner of modifying Christian belief and language to reflect a distinctly African American understanding of legacy and the afterlife is even clearer in the lines of a "Semi-Centennial Hymn," written by African American H. C. Morgan, a deacon of the African Union Society in Newport, Rhode Island, in 1871:

Thy Word for two score years and ten
Has been our sure support,
And for Thy grace we still contend,
All else we count as nought.
The fathers, who in days of yore
Laid here the corner stone,
Have passed away;—their work is o'er:
We're left! but not alone.

The Spirit which in them was found,
In us shall still remain;
Satan may rage—we'll stand our ground
Till the last foe is slain.
They fifty years ago did call
On Thee; Thou said 'twas well:
They fell, dear Lord—so may we fall
Ere the Centennial.

O, praise the Lord for all the past!
Trust Him for all to come,
Our fathers we shall meet at last,
In our Eternal Home;
And when before, the throne we stand,
There waiting for our crown,
When Christ extends to us His hand,
Our praise shall still resound.[21]

Urban Black people placed a high value on connection to others who understood their burdens and realities, past, present, and future. Unity and community were reinforced through song.

To establish and support this unity, Black Americans used church music as discourse. Congregationally they sang to transmit values and support to one another, addressing concerns about education, poverty, family cohesion, economic oppression, and racial unity. Music was art, occupying lyrics like "Bread of heaven, feed me until I want no more," "Lord! What a wretched land is this—that yields us no supply," and "I look for help from thee alone, To thee for succor fly; My son is sick—my darling son—And at the point to die," as the community expressed authentic needs and tragedies of Black struggle.[22] Aside from traditional African American songs, urban Black worshippers increasingly turned to hymnals to supply community language for the exchange of ideas and feelings. They used hymns written by whites, but they also wrote many of their own. Nora Fields Taylor, "a woman of great force and unspotted reputation" was "the author of several songs and small pamphlets," as were numerous other Black men and women who used their lyrical and musical talents to write music, especially for situations relevant to Black experience.[23] Reconstruction era optimism rang out in W. H. Young's hymn:

> Songs of Freedom, join the chorus!
> Sing together with accord;
> Brighter days are now before us—
> Let us sing and praise the Lord;
> Praise the Lord who reigns in heaven,
> On the earth and on the sea;
> Every shackle He has riven,
> He has let the oppressed go free.[24]

Hymns like those of AME pastors Benjamin Tanner and Daniel Payne freely acknowledged hardship and sorrow. Tanner's hymn "Evening" entreated, "As we retrospect the day. . . . In pity, Lord, we pray look down, Our burden'd souls relieve." Payne called on God for source energy saying:

> Give to the blind their sight,
> Bind up the broken heart,
> The erring spirit guide aright,
> And strength to all impart.[25]

The 1892 AMEZ hymnal incorporated several hymns written by African Americans, including Reverend John E. Price's "When the Roll Is Called Again":

> Brother, sister, grow not weary,
> Though you have much toil and pain,
> You shall have a crown of glory
> When the roll is called again.
>
> *When the roll is called again—*
> *When the roll is called again—*
> *Will you meet me—will you meet me*
> *When the roll is called again?*[26]

Songs and hymns like these were the mainstay of urban Black worship life, and in singing them, members of urban Black communities shared hardships and spoke prophetically into Black being.

Talking to God was at the heart of nineteenth-century Black worship. These liturgical conversations flowed in a stream of tradition that expressed thought and feeling as it was experienced. Frederick Douglass recalled that the enslaved "would make the dense old woods, for miles around, reverberate with their wild songs, revealing at once the highest joy and deepest sadness. They would compose and sing as they went along, consulting neither time nor tune. The thought came up, came out—if not in the word, in the sound;—and as frequently in the one as in the other."[27] Filling the pews of border city churches, migrants invigorated the extempore songs and hymns that enfolded two-way conversations with God. Rather than voicing static belief, Black church people in the postemancipation era sang to actively reinterpret Christian faith for their times; their songs became living documents, part of an ongoing realignment with the constantly changing truths of their humanity, safety, family life, work, and freedom. They sang with urgency:

> Increase in us the kindled fire,
> In us the work of faith fulfil.
> By faith we know thee strong to save:
> (Save us, a present Saviour thou!)
> Whatever we hope, by faith we have;
> Future and past subsisting now.[28]

In their humming, swaying, sighing, and singing, they took on a posture of expectation, waiting for a response. Sound is so essential to evoking the spiritual realm in Black religion, and so necessary for a personal and collective connection to the divine, the study of its religious effect has been named "theomusicology."[29] With marked importance, the recording secretary of the Delaware Conference noted during Sabbath Service, "The great Head of the Church favored the Conference and crowded Congregation in attendance with the presence and power of his holy Spirit in an unusual manner on Sabbath day, July 29th, 1866."[30] Amiri Baraka, formerly LeRoi Jones, articulated this vital connection when he said most Black people assume "the Spirit will not descend without song."[31] Singing at church manifested a deeply conversational connection between the congregation and the divine.

Music was a fixed aspect during rites of passage like baptism, marriage, and funeral ceremonies as Black people announced their full civil rights and boldly professed their humanity. Mt. Olivet Baptist African in

New York celebrated a large baptism service, where "Fifty women were immersed in just twenty-five minutes. It took twenty-six minutes to baptize the twenty-six men." *The New York Sun* reported on the celebration songs and style saying:

> The volume of sound with which the great congregation rolled out the full strains of the opening hymn, "Blow, ye, the trumpet blow," was enough to have raised a less emotional congregation to a high state of religious exaltation. It was some time after the "Amen" that closed the song before the undertone of joyful exultation quite subsided. . . . After the closing hymn, "Rock of Ages," had been sung in a mighty chorus that made the great church seem to sway with the harmony, the Rev. Dr. Walker, with his wet garments still upon him, dismissed the congregation with a prayer.

Anticipation for the event spread through the Black community and was "almost enviously commented upon in the Methodist circles." Forty-five minutes before the service began, church doors were locked, every seat was filled, and the ushers had to "dispose properly of the streams of people that came pouring down to the big gray church from the east and west under the shadow of the elevated railroad tracks."[32]

Marriage was celebrated but to varying degrees. African American newspapers ran marriage announcements, occasionally mentioning a church wedding like that of Lula Hooper to Nathaniel Drewry, which "took place at Union Baptist Church [Baltimore] Wednesday evening, April 26th, 1893, at 7:30 o'clock."[33] More often they were married at home. A "Brilliant Wedding" received special attention from the *Afro-American*, which gave details of "the marriage of Miss Lillie E. Moore to Mr. Ernest Taylor." According to the paper:

> It was the most brilliant wedding that has occurred in the Monumental City for a long time. The parlors were tastefully decorated with flowers and plants. While Miss Washington of Newport, R.I., played the wedding march, the bride preceded by six ushers entered the parlor on the arm of her step-father, Mr. Henry Kane, meeting Mr. Taylor under a bell of roses where Rev. Dr. Weaver tied the matrimonial knot. The bride wore a white cotelle silk, trimmed with point a La Plaque lace, cut V neck, and carrying a bouquet of roses. Miss Emma Jones, the bridesmaid, was charmingly attired in fawn cotelle silk. . . . The presents were numerous and elaborate.[34]

This family's affluence later in the century allowed them either to own or rent an instrument, but traditionally a cappella singing made a home marriage ceremony sacred without instruments. Hymns were used for such ceremonies; by 1877 the AME hymnal had a section specifically dedicated to weddings.[35] Urban Black weddings were noticeably less marked than funerals, a fact that points to the prevalence of death in urban Black communities as well as the complexity of Black marriage following emancipation.[36]

Border city Black church records provide details about funerals and frequently include eulogies about the deceased. A dramatic funeral took place at Asbury ME Church when the choir leader died while singing over the body. The record states, "Too much cannot be said of Prof. Bell for he was truly a great man. He led the choir for twenty-five consecutive years. . . . He fell at his post while singing the hymn, "Asleep in Jesus, O How Sweet," over the remains of the Rev. Henry Pickney. The following Sunday his remains laid before the altar."[37] Professor Bell had to have sung with great gusto to lead to such a death; these vivid sights and sounds surely awakened the religious imaginations of those present. African Americans had a variety of hymns for use at funeral and memorial services. In 1886, a typical entry in the Delaware Conference minutes stated, "The order of the day, the Memorial Services[,] was taken up at 11 a.m. The hymn 'Why do we mourn for dying friends' was sung, after which memoirs and remarks were made of the deceased."[38] The organ, too, became more and more a part of the funeral liturgy. In October 1894, Charles Dungee, the longtime organist at Bethel AME Church in Baltimore, requested a raise. The trustees' recorded:

> Balto, Oct. 1st, 1894
>
> New business. A communication from Chas. Dungee asking that his sal[a]ry be raised to $10 per month and he would [play at] all funerals on Sunday and during the week. Motion by Bro. Nid[ealson] that we pay $10 per month with the understanding that he play [on] all funerals. Carried. Bills ordered paid: Chas Dungee $10.00.[39]

The organist's services were desired at all church funerals, which were numerous, sometimes occurring several times per week. Nineteenth-century urban Black communities gave death meaning and celebrated eternal liberation at funerals made more sacred and grand with organ music, solos, and congregational singing.

When talking about the ways nineteenth-century Black musical creativity helped build a counternarrative, especially religious music representative of moral ideals, soul expression, and dignity, it is crucial to remember how embedded Black minstrel music was in mainstream culture at the time. Minstrel shows played nearly every night of the week and allowed white Americans to affirm feelings of white supremacy as they laughed their way through musical misrepresentations of African Americans as inferiors. James Watkins, a Black American formerly enslaved in Maryland, spoke of the degradation this music perpetrated when he said:

> Through the ignorance and the prejudice of a certain portion of this community, we coloured people have been calumniated, and ideas have been disseminated in relation to us, which have no foundation in fact, but have only originated in the malice of people who have made it their business to misrepresent us.... We have public exhibitions in pot-houses and low singing rooms of men who Black their faces, and perform such outlandish antics as were never seen amongst the negroes, and who profess to imitate, but who in reality only caricature men of my race.[40]

Although many African Americans eventually broke into the genre and found opportunity in the industry writing and performing music for a living, it also drew out a deep and disheartening need among many African Americans to perform and create music that countered white supremacy and cultural forms that disparaged Black people. Vaughn A. Booker demonstrates the "transfer of Black middle-class social authority from educated Black Protestant ministers to the world of Black entertainment became possible with the emergence of jazz," but in the nineteenth century, the Black church was the primary sphere where Black people (ministers and otherwise) made music to purposely combat the message of minstrelsy and define themselves as dignified, immensely capable, and vastly above ignorance and the mundane.[41] *The Christian Recorder* highlighted the music of a "well-connected school ... in connection with St. John's Chapel" in Norfolk in 1869 reporting, "The school is penned by singing one of those sacred lyrics that makes the Sabbath school minstrelsy of our country surpass that of the world," noting the superintendent himself accompanied the singers with a melodeon.[42] The marked contrast the *Recorder* made between Sabbath school minstrelsy and secular minstrelsy shows the compelling need many African Americans felt to distance their abilities and identity from the false caricatures of Black people then infiltrating American culture. Getting at the tensions intrinsic to Black performance, Michael Eric Dyson explains, they "felt the need to fend off the white gaze and to recreate a sense of home while forging new expressions in the belly of a racist beast."[43] Music making was key to meaning making; upholding Black humanity and authentic Black experience was at the heart of nineteenth-century Black worship.

SANCTIFYING SOUND

Ella Sheppard, one of the first Jubilee Singers, talked about the group's reluctance to publicly perform the religious songs of their enslaved ancestors on the public stage, saying, "They were sacred to our parents, who used them in their religious worship and shouted over them. . . . It was only after many months that gradually our hearts were opened to the influence of these friends and we began to appreciate the wonderful beauty and power of our songs."[44] In continuity with the secluded worship traditions of the enslaved, nineteenth-century Black churchgoers valued privacy and the ability to sing and worship in their own spaces. In church, African Americans could make music and perform it in their own way; this freedom of expression helped form a barrier against the intrusions of a dehumanizing world to create a sense of emotional privacy while building self-worth and confidence in their freedom expectations. As Nicole Myers Turner puts it, "They sought freedom to worship—soul freedom down to the very core of their being, where nothing could hinder them. They pursued it through gaining control of their worship."[45] Church events like weddings and funerals, commemorative celebrations, musical entertainments, and regular worship services allowed African Americans to exercise psychic resilience as they claimed emotional and expressive liberty over and against a racialized society's bombardment. Marie Stone, a domestic worker in Washington, DC, recalled a memory of her mother in an oral interview saying:

> Pine Grove Baptist Church was the only place I ever saw my mother laugh or seem happy. Even when something was funny to all us children, my aunts, grandmom, daddy—everybody—Mama would just look, say "humph" and turn her head. But down at church she'd be laughing out loud. Or smiling. Things that let you know she could be up some of the time. But it was only at church. Just there.[46]

In church and through song, Black people unpacked the realities of past and present, dealt with trauma authentically, communed with neighbors and ancestors, and met the Lord on Black terms.

Enslaved people worshipped in a "plain brush church house" or deep in the woods, where the sounds of their songs mingled with dirt floors, plain walls or lofty trees, and an upside-down kettle or blankets soaked with water to create a mystical experience. Handshaking and marching, they transformed their surroundings to demarcate space and time that was sacred. It was song that brought this combination of setting, movement, and religious understanding together to make meetings worshipful. Aestheticist Frank Birch Brown explains how factors work collectively to sanctify space, saying, "The aesthetic effect derives from more than meets the eye." What Brown calls "the aesthetic milieu," in this case, worship space, is "constituted not just by *what* is seen but by *how* it is seen—that is, by what it is seen *as*—which depends partly on its whole milieu, including the contexts of perception and various things that we know or think we know."[47] Priest Calbraith Perry described his visit to St. Philip's in Baltimore, sometime around 1873, saying the congregation "worshiped in a small hall over a feed-store on Howard street" and journaled about his experience with them, saying:

> The room gave evidence of care and an attempt at reverence, yet it was cheerless in the extreme. On one side was a large tank, used as a font by a former pastor. . . . The small altar had once been a shopkeeper's counter. An altar frontal spoke of loving hands but poverty of resources. On this . . . diminutive altar were two tiny candlesticks. They were not even as large as those carried by a prominent New York rector in his pocket to his church. . . . Between these candlesticks was a [donated] Black walnut cross as large as the altar.

According to Perry, the room's "peculiarities were forgotten, when the service began in the enjoyment of the hearty responses, the sweet music, the reverence, the unostentatious yet ardent earnestness of the people," and "the enjoyment was not seriously interrupted even by the rats which ran about the floor during the service."[48] Music was key to turning St. Phillip's bare space into a sacred sanctuary, all their own.

Buying and building church structures was a priority for Black people who saw the acquisition of real estate as a democratic right, especially in urban areas where the African American population was rapidly expanding. When new Black churches were inaugurated, music solemnized the ceremony. In 1860, *The Weekly Anglo-African* gave "a brief sketch of the religious ceremonies at the opening of the First Colored American Congregational Church, [New York] . . . in a fine neighborhood . . . very convenient for our colored population . . . especially for the young people living at service." The paper described "the exercises," which "were introduced by Rev. Jas. M. Williams, of Brooklyn, by reading the 8th chapter of 1st Kings and the 84th Psalm.

Then followed singing by the choir, a prayer . . . and more singing."⁴⁹ The 1876 AME hymnal had, for the first time, a section titled "Dedication of Churches & Laying of Corner-stones," demonstrating both the commonplaceness of church building by that time and the demand for hymnody appropriate to sanctify such celebrations.⁵⁰

When possible, nineteenth-century African Americans enhanced the visual stimuli associated with music making to bolster the aesthetic atmosphere of their religious settings. The ring shout's circular shape demonstrates the penchant enslaved people had for combining eye-appealing form to the performance of religious music. Free Black people continued this tradition, especially through the developing role of the church choir. As choirs grew in popularity, African Americans used their presence and placement to enhance the impact of their worship music. The majority of Black choirs probably did not wear robes until at least the end of the nineteenth century due to a lack of means, but they sat in front of the congregation and many times had matching hymnals and sometimes music folders.⁵¹ When AME pastor Reverend T. G. Steward arrived at his new post in Wilmington, Delaware, in 1872, he said the building was "not such as to awaken within me pleasant feelings." It was

> without architectural beauty, of one story, ceiling low, windows small, wretchedly lighted by day and worse at night by its unsightly and inadequate gas fixtures. The interior was in dark colors, and was dirty withal. On the floor were spittoons, saw-dust filled, and around the walls were the head marks of the more than seven sleepers. It had a small loft in front occupied by a choir, led by one Peter Blake, a barber of not the highest reputation, a good musician, however, and faithful in his services.⁵²

Steward's description of the choir's position, in contrast to that of the building, indicates the importance he assigned it as part of the aesthetic milieu. Because the choir was one of the primary focal points of Black church worship, its appearance was a top financial priority. When Shiloh Baptist Church in Newport, Rhode Island, received a fifty-dollar donation, they used it to pay off their organ and furnish the choir with "cane-seat chairs."⁵³ Black Americans signified the value of music in worship by making sure musicians and music-related accessories were pleasing to the eye as well as the ear. As they sanctified worship spaces, setting them apart from all other realms of life and existence as safe, secluded, supportive community institutions, music marked every room, service, and feeling.

SIGNATURE SOUNDS

Congregational Singing

In their early days, Black church music was sung without instrumental accompaniment. Some Black churches practiced a form of "lining out" hymns or psalms, in keeping with the worship traditions from which they emerged. A minister or deacon would sing out one or two lines of a hymn or psalm at a time to be repeated by the congregation, which was easily morphed into an Africanized call-and-response experience. For nonreading members of the congregation, it was practical to hear the words and melody first before singing it back. Often Black song leaders "repeated" the hymn or psalm line in a highly stylized manner, incorporating rhythmic variation and improvisation. The English composer Henry Lowell described his experience listening to African American psalm singing and was surprised at the way they "transformed" the psalms and hymns. He observed, "When the minister gave out his own version of the Psalm, the choir commenced singing so rapidly that the original tune absolutely ceased to exist—in fact, the fine old psalm tune became thoroughly transformed. For a moment, I fancied that not only the choir, but the little congregation intended to get up a dance as part of the service."[54]

Black Methodists and Baptists spontaneously composed hymns and "spiritual songs" during worship. The earliest restrictions on this type of practice seem to have come sometime around 1840, when leaders at Bethel AME in Philadelphia began insisting the congregation sing strictly from the hymnal. Joseph Cox, a member of Bethel, wrote in 1841, "The singing today was not good, there being an opposition because the old people are opposed to note singing. Elymus Johnson, the person appointed by them, is weakly, and the others would not help him. So we had dull music today."[55] AME leaders resolved in 1841 to "strenuously oppose the singing of fug[u]e tunes and hymns of our own composing in our public meetings and congregations."[56] They gleaned this language from their Wesleyan heritage—it was John Wesley who first instructed Methodists to "sing no hymns of your own composing."[57] While white Methodists of the era were also restricting "fugue tunes," a type of song in which harmony and texture were created by the staggering of voice parts, African Americans used the terminology to refer to an Africanized style of singing. Both had the same effect—they obscured the main melody line and made the lyrics hard to discern. As Eileen Southern states in her seminal work on Black music, "It is improbable that the Black congregations were actually singing the kind of 'fugue tunes' popular among whites during the period. More likely, rather, their singing in the polyphonic African tradition produced the same effect upon listeners as did fugal singing—that is, the exotic polyphonic interweaving of melodies obscured the texts of the hymns"[58] Though some Black church leaders, especially AME leaders, worked hard to eliminate Africanized singing in worship services in the 1840s and 1850s, these practices were reinvigorated in the 1860s and 1870s in congregations that added significant numbers of southern migrants to their rolls. This may help explain why Wesleyan language forbidding members to compose their own songs survived under the heading "Of the Spirit and Truth of Singing" in the AME discipline (outlined in the *Book of Discipline*) until 1885, much longer than it did in the MEC Discipline (in *The Doctrines and Discipline of the Methodist Episcopal Church*; shaped by white leadership), which omitted it in 1856.[59]

Choral Music

Choirs developed into, perhaps, the most significant musical element of African American worship services in the nineteenth century. Although both Black and white churches were sometimes resistant to the formation of choirs, they were mostly accepted by the 1840s. When seventy-five African American members of Foundry ME Church in Washington, DC, withdrew in 1836 to form their own church called Asbury ME Church, twenty-two of them sang in the upstart choir.[60] In his historical treatise, AME Bishop Daniel Payne wrote:

> According to the best information obtainable no one now living can say whether or not the introduction of the choir into Bethel, Baltimore, was opposed by any one. On the writer's first visit to Baltimore, in April, 1843, the choir was in popular favor. Its leader was a man by the name of James High. The majority of all of its members were spiritual minded, and therefore conducted the singing with great fervor and effect. They sang "with the spirit and the understanding."[61]

In fact, Bethel's trustees recorded in 1834, that Linus Johnson "having a[ttempted] to raise a choir for the church" was to be informed that the trustees wished to continue in the "old form." The trustees sent Johnson a note "letting him know we are not prepared yet for a singing choir but will give further notice."[62]

When choirs were introduced in Black churches, it was typically at the urging of ministers who anticipated they would learn and lead hymns, thereby adding structure to services. In turn, it was hoped this would stifle the spontaneous creation of congregational song, which, depending on the choir, it sometimes did. Nevertheless, by the postemancipation period, choirs were in good favor and in fact, from the 1870s forward, began to be seen as "evidence" of Black talent and even musical superiority. When African American church choirs performed classical and sacred works, their "mastery of form" was what W. D. Wright has called a "continuous strike against White racism."[63] Black churches held up Black musical achievement within church walls and, as Jackson's history of Asbury ME in Washington, DC, shows, were gratified when their choirs attracted people from outside the church community.[64]

As choirs developed, they began performing anthems by both white and Black composers and sang in parts. A document listing the founding members of Shiloh Baptist Church in Washington, DC, organized in 1854, distinguishes the voice parts of some leading singers:

> James H. Payne was the first superintendent of the Sunday School following the organization of the church. For several years he was chairman of the Trustee Board, chief spokesman, and lay business genius of the group. He was outspoken, exact, plain, and firm. He was the leading tenor voice in the choir. Rebecca Payne was the wife of James H. Payne. She was a leading soprano in the first choir.[65]

In PE churches like St. Mary's in Baltimore, the choir led in chanting and hymn singing during regular services and performed anthems and classical works for special occasions:

> The chants used are Gregorian (Doran and Nottingham), the hymns are set to inspiring tunes, interspersed at night with those familiar to the Methodists, such as "Coronation," "There is a Fountain," or "Nearer, my [G]od to Thee." On High Festivals, more difficult music is rendered, the Communion Services of B. Tours, Monk, Mac Farran, or Schubert, while at the offertory are introduced the "Alleluia Chorus," the Gloria of Mozart's Twelfth Mass, or "Mighty Jehovah."[66]

The fact that African American Episcopalians were singing a combination of Anglican chants, Methodist and Baptist hymns, and classical works demonstrates the versatility and openness of urban Black people to a variety of musical styles and genres, as well as the interchange that existed between denominations.

As the century progressed, youth and children's choirs also began to crop up. Their presence was a means for drawing the young, or parents of the young, into the church and enlivening services. Ebenezer ME Church in Washington formed their junior choir

> in the basement of Isreal [sic] C. M. E. Church, which at that time was located at First and B Streets, S.W. and was our place of worship during the construction of the present Ebenezer M. E. Church building. The Choir was organized to sing for the Epworth League, and was known as the Epworth League Choir, in which capacity it served up to the pastorate of Rev. S. H. Brown, who requested the Choir to sing for the evening services of the Church. . . . The Choir was requested to sing alternately with the Senior Choir, one month in the morning, and one month in the evening, in which manner it is still serving.[67]

As a bishop for the AME Church, Daniel Payne organized "the first celebration of Children's Day" in 1882. During the spring and summer, he "was quite busy . . . preparing . . . odes" for the event.[68] Payne recalled:

> The songs and music, prepared by Rev. L. J. Coppin and myself, were commingled with some of the sweetest in the book, "White Robes." Dr. Tanner, the editor of our Church organ, and Rev. C. S. Smith, Corresponding Secretary of the Sunday School Union, with others, aided us in the celebration. The meeting was enthusiastic, and doubtless seed was sown that shall be productive of great good. In the evening we held another celebration at Ebenezer Church.[69]

Payne's writing efforts and the use of *White Robes*, a "collection of songs, quartets, and choruses for Sunday-schools, devotional meetings, and the home circle" published around 1879, reveal that children that day performed in ensembles and likely sang in parts.[70]

One of the greatest benefits a choir offered to African American churches in the antebellum period was its potential for financial assistance. Repeatedly, as churches found themselves in dire financial straits, they would "get up" a concert. Trinity AME Church in Baltimore gave a concert like many of its day:

> The choir of Trinity church gave a grand concert on Sunday evening last. The exercises which were very interesting, consisted of choruses, solos, quartettes, scripture readings, addresses, etc. Mr. Howard E. Young delivered an interesting address, subject "Music." Mr. Wm. B.

Hamar, a solo entitled "Home so Blessed," after which there was an intermission and the members and friends gave a very liberal collection, during which Mr. Jas. F. Randall sang the following soul stirring songs: "Jesus lover of my Soul" and "Ring the Bells at Heaven's door," which seemed to waft all Christians present many miles on their journey. . . . The collection amounted to nearly $45.00.[71]

When Ebenezer AME Church, Baltimore gave a "financial rally upon the part of the church and the congregation," the *Afro-American* reported, "The choir sustained its reputation and poured forth beautiful and enchanting music which greatly added to the enjoyment of the occasion. A liberal offering during the day was made."[72] Choirs often took on financial responsibility for expenses like purchasing music or keeping the organ in repair. Sometimes they helped the church financially by paying a "room rent" to the trustees for use during rehearsal. The Bethel AME Church choir in Baltimore paid a monthly room rent of $1.50 in 1849 and by 1856, a rent of $2.00 a month.[73] Though choirs in African American urban Black churches began on shaky ground as the "new way" in the 1830s, by the 1860s they were fully accepted as a strong asset for the worship, outreach, and financial mission of churches.

By the end of the century, choirs were a preeminent feature of African American churches, to the point that denominational leaders sometimes felt the need to pull in the reins and temper the choirs' influence. The 1892 AMEZ hymnal committee's vehement preface concerning the priority of congregational singing tells something of the prominence choirs and select groups had come to have in African American churches near the end of the century and how, in many cases, they had become performance groups only:

> The services attending the dedication of Solomon's Temple were rendered still more impressive and grand by the introduction of music. From the account given us in Holy Writ there is every reason to conclude that the whole congregation must have joined in the song of praise which called down upon their heads the blessings of their divine Protector. . . . We cannot think that a part were silent while a "quartette," or select few, were chanting the praises of the world's Redeemer.[74]

Later in the preface the committee was more specific in outlining the role music specialists should play in worship:

What is the duty of the chorister, quartette, or choir?
To lead the congregation in the singing of all the hymns which are read or announced from the pulpit.
Should choirs ever monopolize the service of song in our Churches?
Never, no more than a few should monopolize the prayers of our Churches.
Should anthems and set pieces ever be sung by the choir or quartette alone?
Just before the minister begins his first service, and immediately at the close, a good, appropriate—but spiritual—set piece or anthem will produce a good effect when well rendered by the choir.[75]

As their skill and popularity developed, African American choirs established themselves as a powerful force in African American churches to the happiness of many and the chagrin of some.

Organ Music

Next to the introduction of choirs, an organ was essential to Black worship life in the nineteenth century. About 1857, "An organ for the first time was introduced in connection with the worship of the Church, at St. James [PE, Baltimore]. . . . Reproachful and sneering terms were applied to the Church because of this introduction into the public services of the Church, the 'devil's music box.' Thus, the Church was an early witness for musical accessories in divine service."[76] Although Baltimore's first Black church members to have an organ were upset and aggravated by it, by 1870 members of the Black community were arguing over whose was the biggest and the best. The organ was suddenly emblematic of African American accomplishment. Sharp Street ME Church, Baltimore, for example, claimed in 1870 they were the "First Black church in Baltimore to introduce music on a large scale with the installation of a large organ."[77] The two accounts illustrate the rapid change African Americans experienced in their view of the organ in only thirteen years. After emancipation, Black churches joined in America's fancy for the rapidly developing instrument and eagerly added organs to their places of worship. When Asbury ME Church renovated its building in 1877, then minister E. W. S. Peck "was the first to introduce music in the church by putting in an organ; the older members objected at first, but soon fell in line."[78] Asbury already had a choir and congregational singing, so like most Black churches, this was the first instrumental music they had.

Pipe organs were the church instrument of choice; however, it was more common for African American congregations to have a reed organ since they were more affordable and less complicated to set up. Though it was a smaller instrument, the reed organ could make "a sound as soft as that of a Harmonica [and] could be increased in power to that of a full military band."[79] By the 1870s the reed organ had "better approximation of the [pipe] organ tone quality and, significantly, those of the three other families of tones in a pipe organ: strings, reeds and flutes."[80] The keyboard was split to allow a variety of stop combinations to be used, a situation that encouraged creativity on the part of the player. Reed organs also had a slow attack, meaning "the sound of the reed builds up somewhat slowly after the key is depressed. This [would] lead the performer to [use] *legato fingering,* in which successive notes are played without a break between notes," which would result in a very smooth, connected sound.[81] "Legato fingering" was only used if the organist was trained enough to know what it was and how to do it. Robert F. Gellerman explains that "when the earliest reed organs were being built, musicians wishing to play them were either self-taught or had to rely on instruction books intended for other instruments."[82] It is likely that many of the first African American organists taught themselves and played by ear. Without the use of legato fingering, the sound of the organ was choppy and percussive. For many, if not for all the men and women who took up organ playing in the Black church, "the spirit and the rhythm of African drums remained in the consciousness."[83] Transferring the primordial significance of sacred drums to this powerful, diverse instrument was not a giant leap, since in the right hands it could perform much of the same role. Calling into the spiritual realm with various tempos, techniques, and timbres, early African American organists had a great deal of freedom to make the organ "speak" as they liked.

Later in the century as churches continued to grow in numbers and prosperity, and as the popularity of the reed organ declined, African American churches like Shiloh Baptist in Washington, DC, fitted their buildings with pipe organs. In a typical Reconstruction era account, they proudly recorded, "During Rev. Tayor's pastorate the church greatly increased its membership." Consequently, Shiloh purchased eighteen feet of ground in the rear of the building and enlarged their structure. They also purchased and installed a new pipe organ.[84]

African American poet Josephine Heard wrote "The New Organ" in the 1880s for the dedication of a pipe organ. It shows the impressive effect such instruments had on Black congregations:

> THOU monstrous gilt and rainbow-tinted thing,
> With many as thousand mouthed tuneful throat,

Helps us God's praises here to day to sing,
With happy hearts we raise our joyful note.

What charms thou show'st to our uplifted gaze,
Some mystic hand seems now to lend thee power,
That fillest us with wonder and praise,
And mute we stand and tremble and adore.

Thou seems't almost human in thy tones;
Even he who built thee did not understand—
Sometimes, low, plaintive, then so mirthful,
That thou were peopled by an angel band.

The poem explicitly shows an African understanding of a "mystic hand" assigning sacred power to a central instrument, one that spoke in "almost human . . . tones." "He who built" the organ was assuredly a white man who could "not understand" the significance acquiring this instrument held for a people long denied instruments. In solidarity, African Americans repeatedly pooled resources and spent considerable energy to acquire this one crucial object for their houses of worship. As a sacred symbol, the organ was layered with meaning; it took center stage in the worship circle, gorgeous and powerful as a sign of Black achievement and solidarity.

Singing Schools

As African Americans gained access to education, books, and literacy, some became interested in musical notation and the access it could bring them to hymnody, anthems, classical works, and the popular music of the day. Before emancipation, it was illegal to teach African Americans to read music in places like Wilmington, North Carolina, where St. Paul's Episcopal Church taught the African American choir to sing psalms and hymns by ear only.[85] Singing schools that taught vocal skills and note reading were popular among whites in the early part of the century, and in the North, a few African American singing schools opened. The original rules of the African Union Meeting House in Providence, Rhode Island, make it clear that an African American singing school was already under way in 1821:

> The gallery in the house shall never be occupied for a regular singing school, nor the house for any purpose contrary to the regulations laid down in this pamphlet. . . . As the vestry or school room is calculated for lectures. . . . A singing school shall not be taught in this

room, in the day when the reading school is kept; nor on the evenings of Tuesday, Wednesday and Thursday, during Autumn, Winter, and Spring; when these evenings are wanted for other purposes.[86]

The meetinghouse had "a vestry" to be used for educational purposes. It was "in this room [that] Mr. Wade established his school for instruction in sacred musick two evenings in the week."[87] These schools taught amateur musicians to read music utilizing a method called "shape note" singing, in which note shapes were associated with certain scale degrees, thereby eliminating the need to use sharps, flats, or the various key signatures. Many hymnals and gospel songbooks were produced using shape notes, but no evidence suggests Black churches were using these with any regularity.

The singing school movement had passed the height of its popularity at the time of emancipation; however, Thomas P. Bell, the choir director at Asbury ME Church in Washington, DC, "was the first to organize the Sunday afternoon Singing School" sometime in the late 1860s. Black Americans "from all parts of the city would fill the lecture room of the Church every Sunday afternoon and this continued for years."[88] The 1892 AMEZ hymnal indicates singing schools were still a part of African American church life at the end of the century, or at least that the denominational authorities wanted them to be. The preface instructed, "every church should hold stated singing meetings, for the purpose of rehearsing the tunes for the coming Sabbath, for the general improvement in music; and the whole congregation, with the choir, should attend these meetings."[89] There is no way to know how many congregational members were singing by note in the nineteenth-century Black church, only that there was a push to encourage note reading and rehearsal and that some considered musical education a privilege and priority.

Hymns and Gospel Songs

During and after the Reconstruction period, border city Black churches increasingly published, purchased, and used denominational hymnals and popular gospel songbooks. Even from the days of slavery, hymnals, and the hymns they contained, were considered a privilege to have and read. Belle Caruthers, who was enslaved in Mississippi, recalled, "I found a hymn book one day and spelled out, 'When I Can Read My Title Clear.' I was so happy when I saw that I could really read that I ran around telling all the other slaves."[90] Aside from the Bible, a hymnal was frequently the most common book African Americans wanted to be able to read. Richard Allen, the founder of the AME Church, published the first African

American hymnal, *A Collection of Spiritual Songs and Hymns, Selected from Various Authors*, in 1801.[91] It included "wandering refrains" to be "freely attached to one or more hymns," and it incorporated songs from the African American oral tradition. Sometimes African Americans wrote hymns for conferences, special occasions, or fundraising purposes. For instance, on April 30, 1887, the Daughters of the Conference, part of the Delaware ME Conference, met to discuss business. The minutes from the day state, "The Patron presented and gave an account of printed matter, which had been done for [the] benefit of [the] Association. . . . [The] Secretary presented fifty hymns to [the] Association. . . . On motion by Mrs. A. C. Brinkley, Secretary, traveling expenses and bill of printing were ordered to be paid."[92] It has generally been supposed that African Americans who remained in connection with the MEC (white) used its denomination's hymnal and did not produce hymns of their own. This report, and others like it, indicate that ME African Americans both wrote and collected hymns for worship that were meaningful to them.[93] Significantly, women were involved in the publishing of musical material and the writing of it.

Though African Americans wrote hymns, they nonetheless continued to include hymns written by whites in their hymnals. How and what they chose for these hymnals is what's intriguing. Nineteenth-century hymnals were often very lengthy, including as many as five hundred to a thousand hymns. Relishing the civil right to worship as they pleased, Black Americans choose songs that mattered to them—songs that spoke authentically of their Christian heritage and contained lyrics with deep truth and relevance for their lives. At the Annual Meeting of Colored Ministers of Congregational and Presbyterian Churches held in New York in September 1859, the Advent hymn "Watchman! Tell Us of the Night" by white hymnist Lowell Mason was sung at their Sunday evening meeting at Shiloh Presbyterian Church in New York. This Advent hymn, sung out of season, was a noteworthy choice and warranted mentioning in the New York paper *The Weekly Anglo-African*:

> Watchman! tell us of the night,
> What its signs of promise are;
> Traveler! O'er yon mountain's height,
> See that glory beaming star!
> Watchman! does its beauteous ray
> Aught of joy or hope fore-tell?
> Traveler! yes, it brings the day,
> Promised day of Israel.

> Watchman! tell us of the night,
> For the morning seems to dawn,
> Traveler! darkness takes its flight.
> Doubt and terror are withdrawn.
> Watchman! Let thy wanderings cease.
> Hie thee to thy quiet home:
> Traveler! lo! the Prince of Peace,
> Lo! The Son of God is come.[94]

With millions of African Americans still enslaved, the significance of this hymn's hopefulness, and its biblical allusion to the "promised day of Israel" are obvious. Not surprisingly, the midnight countdown to southern emancipation on January 1, 1863, became known as "Watch Night," or "Freedom's Eve." Singing in unity, the conference goers used Old Testament liberation imagery to proclaim hope and full freedom for all African Americans.

Gospel hymns were new during Reconstruction, and African Americans enjoyed singing these spirited, evangelical songs. Using compound meters (notes subdivided into threes instead of twos) and dotted rhythms (long, short, long, short), gospel songs incorporated "rhythms of life" such as the sounds of a horse and carriage, the railroad, and the battle drums and victory marches of a recently ended war. They were of a simple musical style and used "simple major-key melodies and corresponding simple harmonies" with slow harmonic rhythm (very few chord changes) and "fuller use of chromatic melodies."[95] The musical substance of these songs left a lot of room for creative variation. Revival song leaders such as Ira Sankey, who partnered with Dwight Moody, composed uncomplicated songs with memorable refrains so that the masses of people attending their tent meetings could easily join in. Sankey, who accompanied himself on a traveling reed organ, was so prolific and well known that his songs became known as "Sankeys." The personal and affirming language of gospel songs especially appealed to African Americans. Walter F. Pitts Jr. in his work on Black Baptists states, "During Reconstruction Afro-Baptists sang these new songs, called 'Sankeys,' composed in varied meters. Just as many freed men and women changed their old slave names and former gloomy styles of dress, and took up new social activities, so Black Baptists adopted these white-inspired songs as a symbol of their new free status."[96] Floyd, Zeck, and Ramsey use the metaphor of a sailing ship to express the journey Black musical expression took in the African diaspora—the metaphor fits well when explaining the ways Black people used gospel songs at church. Ramsey notes, "As people moved into new circumstances and had access to new resources, they also needed new tools to help navigate their new situation."[97] Whether because they were symbols of a new life and status or because their message resonated with an African American spirituality, gospel hymnody found a home in African American churches in the second half of the nineteenth century.

Employing Music Specialists

With the development of various choirs, the purchase and installation of organs, the rise of concerts and other musical events, singing school and Sunday school music programs, and the use of hymnals and gospel songbooks, nineteenth-century border city Black churches needed talented musicians to lead their foray into musical endeavors. Generally, it was the choir leader who gave direction to the church's music program. The 1892 AMEZ hymnal committee told churches they could best enhance congregational singing and the worship life of the church "by obtaining the best chorister you can, if possible a devoted Christian, whose duty it should be not only to have charge of the music in Church and in Sabbath-school, but also to teach and drill the people at the stated singing meetings."[98] Choristers were frequently well-educated leaders in their communities and churches, as in the case of Asbury ME Church in Washington, DC, whose choir director and trustee, Benjamin McCoy, was reported to be "one of the early negro educators of the city."[99] By the 1870s the choral program in some African American churches was so developed with its variety of children and adult choirs that an assistant choir director was deemed necessary. In 1872, Asbury's assistant choir director was Joseph Ambush, "a local preacher, a principal of a private school of his own, the assistant chorister of the Asbury Church Choir, and a recording steward of the church, the superintendent of the Public Service of the city and many other things which claimed his attention. He was the greatest tenor singer in the country."[100] Black church histories frequently credit their choirs and choir leaders as one of their greatest assets, as in the case of Ebenezer ME Church in Washington, DC, where "during the pastorate of Rev. William Draper . . . the choir, under the leadership of his son, Professor James E. Draper, attained great notice."[101] Though men often filled the role of chorister, the position was not limited to a man when a woman was best qualified for the job. Emma Ransom, the wife of AME pastor Reverdy C. Ransom, led music at many of the churches where her husband served. After marrying Ransom in 1887, she "assisted her husband in organizing Sunday schools, kindergartens, and youth groups at each church appointment. She encouraged and led efforts to introduce the congregants to Black spirituals as well as classical compositions. Under her guidance, the churches became known for the excellence of

"Newton Stevens Music Teacher, New York." Library of Congress, Prints and Photographs Division, the William Gladstone Collection of African American Photographs, LC-DIG-ppmsca-11054.

their choral music."[102] Choir directors working in nineteenth-century urban Black churches were responsible for leading choirs, overseeing growing and sometimes elaborate music programs, as well as encouraging congregational singing during worship services and Sunday school.

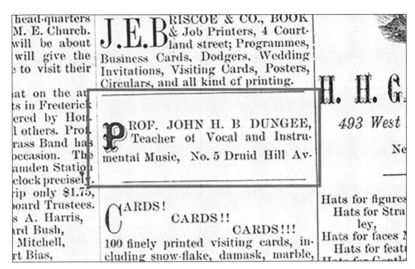

Bethel AME Baltimore's longtime organist Charles Dungee came from a musical family. Black Americans like John H. B. Dungee, likely Charles's father, advertised their services to the Black community, as seen here in the Baltimore *American Citizen*, April 19, 1879. Library of Congress, Washington, DC.

Skilled organists were in high demand, as organ music became characteristic of urban Black worship. As the century progressed, more and more of these players were women. Dr. Susan S. McKinney Steward, an African American medical doctor born in 1848 in New York, "had a talent for music; this she cultivated [,] making it a source of both pleasure and profit. She studied under John Zundel, of Plymouth Church, and for years was organist and choirmaster in the Bridge Street African Methodist Church."[103] Trained organists were usually put on salary and were regularly earning $8.00 to $12.00 a month by the 1880s. The trustees at Plymouth Congregational United Church, Washington, DC, recommended on March 27, 1893, "that, by request of Mrs. Baunaugh, and on account of the many times that she is called upon outside of the regular service of the Church, as organist, that her salary be raised from $8.33 to $10.00 per month."[104] An organ pumper was sometimes employed to pump the crank that maintained the air pressure needed to create sound in certain organs. At Bethel AME Church in Baltimore, an "organ blower" was employed as early as 1864 and as late as 1901.[105] Organists were responsible for accompanying choirs and congregational hymn singing on Sunday mornings. The 1887 AME *Order of Service* directed organists to play a "short prelude . . . immediately after prayer," indicating that by that time, organists also performed solos for worship.[106] Sometimes, as the most trained musician available, the organist was also the choir director, as in the case of McKinney Steward and others. These musicians also contributed to concerts, celebrations, and conferences held by urban Black churches in the nineteenth century.

SPECIAL EVENTS AND CELEBRATIONS

Postemancipation Black congregations loved holding concerts, festivals, "soirees," and commemorative celebrations where music was the main feature or a significant portion of the event. African American newspapers gave details of various church concerts, such as, "The GRAND CONCERT AT the Bridge Street Church, Brooklyn, (postponed on account of the storm) will positively take place NEXT MONDAY EVENING, Dec., 12, 1850"[107] and "Professor G. T. Simpson, the great tenor singer, will give a concert at the Patterson Ave. Baptist Church next Monday night May 1st."[108] All sorts of music was performed at these events, which often featured the church choir, smaller ensembles, or solos by church members. In the 1830s, "the compositions of Bellini, Gluck, Haydn, Mozart, and Rossini were performed with increasing frequency. Every now and then, the music of Black composers was performed—most often, compositions of William Appo, Francis Johnson, and Robert C. Jones. Sometimes a concert was given over primarily to the music of one composer, most frequently Handel."[109] By late in the century, urban Black churches comprised something of a concert circuit for traveling musicians. W. E. B. Du Bois described the phenomenon:

> The favorite entertainment is a concert with solo singing, instrumental music, reciting, and the like. Many performers make a living by appearing at these entertainments in various cities, and often they are persons of training and ability, although not always. So frequent are these and other church exercises that there are few Negro churches which are not open four to seven nights in a week and sometimes one or two afternoons in addition.[110]

Musicians like Baptist minister Henry Jeter and his family performed concerts throughout various cities. On one occasion, "There was an audience of 800 persons at the Nineteenth Street Baptist Church [Washington, DC] to hear the Jeter Family."[111] African American church concerts were a well-established tradition by the end of the century; they were sponsored by a variety of organizations and continued to be a source of income for border city Black congregations (and later, for Black musicians). Urban Black churches were the center of African American social and cultural activity. As such, they hosted a

Henry N. Jeter and family. Courtesy of the Schomburg Center for Research in Black Culture, Jean Blackwell Hutson Research and Reference Division, New York Public Library, https://digitalcollections.nypl.org/items/510d47df-ac40-a3d9-e040-e00a18064a99.

variety of African American musical presentations, sometimes sacred, sometimes not, to benefit the spiritual or financial missions of their congregations.

Black Americans held an abundance of commemorative celebrations to honor the signing of the Emancipation Proclamation, the addition of the Thirteenth Amendment, American independence, and various denominational and racial landmarks such as the founding of African American churches. Thankfulness was the primary focus of the New Jersey AME Conference's American Independence Centennial celebration. Claiming they were "alive to the religious, intellectual and political interests of its people," the conference announced:

> The fourth of July, 1876, should be appropriately celebrated by all of our churches and people by devout thanksgiving to Almighty God by special religious services and liberal offerings; therefore be it, *Resolved*, That the thanksgiving service commence on the first day of July, 1876, and close on the fourth day, to be celebrated at such times and places as may best suit the convenience of the societies and churches.[112]

African Americans embraced patriotism and the music that expressed it. On July 4, 1879, Sharp Street ME in Baltimore "spared no pains" to engage "Prof. Johnson's celebrated Brass Band" to greet the estimated two thousand excursioners expected to board the Baltimore and Ohio Railroad at Camden Station for the Grand Excursion to Frederick City—"one of the most delightful trips ever offered to the Colored Citizens of Baltimore . . . [arranged] for the purpose of visiting their friends at Frederick."[113] At one postwar celebration, Black people and white people assembled to hear a program of speeches and band music. At its close, "there suddenly arose, close beside the platform, a strong male voice (but rather cracked and elderly), into which two women's voices instantly blended, singing . . . 'My Country, 'tis of thee, Sweet land of liberty, Of thee I sing!'" Some whites started to join the impromptu singing of these Black Americans, but Colonel Higginson waved them to silence. Describing the feeling of the movement he declared, "I never saw anything so electric; it made all other words cheap; it seemed the choked voice of a race at last unloosed. Nothing could be more wonderfully unconscious; art could not have dreamed of a tribute to the day of jubilee that should be so affecting; history will not believe it."[114] At the evening service of the AMEZ Centennial service in 1896, "My Country 'Tis of Thee" was sung by the entire congregation. Placed at the beginning of the service, it was prefaced only by Handel's "Hallelujah Chorus" and prayer. The dramatic placement of this patriotic hymn in the order of service signifies how elemental it was to African Americans to gather and sing about Black democracy; the choice to sing this patriotic song in church right after singing, "the Lord God omnipotent reigns . . . King of Kings" speaks to the theological and historical link between Black religion and Black citizenship.

At African American festivals and commemorative events, celebration and song were inseparable companions. The 1877 edition of the AME hymnal clearly demonstrates this connection in a hymn called "Freedom's Morn" under the heading "Anniversary of Freedom." The hymn, written by W. H. Young and sung to the same tune as "My Country 'Tis of Thee," demonstrates the exultation African Americans felt at being able to lift their voices in freedom:

> All hail! Fair Freedom's morn,
> When Afric's sons were born,
> We bless this day.
> From slavery we are freed,
> No more our hearts will bleed—
> Lord, make us free indeed.
> To Thee we pray.

> Bless'd day of liberty,
> We raise our songs to thee,
> Day of the free;
> Our voices loud we raise,
> In freedom's joyful lays,
> In songs of joy and praise,
> O God to thee.[115]

Whether for entertainment, financial gain, celebration, or commemoration, musical performance was core to nineteenth-century urban Black church life.

Outdoor Religious Meetings

Camp meetings, a continuation of early African American Christian tradition, remained a vibrant element of worship life in the mid-Atlantic region, though after emancipation they evolved into events highlighting Black musical prowess, especially before whites. Unfortunately, to a public saturated with Black minstrelsy, authentic Black performance at camp meetings became "highly ambiguous," as spectators regularly heard spirituals, jubilee songs, and music by whites commingled by both Black and white performers. Eric Lott explains how this mixed repertoire combined with the association of Black faces to minstrelsy resulted in confounding the notion of a distinctive African American people's tradition.[116] According to *The New York Herald* in August 1873, "White auditors poured in" to the colored camp meeting hosted by New York's African ME Church "and left the colored portion of the congregation nowhere." The pastor took the opportunity to raise money to pay off the church. After his sermon and call for an offering, Mr. Oliver

> leaned over to an enclosed space that was just below the stand, which was filled with a collection of feminine colored beauty, and said, "Start the music." The leading soprano of this choir was a young lady, a little off-color, attired fashionably in white. She wore VIOLET KID GLOVES, and beat time with a fashionably constructed parasol. The choir was strengthened by the voices of the ministers on the platform, with the exception of Mr. Oliver, who left to refresh his inner man at the refreshment tent. The singing drew the crowds from all parts of the grove.... The hymn that was sung may be judged of from the following specimen verses:—"Said Jesus, Lo! I am with you in every trying hour, And though thou art deficient, I am the God of power.... Sometimes I feel discouraged and think my word in vain, But then the

holy spirit revives my soul again...." This was sung with all their mortal powers, voice, head, feet and body, all entuned for the occasion.[117]

On September 7, 1874, *The New York Herald* reported on "A Colored Camp Meeting" at Walnut Grove on Staten Island sponsored by the Zion Colored Methodist Episcopal Church. Over five hundred people, "including no small sprinkling of whites," from New York City and Staten Island, as well as other parts of New York and New Jersey, came "determined to mingle rural enjoyment with religious exercise.... The hymns rung out with all the old melody peculiar to the colored race and sounded curiously in this open space with the heavens above and the trees waving a faint accompaniment to the song of praise and peace. There was something inspiring in the scene and one could not help but feeling better for the experience."[118]

Leaders like Reverend Jacob Thomas and Deacon Philips, "a colored man of no small activity" from Zion ME in New York, worked hard at "all the multitudinous details which are necessary" to plan and pull together elaborate camp meetings. They also delineated what type of music was appropriate for what type of event, whether Sabbath day hymn or camp meeting song. When assembling the 1877 AME hymnal, Bishop Henry McNeal Turner included under the heading "Revivals," "a large number of old 'Zion songs' ... to accommodate even the most illiterate." Turner called these songs for camp meetings "good old soul-inspiring songs" both "time honored" and "precious." Nevertheless, Turner included certain choices in his hymnal as alternatives to the "spiritual songs" he deemed "devoid of both sense and reason;... some [of which] are absolutely false and vulgar," apparently common at camp meetings.[119] Frequently, camp meeting songs had refrains and were overall more repetitive in style, following suit with traditional African American music. For example, hymn number 1046 in Turner's hymnal makes use of repetitive phrases like "by and by":

> Our bondage it shall end, by and by,
> From Egypt's yoke set free;
> Hail the glorious jubilee,
> And to Canaan we'll return, by and by.
>
> Our Deliverer he shall come, by and by,
> And our sorrows have an end,
> With our threescore years and ten,
> And vast glory crown the day, by and by.[120]

Traditional African American songs thrived among urban Black people during these summer camp meetings, which were sanctioned by church leaders and celebrated by the Black community.

"Bush meetings" still cropped up throughout the century and may have served as an alternative space for ever persistent authentic Black musical expression, as camp meetings were co-opted by whites. AME Minister Thomas Henry and others like him recounted a bush meeting "in a woods near Long's school house. We had all the benches from the school house in the woods."[121] Darius Stokes was "declared 'rebellious' for holding a 'bush meeting' without permission of the elder of the church and was suspended for six months."[122] His case and others like it suggest bush meetings were a private outlet for Black expression.

The signature sounds rising from postemancipation era Black churches were self-defining and space sanctifying. Music was central to the reidentification process Black Americans explored through community and the new stories they shaped about a collective identity. When they took hold of civil rights like marrying and acquiring real estate, they marked those powerful moments with song. They nurtured Black musical achievement and put it on display at concerts and camp meetings as a form of resistance. Nineteenth-century Black churchgoers chose from an array of historical and modern music, liturgical options, and whatever felt right. When they disagreed over what style of worship best represented who they were, they struggled through singing to find solidarity.

Chapter Two

STABILIZING STRUCTURES AND SPONTANEOUS SONG

The Case of Bethel African Methodist Episcopal Church, Baltimore

In September 1872, Reverend George Watkins, the pastor of Bethel AME Church in Baltimore, reached his breaking point. At an official board meeting, Watkins addressed the issue of class meetings, which after the preceding Sunday, he could no longer ignore. Many of the board members were class leaders too; Brothers Roberts and Burk were the worst offenders. Roberts's and Burk's classes met on Sunday evening and let out so late that the dismissal conflicted with the beginning of the evening church service. Steam pouring out his ears, Watkins characterized the situation as "shamefull" and then "went into quite a Lenthy Lecture to the Leaders generally about the maner and time of Leading, which was listened to with marked attention." In addition to the "many things said," Watkins especially highlighted that "there was some of the Leaders who drank too much whiskey" and "made some very pertinent remarks with regard to the maner and Selections of hymns in Class."[1]

Watkins's admonishment to the class leaders reflects a mounting struggle between pastor and people over what was important to them. The 1870s were intense years at Bethel as the church attempted to meet the needs of a swelling and struggling congregation. Black church leaders in Baltimore were faced with the challenge of helping masses of migrants pursue homes, work, education, and dignified community. This messy influx of social

Bethel AME Church, Baltimore, ca. 1855. Courtesy of the City of Baltimore.

problems, combined with the community's passionate swell of expectations for full democratic freedom, swirled within the worship center and at times incited pastors like George Watkins to batten down the hatches to gain some control over perceived chaos. Their rigidity only raised the sails of fresh dreams Bethel's ordinary men and women held for full egalitarian rights in civic and religious society. This case study accentuates the ways laypeople used church as a free space to build courage and assert desires when leaders tried to enforce rules and restrictions that did not suit their needs. This back-and-forth negotiation of values and community identity often expressed itself through debates over worship style.

UNDERSTANDING THE PLAYERS

Looking at some of the people who made up Bethel's congregation and leadership gives insight into generational and historical lines that showed up during Reconstruction. Like a keel in the vessel of Bethel's worship history, ancestral stories are a foundational part of Bethel's voyage through struggles and identity building. Some of the satellite concerns members expressed while practicing full citizenship enlighten us as to who filled Bethel's sanctuary and what they brought to church with them. Worship life may appear ancillary to the more pressing matters of reconstructing Black life in the 1870s, but as the story moves along, background pieces will come together to illustrate its centrality.

Bethel held a significant place in the Black community from its beginnings, and as such, many important events in nineteenth-century Black life played out inside her walls. The church was regularly assigned some of the most educated and accomplished African American pastors. Daniel Payne, an AME bishop during the postemancipation era, cut his pastoral teeth at Bethel in the 1840s. Trained at the Lutheran Seminary in Gettysburg, he had a strong taste for European sacred music and formality in worship; his long ministry and persistent work influenced the denomination and set a tone for Bethel while he was there. Among his top priorities were to eliminate music and worship practices he saw as the "degraded" outgrowth of Black religious life during slavery.

Payne was a complex character. He was known as snooty and lacked the kind of empathy and finesse that would win friends who did not share his views and cultural background. As he said himself, the people at Bethel "had no fault to find with my character, but that I had too fine a carpet on my floor, and was too proud; that if one of the members should ask me to take tea with them, I would not; and lastly, that I would not let them sing their 'spiritual songs.'"[2] In another account, he reports it was because he would not let them sing "the cornfield ditties."[3] Today we might wonder if Payne was somewhere on the spectrum; his blindness to his social deficits and his seeming inability to see how others might interpret events gave him a harshness that seems incompatible with his race-conscious self-sacrifice and near savant ability to organize a massive, growing network of AME churches. He founded multiple schools, including Wilberforce University, identified men and women[4] with potential and interest in becoming ministers and teachers, and established infrastructure in Black communities that would encourage autonomy and the highest access to learning, earning, and spiritual growth.

George Watkins, the heated pastor at the start of our story, was part of the nuclei of foundational leaders Bishop Daniel Payne used to nurture and stabilize the AME during Reconstruction. He had his doctor of divinity before 1867, and just after Virginia's emancipation he was transferred to the new Virginia Conference as a key AME leader charged with establishing the network of churches there.[5] At their first session, the conference members resolved "to draw up an address to our people in the state of Virginia congratulating them upon their recent success, and in the advanced position they have been placed in the several Acts of Congress."[6] It was time to put AME boots on the ground. Payne assigned Watkins as presiding elder of the Norfolk District and pastor at St. John's Chapel in 1866. In his leadership role Watkins handled numerous structuring tasks for the denomination, including the deeding of church property and the ordination of ministers like Israel La Fayette Butt.[7]

Watkins could be terse and exacting, but like Payne he was dedicated and self-sacrificing. As a young AME minister in a Baltimore mission church, Henry McNeal Turner, later Bishop Henry McNeal Turner, told the story of "a young gentleman, a member of his church, by the name of Mr. Watkins, now the Rev. George T. Watkins, D. D.," who "had complimented his thought and oratory but had severely criticised his knowledge of grammar." It is not surprising Watkins zeroed in on Turner's language deficits. He was trained in precise grammar and diction by his father, who demanded inflection "so signally precise that every example in etymology syntax and prosody had to be given as correctly as a sound upon a keyboard." He later became McNeal's teacher, giving four years to training McNeal in Latin.[8]

Born the second of seven children to William Watkins Jr. and Henrietta Russell in 1828, Reverend Watkins was destined to be educated and race conscious. His father, William, was a teacher and minister who held various other occupations, including "self taught practitioner of medicine." His grandfather, William Sr., was a blacksmith and founding trustee for Sharp Street ME in Baltimore around 1810. William Watkins Jr. founded Watkins Academy for Negro Youth, where he taught numerous men and women, including his own children, several who became teachers there.[9] In an August 1836 lecture to the American Moral Reform Society in Philadelphia, he asserted, "Give the rising generation a good education and you instruct them in and qualify them for all the duties of life . . . and then when liberty, in the full sense of the term, shall be conferred upon them, they will thoroughly understand its nature, duly appreciate its value, and contribute efficiently to its inviolable preservation."[10] At the time, his was the first school for African Americans in Baltimore. William was extremely active in the abolition movement and ardently protested African colonization, which he fought to the point of opposing his mentor and Bethel's first pastor, Daniel Coker. This is the multigenerational atmosphere of resistance through education, protest, and religion that nurtured and shaped George T. Watkins.

While ministers were concerning themselves with education and organization, structurization and stability, burying and baptizing, and the frenzy and formality of worship, others managed Bethel's building, parsonage, and mission church properties as well as some of the practical and moral concerns of the members. Women were at the helm of church work and identity building at Bethel, raising money, organizing events, and pooling resources to care for the community. "Let Mt. Zion rejoice. Let the Daughters of Judah be glad" was the motto for the King's Daughters, who made home visits to 265 people during a single quarter.[11] Women working together was characteristic of Black church life, and as Alexis Wells-Oghoghomeh shows, many "encountered Christianity primarily through their mothers' and grandmothers' religious experience and memories."[12] Women like Caroline White were part of defining the church's executive character and civil power during Reconstruction by bringing their cases before the stewards. Hearing her case on April 22, 1871, the lay leaders resolved, "On Motion Sister Caroline White will be allowed permission to pursue her claim against the Member of this Church who owes her house rent and will not pay." White was a property holder with more at stake than just rent. By coming before the church, she and others like her legitimized their propriety and livelihood—in Baltimore particularly, where women were frequently accused of running brothels. Historian Katie M. Hemphill's work demonstrates "Bawdy house charges, like all criminal charges, were political, and they could be used to police women's sexuality and presence in public space even when the women in question were not actually sex workers. Black women were especially vulnerable to this type of policing."[13] Women like White used the church system at Bethel to claim status as well as to establish a trail of evidence, since ministers often went to the civil courts to speak on behalf of their members.[14] By stepping forward in such ways, the women of Bethel methodically carved out and held dignified social and cultural space for Black women in Baltimore and within the church community.

They also asserted themselves at church to clarify status and claim marital rights, as in the case of Anna Staten, who according to Bethel's board of stewards, "presented a very Serious Charge . . . against Sarah Cottman for Illegal Matrimony In that She Said Sarah Cottman did in the Month of October 1873 Enter Into Wedlock with James Staten Who is her (Anna Staten) Lawful husband." Not taking things lightly, the stewards noted, "The Case was Set for Trial on Friday Evening next Dec. 5th 1873 at 8 ½ O clk the Pastor being duly

Summoned."[15] Emancipation created an ambiguous set of interpretations for the formerly enslaved whose marital options ranged from honoring their former master's pronouncement of marriage to civil-sanctioned marriage, with a wide range of common-law options in between. Women at Bethel boldly took part in renegotiating Black marriage, asserting how it would be "remade in meaningful ways for newly sovereign individuals, couples, families, and communities."[16] After hearing all the parties and supporting testimony, the following week, "The Committee appointed to Try the Cause between Sarah Cottman and Anna Staten Rendered a verdict—that . . . Sarah Cottman was guilty of the facts charged. The Pastor declared her Expelled from the Church."[17]

Salt of the earth men like Isaac Meyers,[18] the longtime secretary for Bethel's trustees, and John H. Murphy,[19] who rose to leadership as Sunday school superintendent, kept the church running. Myers was a caulker who headed the African American labor movement in Baltimore, eventually becoming president of the (Colored) National Labor Union, and Murphy was a whitewasher who began attending Bethel as a young newlywed not long after he was emancipated by the Emancipation Proclamation. He eventually borrowed money from his wife, Martha Elizabeth Howard, to buy a printing press and start the weekly church publication *The Sunday School Helper*. Later he started the *Afro-American* newspaper, still in publication today. Men like Myers and Murphy saw to everyday needs, like ordering camphene for the oil lamps, ensuring that the privy was cleaned, paying the janitor and organist, printing the church newsletter, and hiring workers to tend to building maintenance. Their common sense, life experiences, and ingenuity were the lifeblood of church existence and rendered them influence as well as church member comradery and trust.

While continuing to highlight the diverse array of characters who filled the pews of Bethel in the 1860s and '70s would give even greater scope to the story, the point here is to draw attention to how important nuances are often left out of the nineteenth-century Black church narrative. Depending on the belief that educated Black men in ministry oppressed their congregations and forced them into straight lines overshadows the stories of so many resilient and self-aware Black people who stood for liberty, humanity, and creativity, especially in the shared social space many felt most invested in—the church. It also discounts the genuine Black consciousness many of these Black ministers felt, as in the case of George Watkins, whose generational understanding of the link between ministry and democracy was deeply rooted in his upbringing and a long transference of African values, particularly the value of education and learning. From its beginnings Bethel was composed of every kind of African American: enslaved and free, druggist and drayman, educated and illiterate, men and women, children and "the aged." In an era of pew rents, Bethel's stewards and class leaders on January 6 (Epiphany Sunday) 1871, endorsed "the action of the Trustees in providing for the Seating of the Congregation indiscriminately."[20] The story of Reconstruction era Bethel AME Church in Baltimore is the story of how members of the Black community navigated or mitigated differences of values and priorities across class and gender lines, while simultaneously creating lives in opposition to white narratives and mere survival.

Throughout the nineteenth century, Bethel's records reflect a continual struggle between the laity and those in positions of power—a struggle sometimes demonstrated by outward conflict but more typically by unstated resistance. Bethel's members showed a keen sense of respect for their pastors while maintaining a strong sense of self-confidence and self-awareness as individuals. AME organizational structure fostered an environment where middle management lay leaders wafted between loyalties to pastor and loyalties to laity. Certainly true in Bethel's case, class leaders, stewards, and trustees regularly demonstrated a desire to get along with the pastor while pleasing the church members under their care. At times, pastor and people were at odds, and lay leaders took up the mission to steer a course between the two. At the heart of Baltimore's Black community, Bethel provided a rich space for Black people to cultivate their civic capacities.

HISTORICAL BACKGROUND—A TRADITION OF RESTRICTION AND RESISTANCE

The question of musical style in worship was an ongoing battle at Bethel, and though the variance between pastor and people on this issue was pronounced in the 1870s, when migrants were filling the church, the difficulties began much earlier. When Daniel Payne was Bethel's pastor in 1849, he inflamed many of his congregation with the changes he made by adding instruments and structure to public worship, hosting sacred music concerts, and eliminating Africanized worship practices. Resistance to these changes culminated during a church meeting where five trustees were impeached. Mrs. Serina Richfield and a female cohort literally attacked Payne and church leader Darius Stokes with a club, "attempting to beat the Pastor at the very Altar."[21] Little is known about Serina and her friend other than they were "infuriated" and came to the church meeting armed with "cudgel and slug shot." When the lay leaders were pronounced removed, Serina stood up and said, "It is enough" and headed up front to attack. Payne claimed he managed to dodge "the blow, upon the sleeve-top of my thick overcoat, which was made to stand up at the shoulder after the fashion of that day," while the other women succeeded with Stokes, "laying him almost speechless in his blood." Payne recorded, "This assault produced the most terrible excitement, which brought in the city guards, who arrested the assailants and a few of their prominent abettors, and threw them into the watch-house, from which their friends soon bailed them." He minimized the number of church members who left Bethel due to the conflict, but it was no small dent in Bethel's membership—several hundred left the church. His anger is felt in the way he scratched numerous members' names out of the roll book, marking them "expelled for rebellion." Payne called several of these ex-members "ringleaders," including John Chesley, who was declared "one of the most violent, one of the chiefs," and Gilbert Peken, who went down in history as "a useless man at best."[22] The argument eventually landed in court, and in February 1850 the church compensated Darius Stokes $17.88 "on account of a false suit entered against him by [Joel] C[a]rmack, Krius and others."[23]

If left with only Payne's account of the situation at Bethel in 1849 and 1850, it is easy to assume a handful of fractious church members, who did not like Payne and were fighting for power, single-handedly created this embarrassing church conflict. Martha Jones's deep exploration of the *Bethel Church v. Carmack* case reveals temporal control was an important element in the upset; however, her legal study necessarily omits aspects of emotion and resistance the case involved, as disagreements over worship style would be irrelevant in court.[24] Bethel's struggle played out at home and in court and left fissures of disagreement still to be settled in the 1870s. As crucial as exercising rights in court was to Bethel's citizenship development, it is only one aspect of the complexity of ideas, faith, and values stewing in the sanctuary.

The view from inside reveals that many strong individuals were simply unwilling to give up the modes of religious expression they considered essential to their happiness and welfare. The clash between Payne and his church members was deeply rooted in a fight for cultural identity. In 1848, not long before the dramatic attack, Nathaniel Peck, a local preacher who led two classes at Bethel numbering over 150 members each, left because he could no longer tolerate what he believed were Payne's harsh and unnecessary changes. He and his followers started the First Colored Methodist Protestant Church in Baltimore.[25] If there is any temptation to lay the burden of conflict on a difference between enslaved and free or between southern and northern religious music preferences, it should be noted that Peck, originally from Baltimore, was listed in Bethel's church membership rolls as "free" in 1815.[26] As one of the founding members of Bethel, Peck would have heard Bethel's first minister, Daniel Coker, say to Bethel's congregation, "We as a band of brethren, shall sit down under our own vine to worship, and none to make us afraid."[27] Bolstered by these words, Peck and his followers were not intimidated in matters of worship, even from within.

The heart of the conflict at Bethel in the late 1840s was over Payne's efforts to "modify the extravagances" in worship. He recorded the lyrics of some of the "spiritual songs" or "cornfield ditties" he found so offensive:

> Ashes to ashes, dust to dust;
> If God won't have us the devil must.

and

> I was way over there where the coffin fell;
> I heard that sinner as he screamed in hell.[28]

Though he was greatly disturbed by the primitive and "heathenish" language used in such songs, Payne was most distraught over the "singing and praying bands" where these songs were sung.

An African American variation on the Methodist class meeting, singing and praying bands among Black Methodists grew out of the Invisible Institution.[29] In an antislavery work published in 1857, John Dixon, a white Methodist preacher, abolitionist, and native of Maryland, described a typical meeting of enslaved Methodists saying:

> The colored exhorter or leader calls on two or three in succession to pray, filling up the intervals with singing tunes and words composed by themselves. At a given signal of the leader, the men will take off their jackets, hang up their hats, and tie up their heads with handkerchiefs; the women will tighten their turbans; and the company will then form a circle around the singer, and jump and bawl to their heart's content, the women always making more noise than the men.[30]

Writing in the 1880s, Payne recounted, "These 'Bands' I have had to encounter in many places," including his "early labors in Baltimore." His portrayal of a praying and singing band bears noticeable resemblance to Dixon's description. Though agitated and condescending, Payne nonetheless provided a rich, colorful description of singing band worship:

> To indulge in such songs from eight to ten and half-past ten at night was the chief employment of these "Bands." Prayer was only

a secondary thing, and this was rude and extravagant to the last degree. The man who had the most powerful pair of lungs was the one who made the best prayer, and he could be heard a square off. He who could sing loudest and longest led the "Band," having his loins girded and a handkerchief in hand with which he kept time, while his feet resounded on the floor like the drumsticks of a bass drum. In some places it was the custom to begin these dances after every night service and keep it up till midnight, sometimes singing and dancing alternately—a short prayer and a long dance. Some one has even called it the "Voudoo Dance."[31]

Payne's disdain for the activities of the bands and his insistence that they cease were his major source of conflict with the people of Bethel. He believed leaders needed to "speak against" and "resist" "these evils," even to the point of excommunicating unruly members—which is exactly what he did in Baltimore.

Aside from fiercely condemning the freestyle singing and worship of his congregants, Payne vigorously enforced adherence to hymn singing strictly from the hymnal and led by the choir. He introduced instrumental music and sacred music concerts to Bethel in the spring 1849, when he "resolved to get up" Bethel's first musical "soiree" to raise funds for the church. He brought musicians from outside the church to provide the featured entertainment and composed the lyrics to all the songs performed. These lyrics were set to music by James Fleet, who Payne called, "the ablest colored musician then in the District of Columbia." Fleet, Eliza Euston, and Fannie Fisher sang accompanied by James Wormley[32] on bass viol (cello) and Hermion Fleet on piano, flute, and guitar alternatively. Payne refers to the group as a quartette but mentions only three singers, suggesting perhaps, he sang the fourth part. Later he arranged for a "second grand concert . . . prepared and conducted by William Appo," at a time when "there were but few who could compare with him in scientific acquaintance with music." Elizabeth Taylor Greenfield, an opera singer known as "the Black Swan," sang all the solos accompanied by seven violins. James Trotter would later recall Appo and Greenfield in his book on "remarkable musicians of the colored race," saying, "Few, if any, of the large number of musical students of these better times, can realize the vast difficulties that on every hand met the colored musician at the time when Mr. Appo and . . . others elsewhere mentioned began their ambitious, toilsome careers."[33] Inspired and seeking to inspire, Payne would later recall, "Until this concert of stringed instruments not one of us knew that the violin could be used with great effect in the service of the Lord."[34]

In conjunction with the concerts of 1849 (which helped Bethel raise significant funds for the new building they purchased under Payne's leadership), Payne introduced instrumental accompaniment to Sunday morning services. Bethel did not purchase an organ then, but the trustees paid five dollars "for hire of Piano forte" in January 1849, which was a shocking enough addition to the previously unaccompanied congregational singing.[35] In early 1850, Thomas Bradford was paid six dollars for a guitar "used in aid of the church."[36] While Payne's changes may seem subtle, they sent shockwaves through the congregation in 1848 and 1849, leading to the "rebellion."

Though Payne portrayed his musical reforms at Bethel as lasting, this is only partially true. In 1851, not long after Payne left, Darius Stokes, the man harmed in the attack, was expelled from the church, and his class was "given to Brother Washington."[37] His name is blotted out of the church membership roll so fiercely one can hardly avoid noticing how gleefully it was done. With the brazen enforcers of formality gone, Bethel's members reinvigorated their singing and praying band traditions and maintained authentic expressions of Black identity through music and worship. While in Baltimore in the 1850s Fredrika Bremer, a Swedish traveler, visited "a Methodist church of free negroes"—quite possibly Bethel. Her account highlights several telltale Africanized forms of expression, including the preacher's "talent of improvisation" and knack for "applying theoretical truths to the occurrences of daily life." She described the assembly as "a tempestuous sea," explaining that "one heard only the cry, 'Yes, yes!' 'Farewell! forever!' 'Yes, amen!' 'Nevermind!' 'Go along!' 'Oh God!' 'Farewell!' 'Amen, amen!' etc." She observed that "besides these convulsive groans, cries and howls, the assembly was ready for any extravagance, whatever it might have been, if the preacher had willed it."[38] Despite Bremer's racial bias and inability to understand the sophisticated ability these worshippers displayed as they simultaneously accessed emotion, thought, body, and creativity in communal space, her account reveals Baltimore's Methodists still favored, and were further crafting, the "homiletical musicality" Braxton Shelley calls "tuning up." The sonic escalation Bremer describes here displays several elements never eradicated from Bethel's worship: call-and-response, communal participation, and a cycle of rhythmic and melodic inflections. Shelley's work reveals that Black preaching as Bremer described creates a moment "that affirms the parishioners' of the presence and power of God in their lives." He argues, "Tuning up as an aesthetic practice is a form of thought" and cannot be separated from other "sonic ritual acts that shape Black worship." The movement between singing and tuning up "transfigures the congregation's religious experience."[39] The value Bethel's

Organ used at Bethel Church, ca. 1864–1874. Courtesy Bethel AME Church, Baltimore, and the Frederick Douglass–Isaac Myers Maritime Park, Baltimore. Used with permission of Philip J. Merrill, Nanny Jack & Company, LLC.

members placed on this tool for understanding is tightly woven into their historical identity.

In matters of formality and structure in music, Bethel's members increasingly moderated denominational and pastoral ambitions, choosing what served them and ignoring what did not. They hosted a few musical concerts and events during the 1850s and 1860s for fundraising purposes, mostly featuring the choir or musical members of the congregation like Thomas Bradford and his family.[40] In about 1857, St. James PE Church, a neighboring African American congregation, introduced an organ into its services, and it was considered a real "novelty" in the city at the time.[41] A few years later Bethel followed suit. Payne recorded in his *History of the African Methodist Episcopal Church*, "The introduction of the organ into Bethel, Baltimore, was during the pastorate of Reverend Savage L. Hammonds, in the year 1864. The last and present organ was put in under the administration of Reverend George Watkins, D. D., in the year 1872. It cost $2,500, and was built by Pomplitz, of Baltimore, Md."[42] Few records survive to tell what transpired at Bethel during the Civil War years, simply because war-related problems created great disruptions, as in 1863, when "Baltimore was threatened by an invasion of the Confederate Army. Every able bodied colored man was arrested by the police and carried to the outskirts of the city to assist the United States Government in throwing up breast-works. Reverend A. W. Wayman, who was pastor of Bethel Church at the time, was among those arrested." After the arrest, James Handy, then a member of Bethel and later its pastor, visited "the church on Sunday, and found it deserted, so far as men were concerned. The churches were all deserted."[43] Despite sparse record-keeping in these years, it is clear the congregation allowed a more structured Sunday morning music and worship format while maintaining many of their cherished musical expressions on the sidelines.

RECONSTRUCTION ERA REPRESSION AND REFORMS

Understanding the conflict over music and worship that transpired between Payne and the members of Bethel in the late 1840s and early 1850s sets the stage for understanding why these issues erupted again during the 1870s. Twenty years after Payne's departure—when emancipation and Reconstruction presented exceptional new social and cultural issues to border city Black communities like Baltimore—Bethel blurred sacred and profane imagination more than ever. Here Black Baltimoreans found solidarity, refuge, validation, and dignity as they sought full realization of their democratic dreams. Here it was possible to give expression to experience—literally creating a shared artistic and spiritual response to the harsh realities outside. Extemporaneous and emotionally laden religious music and worship were always near the surface at Bethel, and now they were invigorated as more and more southerners made their way North and joined the community. As they looked for work and safe housing among competitive forces, provided for families, encountered rigorous racism, and struggled to realize government failure and the need for a national community of Black people, they looked deep into their collective heritage and found a profound voice of unity to sing through the struggle.

From 1872 through 1877, the heart of the Reconstruction era, Bethel's ministers, with the support of the Methodist ministers of the city, aggressively began shaping worship services to reflect the respectability and decorum fundamental to their notions of "uplifting the race." Within the first six months of his tenure at Bethel, Watkins was indoctrinating his stewards and class leaders with the need for order and discipline. A man later described by Isaac Myers, the articulate and careful secretary for the trustees, as "a learned and eloquent speaker" who was "not polished in ordinary conversation," Watkins struggled to make allies of his leaders.[44] In July 1872, scarcely two months after his arrival, Watkins was not at all reluctant to put his class leaders in their place when "he remarked too much Irregularity on the part of the Leaders was bound to have a very bad effect on the punctual attendance of the members" and "said a Leader who would retain his members untill Eleven O'Clk was of itself proof of his incompetency." Watkins used the Methodist mantra of "perfection" in his lecture to the leaders, telling them their spiritual health would certainly be hindered by their lack of discipline and punctuality. In turn, their spiritual weakness would affect the health of the entire church.[45] The reason the classes were letting out so late was because of their singing.

As the months passed, Watkins introduced more and more changes to morning services. In early 1873 Watkins called upon the trustees and stewards of the church to head a campaign to purchase a new organ for Bethel. In September of that year, he informed them the organ was "near about done and would cost twenty-five hundred dollars or twenty-one hundred dollars and our old Organ. The terms of agreement between the trustees and the Contractor was $1,000 dollars when the same was completed." The high cost of the organ confirms that Watkins sought to install Bethel's first pipe organ, since the most expensive reed organs of the time cost under $900.[46] This put a considerable strain on the church, which rarely had more than $150 in its budget during this time; however, the ever progressive Watkins did not hesitate to use his eloquence to convince the leaders of their obligation to ensure that the new instrument would find its home at Bethel. Secretary Gaines recorded:

> After some further detail[ed] statements[,] the action of the trustees was made known to the Effect that Each one would Subscribe five dollars to be paid on the day the Organ was placed in the Church. They respectfully asked the Concur[r]ence of the Official Board by their doing Likewise. The Pastor made quite an interesting Speech in favor of the Object Soliciting all to act and then [proposing] Such as could not Subscribe to 5-4-3-2[,] let them contribute one, going further at considerable len[g]th upon the duties of Officers as well as members to the Church of Christ. On motion the proposition of the Trustees be received, carried and on motion the proposition was unanimously adopted.[47]

Watkins was the major proponent of the organ purchase, but there were "a number of petitions praying that the trustees might get an organ in the church com[me]nsurate to her capacity."[48]

Bethel joined in America's organ fancy and the Black community's race to acquire "the best." Their organ was six or seven years old, and at least

In 1873, Bethel commissioned the building of a pipe organ for their church from Baltimore organ manufacturer Pomplitz & Co. Advertisement from *The Baltimore Sun*, September 12, 1854.

some of her members were ready for the power and brilliance a pipe organ could provide. Watkins called "the attention of the entire church and congregation to the importance of cooperation to succeed," saying it was most desirable to have the purchase "completed by annual conference." Besides the obvious bragging rights Watkins would gain by securing the organ's purchase by the annual conference in 1874, he knew he would be leaving Bethel that summer.[49]

The choir was in existence long before Watkins arrived, but in the 1870s, Bethel's ministers began using the choir to shape the structure and style of Sunday services. The choir used hymnals to lead hymns like "Try Us O God" and "O for a Closer Walk with God."[50] The ministers' insistence that the choir lead strophic hymnody, meaning each verse sung to the same music, eliminated the antiphonal psalm singing that was practiced and most improvisational call-and-response singing.

As a result, the choir's role at Bethel increasingly became more prominent, and in July 1873 a debate over how important that role was is detected in the official board's record. While discussing plans for an upcoming camp meeting, the secretary asked if the General Committee on Camp Meeting had made any plans to "accommodate the choir to and from camp," and if not, what arrangements did the board plan to make? After "quite a discussion among the Brethren," a motion was made to provide ten tickets "for the use of the choir to and from camp." However, "after much discussion, the motion was lost."[51] The board remained resistant to the choir's growing prominence and used their voting and financial power to restrict the choir as an official representative of the church.

Church leaders too were encouraged to set the example by singing from hymnals during worship services. Reverend W. S. Lankford, Watkins's predecessor, "announced that He was prepared to Serve the brethren with Hymn Books and discipline and disposed of Several by his request" at one of his first stewards' meetings. Lankford's strong insistence on singing by the book clearly demonstrates his desire to suppress the improvisational and spontaneous singing of his congregation. Bishop Payne held powerful sway over denominational leaders, such as Watkins and Lankford. He told them:

> Few of our people can read our hymn-books correctly. This circumstance tends to introduce disorder and confusion in our singing; the great majority, not being able to use our hymn-books, make fugue tunes for themselves, and these fugue tunes are always transcripts of low thoughts, ignorance and superstition, hence, confusion in singing. Their language used in prayer is also characteristic of the want of education, being almost always incorrect, and when it is, only by mere chance. And for the want of good language they cannot express, to the edification of the Church, their own good thoughts, hence confusion in prayer.[52]

These efforts make it plain that at least until 1874, Bethel's members still sang extemporaneously and by ear during worship. Leadership's desire to use only officially sanctioned hymns from the AME hymnal stemmed from a belief that the "fugue singing" of their congregants was "incorrect" and confusing—a hindrance to the well-being of the church.

It is important to notice, however, that not all church leaders fell in step with Payne's attitudes. Bishop Henry McNeal Turner assembled the first AME hymnal published after the Civil War and made a great effort to include some of the "old Zion songs," although he admitted in the preface this choice "may elicit the disapproval of some of our poetic neologists." He reminded those who might not approve of the hymnal's "good old soul-inspiring songs" that they "must remember we have a wide spread custom of singing on revival occasions, especially, what is commonly called spiritual songs."[53] Turner's hymnal, first published in 1876, included a few original hymns by African Methodists, including one by James Handy who became Bethel's pastor in 1875.[54]

The reactions of Bethel's organist give more evidence of the intensified structuring of church singing and services. In 1870, the stewards paid Joseph Ockermy $20 per quarter to play the organ and $2.50 a month to William Taylor the "organ blower."[55] In his book *Highly Musical People*, Trotter put Ockermy in a list of those who did not understand "music as a science" but as one who "in spite of obstacles that would seem to be insurmountable, obtained a fair musical education" and "exhibited an artistic skill and general æsthetic love and taste" for music.[56] His pay was increased to $25 once Watkins was on the scene in 1872. Paying musical leaders gave pastors more power to control how and when music would be performed. Ockermy remained on the job for ten years, playing for Sunday service as well as funerals and other official church services. By 1880, though, Ockermy, feeling his responsibilities had greatly increased, requested "an increase of sallery to $200.00." With only $52.83 in hand at the end of their meeting, it is no surprise the stewards refused to give Ockermy or the organ blower a raise. The constancy of choir rehearsals, music preparations for each service, answering the demands of the pastors (and no doubt the complaints of members), and a failed attempt at negotiating a raise caused Bethel's longtime organist to call it quits.

Pastor W. S. Lankford arrived at Bethel in 1874 and continued Watkins's reforms to public worship. In December 1874 he "called the attention of the board to the fact of the Irregularity of Our System of ushers." He asserted that every aisle needed to be "g[ua]rded with an usher on all occasions of Divine Service." Lankford's concerns about the "irregularity" of the ushering system seem to be linked to maintaining order and decorum during services; Lankford was working to control the physical movement and spontaneity members expressed in the church aisles. Zilpha Elaw, a self-appointed Black female preacher who frequently preached in and around Baltimore, recounted that camp meeting–style worship manifested itself inside Black church walls despite "the polish of the minister, the respectability of the congregation, or the regularity and method of its services." Elaw, whose own spiritual narrative included a "trance of ecstasy" in which she "sank down upon the ground, and laid . . . prostrate," described one such service, possibly at Bethel:

> The excess of their emotions were such, that the order of worship was suspended; for some were calling upon the name of the Lord, some were groaning to receive the atonement of Jesus, while others were rejoicing in his salvation and giving glory to God. Our services were not unfrequently interrupted by scenes of this description; for the operation of the Holy Ghost can no more be circumscribed within the limits of man's arrangement, than the wind and rain and sunshine can be restricted to man's time and opportunities.

In keeping with both her Methodist and African American religious heritage, Elaw reminded church leaders that although "order in divine worship and in the house of God is graceful and appropriate, . . . the life and power of religion" is greater than any attempt to suppress it.[57] Regardless of where Bethel's trustees stood on the issue of extemporaneous musical and bodily expression, they liked the fact that individuals had to be "especially deputized to act the part of ushers" and in time agreed the ushers, as well as class leaders and trustees, would wear white gloves and corsages to reinforce the importance and distinctiveness of their role in managing order in the sanctuary.[58]

HOW IT PLAYED OUT

As Sunday morning service became more and more structured, it was in the singing and praying bands that Bethel's members sang freely. The Africanized worship of these bands persisted for decades, despite attempts to squelch it. As bishop, in 1891 Payne begrudgingly wrote that many local pastors claimed they "could not succeed in restraining" the singing bands. At Bethel and elsewhere band worship was "regarded as the essence of religion."[59] Watkins was continually irked by his inability to control the bands and their worship. In board meetings, he reprimanded class leaders for their failure to respect decorum, telling them he was displeased with "the mode, man[n]er and spirit of conducting our Prayer Meetings" and complaining "that Some tried to see how much Louder some could sing than others."[60] Watkins's criticism of the singing bands make it sound as though little had changed since Payne was there decades earlier.

By the end of 1872, the chasm between pastor and people was growing to great proportions. Watkins's continual disrespect for the spirituality and dignity of his people, in tandem with his open disgust for their music and worship, was met with indignation. In one stewards' meeting, "the Pastor Stated that in all his ministerial Service he had for the first time been insulted by an assistant Leader."[61] The offender was assistant to George Murry, a class leader since the 1840s, and

> after a Statement of the manner in which he [the pastor] was insulted by James Grey he announced that the said James Grey be and the Same is hereby, Suspended from leading in any class of this Church for three months and until he shall have made the nessecery appology [sic] for the insulting remark on the occasion referred to and untill [sic] he can at least have common politeness for the Pastor.[62]

The next month, Watkins claimed, "he had been the recipient of more insulting notes Since he had presided here than in all of his Life before and they were mainly from the members of the Bands with their signatures to them."[63] Apparently, the band members pushed back when Watkins instituted reforms, and they were self-assured enough to sign their names to their rebuff.

Watkins did little to endear himself to Bethel's membership and could not help being overshadowed by his predecessor, the Reverend W. R. Revels, whose "giant mind, indom[it]able will and daunting perseverance" won the affection of the congregation. In a garrulous "mode of expression" given by secretary of the board, Causman H. Gaines, Revels was credited with "giving tone and character to this people, permeating its influence throughout the Len[g]th and breadth of this our City and State."[64] Unlike Watkins, and later Lankford, Revels accepted the worship status quo and valued the desires and preferences of all Bethel's people.

The core of Watkins's problem with his congregation is most evident in his remarks about revivals to the board on November 21, 1873. He saddled members with "preventing the manifestation of the Spirit of God" at Bethel. Still perturbed by the unruly worship of the bands, he argued the spirit failed to visit the church when there "was too much self confidence into Bands in our Societies."[65] Watkins's word choice provides a telling look into the struggle: he believed his church members were too confident, resisting proper lines of authority. The singing bands continually disregarded the pastor's regulations about music and time, determining for themselves when and where they would submit. By emphasizing their self-confidence, Watkins gives a sense of their determination in asserting their desires, which gets to the heart of real issues over music and worship. It was an issue of identity. Bethel's members fought for their right to full freedom of expression and boldly resisted any authority that tried to suppress it.

The character of Bethel's worship was in many ways worked out through the minds and behaviors of class leaders who migrated between pastoral authority and popular opinion. In the Methodist framework, class leaders held authority over their classes; leaders regularly met with classes to advise, reprove, and encourage the members under their care. The class leaders collected funds from their members and met with the pastor and stewards to submit the money and report on the spiritual and physical condition of their members. Most took these civic responsibilities seriously and formed alliances with their members while also striving to fall in line with pastoral leading.

Bradbury Roberts straddled this leadership line in December 1873. At a board meeting the pastor announced, "There were members of this Board who walked with Members of this Church knowing them to be partakers in intoxicating Liquors and who failed to report them."[66] Offenses like drinking could get a member thrown out of the community, but leaders sometimes overlooked these stringent rules. By a vote, the pastor tested "the knowledge of the board" and determined Brother Roberts, a class leader since the 1840s,[67] was especially guilty of ignoring certain transgressions. Handling the situation delicately, Roberts "made a very wise statement in Explanation of his position," which extinguished the pastor's criticism for the time being.[68] Class leaders held the precarious position of mediator between pastor and people, a balancing act that required diplomacy and sometimes a bit of feigned naïveté. Certain classes, or bands, had more freedom to sing their spiritual songs than others because their leaders were permissive and accommodating.

At Bethel in the 1870s, the class leaders who were especially loved by their members had repeated troubles with the pastor. In August 1872, the pastor reprimanded Stephen Glascow, whose class purportedly numbered seventy-two by 1870, for being a "gate keeper at a danc[e] picnic or something of the kind."[69] Glascow "replied it was true had had done so[,] but seemed not to comprehend the enormity of the offense." As superintendent of the Leachville mission, Glascow believed he was helping the members there.[70]

The culmination of worship reform at Bethel came in November 1874, when then pastor W. S. Lankford told the board the city's "colored Methodist ministers" at their weekly preachers' meeting had "Inaugurated a Movement for the better regulating of the Band Societies." He informed them the preachers "desired an Expression from the Board as to the Merrits or demerits of the Issue which is to oppose the present mode of Band Singing and then with the unity of [the] Entire Col'd Methodist Ministry In this City to Either reform it or [Extinguish] It." In response, the board members offered their "hearty Cooperation In their Efforts to regulate the band Societies In accordance with Discipline and Order."[71] They endorsed specific resolutions made by the ministers to reform the singing bands, however, not without "an Earnest Exchange of views as to the best means of carrying into Effect the Spirit of the resolutions."[72] Though none of the resolutions are preserved, the secretary revealed in his notes that a primary concern was that Sunday prayer and singing meetings should be sponsored only by the church and not by separate bands. After much discussion, "it was finally concluded that as a separate Band Meeting for Sabbath morning had heretofore been announced from the pulpit It would no Longer be tolerated or announced from the pulpit" and that there was to be "no Other prayer Meeting but Church Prayer meeting."[73]

Concerned about reactions, Charles H. Dorsey proposed "that so much of the proceeding minutes to the meeting as it relates to the Sunday morning Prayer meeting be stricken Out." His motion was lost by a vote of ten to thirteen, so records of the conversation remain.[74] While the board unanimously agreed the Sunday morning singing bands should be discontinued, they were almost split on the issue of whether to keep a record of their participation in the decision. The board predicted an upset in the church; quite a few did not want to be held responsible.

From this point on, music sanctioned by the pastor and a service held "according to discipline" became the trademarks of Bethel Church. Bolstered by their peers and backed by the church's official board, George Watkins and W. S. Lankford changed the face of Bethel's Sunday morning worship during the 1870s. Their stern policies and aggressive leadership styles ensured that only music the AME leadership considered "elevating," appropriate, and "respectable" would be used and performed in official church meetings.

EXERCISING RELIGIOUS FREEDOM THROUGH MUSICAL ALTERNATIVES

Bethel's members found ways to continue singing the music that held spiritual power for them. Evidence indicates that class leader Stephen Glascow, and perhaps others, continued allowing his class members to worship in an exuberant and noisy way, despite the resolution to reform band singing made by Baltimore's Black Methodist ministers and endorsed by Bethel's board. On March 5, 1875, James Henson's name was "Inserted on the Leader's Roll in place of Bro. Stephen Glascow—removed." Referring to the action of disciplining Glascow and his class by removing their leader, Lankford told the board that "a reformation in the Church was absolutely a necessity or the Church would ultimately Fall." Still not completely convinced of Lankford's view, "the Brethren Freely discussed the Cause pro or Con."[75] Three weeks later, the members of the class formerly led by Glascow "turned out Strong" for a meeting with the pastor, where they "urgently appealed for the retention of their former Leader Bro. Steven Glascow, Promising In which Event to do their very best to redeem their former standing upon such." Evidently feeling he had made some headway with the members, Lankford "consented to keep Bro. Glascow on Trial as Leader."[76] While free expressions of worship were rigorously put down during official church meetings, Bethel's members morphed the Methodist system into a democratic one, creating and accessing multiple worship options. Under the umbrella of the church, members deftly navigated a variety of church gatherings to participate in both new and old cultural expressions. Like an artist's palette, mission churches, home gatherings, bush meetings, and Sunday worship were the colorful worship venues Bethel's members chose from as they painted new pictures of themselves as free people.

MISSION CHURCHES

As "unruliness" simmered down at Bethel, it oozed out in Bethel's mission churches. Because of its rapid growth in the 1870s, the church known to many as "Mother Bethel" founded several new missions, including Mt. Zion, Leachville, and Trinity. On June 22, 1877, Handy, now Bethel's pastor, "called the attention of the board to a very formidable Complaint in the form of Signed petitions from the property holders in the neighborhood of Mt. Zion against the present mode of worship." The petitioners who called the bands a "menace" threatened to ask the court for an injunction, resulting in Handy's decision to, at least temporarily, "suspend operation of the bands" at Mt. Zion.[77] The mission churches, although under the direction of Bethel's leaders, operated mostly autonomously. Created for the overflow of Bethel's members and the convenience of those living in different areas of the city, mission churches were an alternative. Out from under the constant eye of AME's most trained pastors, those who freely composed religious music and continued practices such as the ring shout, call-and-response, and the singing of spirituals could worship without rebuke. While still in connection with Bethel, the mission churches allowed Bethel's members to self-separate according to worship preferences, even while sharing a common cup.

FEMALE IDENTITY AND RESISTANCE

Despite their control of official meetings such as Sunday service and class meetings, Bethel's pastors could do nothing to prevent worship meetings held by individual members of their congregation. Women especially kept a long tradition of holding meetings in their homes. Handy "was carried to Sunday School" by his grandmother when he was five years old and maintained he was "a member of Bethel Sunday School ever since." He later recorded his remembrance of some of Bethel's women:

> Annie Dickerson was one of the pillars of Bethel Church, in Baltimore. She took under her care and instruction all of the new female converts and indoctrinated them in the duties they owed to their God and to their church. She could be seen every Sabbath at her place in the church, the amen corner, before the hour for public worship, with a large number of young women around her, she exhorting, and her assistant, Miss Mary Ann Prout, who was the teacher of small children in the day school, read the Bible and Sister Dickerson explained the Scriptures to them.

He also recalled, "Doritha Hill, the wife of Stephen Hill, was of great assistance to the infant organization in Baltimore. She was a remarkably good singer, and frequently, in the absence of her husband, led class meeting. She held at her house prayer meeting, once each week, and a band of sisters every fortnight, in which she catechised, exhorted and assisted them in their religious duties."[78] "Old Elizabeth," a Methodist female preacher in Baltimore during the early to mid-nineteenth century, told of a meeting at the home of a poor widow "which was situated in one of the lowest and worst streets in Baltimore." Sometime during the evening, a watchman came to break up the meeting, saying a complaint had been made "that the people round here cannot sleep for the racket." Elizabeth replied, "A good racket is better than a bad racket" and asked why they should be punished "for praising God, our Maker?"[79] Some class leaders visited another of her meetings and asserted she was "holding meetings contrary to discipline—being a woman," but they did not stop her.[80] As the nineteenth century progressed, Bethel's women founded circles and societies such as Society Lilly of the Valley, Daughters of Zion, the King's Daughters, the Ladies' Church Aid Society, the Ladies' Mite Missionary Society and numerous others, which met in private homes.[81] There women met safely together for worship and prayer while attending to authorized activities such as sewing, church suppers, and fundraisers.

Women at Bethel were emboldened by the Holiness movement with its doctrine of entire sanctification and emphasis on expressive worship. The movement's broad female base and home meeting format promoted an emotional and bodily worship practice that neatly aligned with the African sensibilities and interests of many of Bethel's members; it created a synchronized theology and a distinctive worship practice away from scrutinizing eyes and reminiscent of the Invisible Institution's liberating impetuses. Like the smallest doll in a Matryoshka set, Holiness women were the soul of Mother Bethel, aligning Christian worship with historical memory to create meaning and preserve their African identity outside of racist and paternalistic enforcements.

In 1843 Phoebe Palmer published *The Way of Holiness* and recorded that she was troubled by a bland, solemn worship service she attended, noting, "There was an apathy, a feeling of irresponsibility manifested by the congregation, that were really painful to me to witness." Going on about the congregation's singing she said, "I do feel persuaded that there is not only moral unseemliness, but Scriptural impropriety, in the listlessness of demeanor indulged in by various denominations of the present day." In many instances during prayer, Palmer was "perhaps the only one in the whole assembly besides the minister, who like God's ancient servant, was kneeling, and with outstretched hands supplicating the mercy-seat."[82] Palmer criticized decorous worship services absent of emotion and bodily movement and developed a theology of holiness founded on passionate worship of God. Her words and developing theology were timed perfectly to provide pressure release for the boiling hot issues of music and worship in the AME.

Black women were, in fact, preaching the same doctrine of holiness to at least some of Bethel's members well before Palmer's movement took shape. Zilpha Elaw preached sanctification in Baltimore in the 1830s. The freedom and confidence of her message was especially appealing to women, who gathered to sing, pray, and pursue holiness. Elaw explains, "I had an extensive circle of young ladies who were constant attendants upon my ministry.... These manifested great diligence in their pursuit of the higher attainments of experimental spirituality."[83] Julia Foote, an African American woman who professed entire sanctification, began her preaching ministry in and out of MEC, AME, and AMEZ circles in the 1840s. In her autobiography, Foote recorded in August 1849 that she received "a pressing invitation from Rev. Daniel Paine [Payne] ... to visit Baltimore, which I accepted" and noted in fall 1849, "We remained some time in Baltimore, laboring mostly in Brother Paine's charge."[84] Foote described her time there, saying, "We attended meetings and visited from house to house." In one instance, "After class-meeting, a good many came to me, asking questions about sanctification; others stood off in groups, talking, while a few followed me to my boarding-house," while in another city "the church became much aroused" after she spoke.[85] After one confrontation with a minister, she "involuntarily burst forth" and sang, "My soul is full of glory inspiring my tongue, Could I meet with angels I would sing them a song. . . . Though my gifts were but small, I could not be shaken by what man might think or say."[86] Foote's work invigorated the natural religious expression of Bethel's laypeople during Payne's pastorate, when he was away from the pulpit, and established a tradition of resistance Bethel's women called up in the 1870s, when ministers forced strident reforms into Sunday worship practices.

During Reconstruction, the same year Baltimore's Methodist ministers made their resolution to reform the singing and praying bands, the Holiness movement's efforts again penetrated Bethel. At a board meeting in January 1874, "The Pastor made a very important Statement to the Effect that Several Ladies (White) belonging to the M. E. Church had waited upon him for the consultation with a view to holding a series of meetings for the promotion of Holiness." The Methodist ladies planned to make a "thorough Canvass of the City In Order to find out the Sabbath School Interest" among African American Methodists.[87] Lankford could not have known how far the Holiness movement would extend within his own church, but in the 1870s, as Methodist churches became more straightlaced, Bethel's Holiness women met at home to practice the ecstatic worship forbidden in Bethel's sanctuary.

BUSH MEETINGS

Bethel's members continued the outdoor practice of worshipping in open air and "hush harbor" gatherings well into the late 1870s and '80s. When formerly enslaved Clara Davis moved to the city she declared:

> You can have de busses an' street cars an' hot pavements en' high buildin' 'caze I ain't got no use for 'em no way. But I'll tell you what I does want. I wants my ole cotton bed an' de moonlight nights a shinin' through de willow trees an' de cool grass under my feets as I runned aron' ketchin' lightnin' bugs. . . . I wants to walk de paths

th'ew de woods an' see de rabbits an' watch de birds an' listen to frogs at night.[88]

"Uncle John," a class leader, remembered how when he and his wife were enslaved, they favored the outdoors for worship. He said, "Nancy had been praying for a long time. She used to go away off in the woods to pray. I went in the woods many times to pray; I thought I could pray better in the swamp."[89] As in the singing bands and Holiness meetings, women had greater freedom to lead out in bush meetings. Julia Foote "assisted in a bush meeting" where "the Lord met the people in great power," and she remarked, "I doubt not there are many souls in glory to-day praising God for that meeting."[90] In 1872, at one of Bethel's official board meetings, "Bro. Squirell made a statement that he purposed holding a Bush Meeting on Sunday week next and wanted to Raise the means necessary to Chartering the Cars which was 100 dollars." Watkins was brand new to Bethel, so he said nothing to the proposition. Apparently, there was some awareness of his disapproval, however, since "There being no disposition to Open the Subject the motion to adjourn was put and carried."[91] One can almost feel the tension in the room when Brother Squirrel naïvely approached the taboo subject; the board members and pastor not only refused to respond but also abruptly ended their meeting.

On July 4, 1878, Bethel's pastor, J. W. Becker ordered his leaders not to participate in a bush meeting to be held by Samuel Ferguson at Fallen Spring on July 7, 1878. Becker commanded the "Local Preachers of Bethel AME Church not to accept any appointment to preach at that Grove on above named date July 4th, 1878."[92] These outdoor meetings were not merely quaint observations of religious traditions gone by but rather a place for genuine religious expression. Daniel Payne was shocked by "a singing and clapping ring" he witnessed at a bush meeting that same year. At Payne's urging the pastor in charge went and stopped their dancing, but they "remained singing and rocking their bodies to and fro," which "they did for about fifteen minutes." Still unsettled, Payne "then went, and taking their leader by the arm requested him to desist and to sit down and sing in a rational manner." The people then "broke up their ring; but would not sit down, and walked sullenly away." The music leader was bold enough to counter Payne and promote the manner of singing at bush meetings telling him, "The Spirit of God works upon people in different ways." In 1888 Payne was still complaining about the continuance of bush meetings among AME members.[93] While Bethel's pastors might be able to keep their leaders from contributing to bush meetings in an official capacity, they could not keep the meetings from being held or their members from participating.

FINANCIAL CONTROL AS RESISTANCE

Later records indicate that even with the changes made to Bethel's official services in the 1870s, bubbles of opposition still popped up until at least the turn of the century. In 1881, Handy's daughter was the church organist. At a board meeting, Handy raised the issue of his daughter's pay being $2.00 short, although she had obtained "the consent of a majority of the Board of Trustees" to be gone one Sunday and should have been paid while away. After discussion, it was revealed that Miss Handy "had not received consent of a majority of the Board" to be absent. According to the secretary, "considerable time was devoted to the discussion," and in the end, Miss Handy was not paid.[94] Though subtle, it hardly seems insignificant that the trustees took this opportunity to demonstrate their authority over Miss Handy, the pastor's daughter. In another instance James Dungee, the choir leader in 1891, moved the organ to accommodate a special service or concert. That week, the trustees agreed that Dungee should "be informed that the next time he wants something done that he first get the approval of the trustees."[95] When James Davage the chorister sent a "communication" to the board in 1897 requesting monthly compensation, it was "opposed vigorously" by Nimrod Westcott, one of the oldest and longest standing members of the board. The position of leading the choir had always been a volunteer role, and much of the board wanted to keep it that way. Ultimately, the board refused to put Davage on salary.[96] These episodes may seem inconsequential, yet other than issues related to church property, the trustees' records rarely demonstrated any real assertion of power over others—only in the case of the church's musical activities.

As much as Bethel's pastors wanted their well-known church to exemplify the elevated and suitable music they felt would dignify their people, in 1901 the congregation and choir were still singing by ear rather than by note. Although in the 1870s the pastors bolstered the choir and encouraged the use of hymnbooks for hymn singing, their efforts created more of a façade than an actual change. Apparently so few members owned hymnals that all singing was left to the choir, with members following along as they could. In January 1901, "the condition of the choir came before the board," and a committee of three trustees was formed to "make such recommendations to the board as would add to the improvement of the choir."[97] The committee proposed "the continuation of a Choir and not [for] the introduction of congregational singing exclusively." They further recommended a "reorganization of the choir with a combination Leader who can play the Organ, Instruct and Lead." If this was not possible and the choir was discontinued, the trustees would "be required to place racks on the back of the benches and supply the church with books for singing purposes."[98] Charles Dungee, Bethel's organist of several years, made application for the new combined position and was offered a contract stating that, among other things, he was "to teach the art of Music to the members of the choir, beginning with the rudimentary principles so that every member of the choir be trained to sing strictly by notes."[99] A year after Dungee took the position, he was the subject of discussion at the trustees' February meeting, as some felt "it has been evident that the progress of the choir has not been satisfactory." According to the pastor, Dungee violated the contract because he had not reorganized the choir or taught them music. Dungee was released as choir leader but remained as organist until his death many years later.[100] Even in the late 1930s Bethel was paying Dungee's widow a small pension.[101] Whether Dungee refused to follow the contract or whether he simply lacked the skills needed to fill the order, he managed to avert the push for note reading and stay the course with whatever the music and worship norm was. Despite his failure to honor the terms of his agreement, Dungee continued at Bethel, where he evidently was appreciated and well loved.

Bethel's people created and perpetuated religious music that survived even the most rigorous attempts of AME pastors to eradicate it. While submitting to the authority of their pastor, church leaders and musicians found ways to stifle and at times ignore mandates to continue with their traditional forms of worship. They discovered alternative ways to maintain their spiritual identities and dignity within the boundaries of the AME church, using it as a space to practice citizenship and democratic governance. Even where the church's worship was reformed, it was infused with the genuine character and reality of Bethel's members and their experiences. Bethel's pastors held power over their members, and several were not afraid to threaten, coerce, or browbeat those under them to shape a model church in which AME notions about music and worship could be on display. They were often disappointed. Great numbers of Bethel's members had the wherewithal to pursue their longings and break free from repressive forces within their own church; they developed imaginative options and practiced asserting their rights to free bodies and free expression as they organized themselves within a useful, though sometimes restrictive system.

Chapter Three

EDUCATION, EMPOWERMENT, AND ESSENTIAL MUSIC IN THE FIRST FREEDOM SCHOOLS

The Case of Zoar Methodist Episcopal Church, Philadelphia

On April 24, 1870, pedestrians turned off Brown Street, opened the short, black, wrought iron gate, and moved their way into the narrow three-story red brick building that was Zoar ME Church to attend the twenty-eighth anniversary commemoration of the founding of their Sabbath school. Men with muttonchops and waistcoats, women and children in their bonnets and bows—they surely entered a festive scene. Nestled between C. W. Kramer's Light Carriage and Wagon Factory and a livery stable, the modest but sturdy church, built in 1833, was alive with enthusiasm for this commemorative service. An organ "commensurate with the building" stood before attendees as they entered the wooden-floored sanctuary.[1] The ladies' circles made bunting, most certainly lined with trimmings purchased from the Black female business owners Hannah W. Mead and Amelia E. Mills of Mead & Mills Dry Goods, which they hung liberally about the room. This was purely a celebration of Black culture and accomplishment.

So much feeling was behind this event, as indicated by the preparations, including the three and a half by five–inch, eight-page pamphlet created to accompany the service. The church's Sabbath school concert was far more than a celebration of moral training; it was a celebration of Black resistance to greater society's denial of their right to education. Zoar's Sabbath school, like so many

Zoar ME Church, built 1838. Original watercolor "For Sale" advertisement, 1884. Courtesy of the Library Company of Philadelphia.

African American Sabbath schools, was the imminent training ground for African Americans learning to read. It was also a space for formerly enslaved and free adults to learn and utilize skills and tools of governance, business, and leadership. Notably, these values and accomplishments were commemorated through a service of songs—songs embedded with symbolic meaning.

This case study portrays an African American congregation that uniquely minimized class stratification and the internalized racism of uplift ideology. The story of Zoar ME Church also demonstrates how some African American congregations played out various forms of resistance while nonetheless maintaining ties with a white-led denomination. Through negotiated meanings and subversive tactics, Zoar's members fought racism and achieved their goals by using resources available through their denomination and mainstream culture. They artfully wielded the musical learning methods available in the MEC's Sunday school materials and the popular gospel songs of the day for this purpose. How they sang and ritualized their accomplishment was an authentic expression of Blackness.

HOW IT STARTED

The well-told story of how Absalom Jones and Richard Allen led a group of African Americans out of St. George's ME Church in Philadelphia sometime around 1787[2] and went on to form a new and separate African American denomination generally omits the account of the small group who did not agree with their decision to leave, so stayed behind. Although they opted to stay in connection with St. George's, this group organized for separate Sunday worship under the auspices of a mission church known as Zoar. It bears significant weight that when Zoar's members officially named their church they called it African Zoar Methodist Episcopal Church to reflect their self-conscious identification with Africa[3] and Zoar,[4] after the city Lot fled to when God destroyed Sodom and Gomorrah. The deliberateness of this choice should not be overlooked.

Zoar's members reacted in the same manner as the followers of Allen and Jones—by pulling away from the white congregation to meet on their own though still under the umbrella of St. George's and the Philadelphia ME Conference. Little attention has been given to their history because no new movement was formed and, frankly, because its early records and activities were intertwined with a white church that deemed it insignificant.[5] As "the oldest continuing Black United Methodist church in the United States," their decision to stay within the borders of the MEC cost them the respect of some of their Black Methodist peers and made them vulnerable to the charge that they willingly subjugated themselves to whites.[6]

A deeper look reveals that Zoar's members were advocates for change and maintained a clear Black consciousness. On May 9, 1822, Robert Green,[7] a member of Zoar known for accessing his legal rights in court, wrote a letter to the MEC bishops and conference stating, "That after being a member of Methodist Society upwards of thirty years and a Trustee a[nd] member of Zoar Church and after applying to Conference for the liberty of Transacting our own Temporal business in Zoar Church which they readily granted to us 21st May 1821, I was fully disowned by Mr. James Smith. I lay this before [you] for your consideration."[8] The record is unclear as to how Green's case was resolved, but it is known that this same James Smith, a white proslavery minister from Virginia who played a key role in the agitation with Richard Allen and Bethel's separation from the MEC,

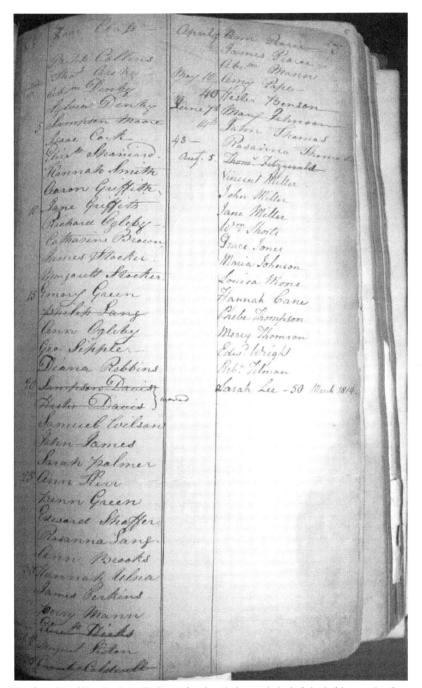

List of members of "Zoar Class," 1818. This list was found upside down at the back of a book of class members from St. George's MEC for the same year. Courtesy of Historic St. George's Museum & Archives, Philadelphia.

was expelled from ministry in 1839,[9] quite likely for his indiscreet heavy-handedness with African Americans. Members of Zoar, people like Green, were not passive in their relationship with the MEC and asserted their right to call out racism and govern themselves. They separated for worship, but they maintained their connection with the MEC, believing God would use them as agents of reform from within. Zoar's members were firmly tied to their American Methodist heritage, which began as an egalitarian movement, initially opposed slavery, cultivated lay leaders, and ministered to social needs. They refused to abandon the communal identity and spiritual memory Methodism had helped them foster.

Early on, members of Zoar were active in providing service to the Black community and in voicing the rights of Black Americans. Zoar's stewards' records are exceptional in that they are filled with a noticeably large number of instances in which the stewards gave money or material goods to those who needed them. They were expedient in sharing money from the "poor fund" with a brother or sister in dire circumstances,[10] formed committees to "raise provision groceries, or monies" or provide "a suit of clothes and a good Christmas dinner" for those in need,[11] allowed members from other churches "to stand inside of the church and ask alms from the congregation as they passed"[12] and set aside certain days "to collect money for the yellow fever sufferers in the South"[13] or "to give a dinner for the aged members on Thanksgiving Day."[14] As early as 1826, Zoar organized two mutual aid societies for the benefit of their community: Beneficial Philanthropic Sons of Zoar and the Female Beneficial Philanthropic Society of Zoar.[15] Perhaps most telling is Zoar's connection with the Underground Railroad, which commenced in 1838.[16] Consistent with their history, in the years following the Civil War when southern migrants were flooding Philadelphia, the members of Zoar molded their ministry to meet the needs of the Black community.

Located in Philadelphia, Zoar rose as a prominent Black church in the heart of the Black community well before emancipation brought masses of migrants to their doors. They had a pedigree similar to their Bethel peers', but into the 1870s and '80s, they managed a more moderate worship style than neighboring Bethel AME and others under the influence of Daniel Payne (now an AME bishop) and his musical reforms among African American churches. Zoar created a cultural space in Philadelphia where the formerly enslaved felt greater acceptance and a sense of belonging. By choosing music that rallied all members and by relaxing middle-class concerns about "elevating the race" through a cultivated European musical tradition, the church negotiated a broader sense of unity and equalized their mutual desires for education, community, and meaningful worship. Rather than scorning what some educated Black people deemed the lowbrow tastes of their southern-born members, leadership at Zoar focused on musical common ground, and the migrants who joined them expressed comfort and ownership in their worship.

MUSIC AND WORSHIP CULTURE AT ZOAR

Zoar's musical activities bring to light how Zoar's people fashioned a religious life that was uniquely theirs even when they followed typical MEC formats and musical choices for public services. Unlike some Black churches from this period, there is no indication that Zoar suffered dissension over what kind of songs to sing or how they were sung. As W. C. Dickerson wrote in his "History of Zoar Methodist Episcopal Church. No. 7" at the end of his pastoral appointment in 1879, "I leave 317 full members and not a Jordon strain[17] amongst them."[18] This apparent peacefulness over music in public worship and the use of the MEC hymnal does not mean that these African American were trying to be like whites or that little that was African survived in their music making. In fact, these congregants first began meeting separately from the white members of St. George's so they might "sing, pray, and worship with a sense of free participation and unhampered expression."[19]

Many of the songs and hymns Zoar chose for worship were birthed in the First and Second Great Awakenings; they are the same living documents the enslaved absorbed and drew from as they created the spirituals. The Methodist and Baptist movements and music of this era activated the religious imaginations and converged with the realities of both free and enslaved African Americans and inspired them to embrace Christianity in ways they had not previously. In the words of Richard Allen, "The Methodists were the first people that brought glad tidings to the coloured people. I feel thankful that ever I heard a Methodist preach. We are beholden to the Methodists, under God, for the light of the Gospel we enjoy."[20] African American Methodists considered the songs of the movement their cultural possession.

In 1801, Allen published his *Spiritual Songs and Hymns* in Philadelphia, and it was very likely used at Zoar. It reflected the priorities and preferences of African Americans and included items like "wandering refrains" and other musical devices supportive of an African-infused worship style that encouraged freedom and informality in services. The complaints of Philadelphian white Methodist leaders confirm that African Americans worshipped in their own way. John Fanning Watson ranted, "We have too, a growing evil, in the practice of singing in our places of public and society worship, *merry* airs, adapted from old *songs*, to hymns of our composing: often miserable as poetry, and senseless as matter. . . . Most frequently [these hymns are] composed and first sung by the illiterate *Blacks* of the society."[21] Once they separated from St. George's, Zoar's members freely embraced the right to express themselves in worship. Though they were supplied with white ministers by the MEC, those ministers often did not attend services and left the preaching and flow of worship to Black lay preachers. Jeffrey Beulah and the well-known Harry Hoosier who traveled and preached with Francis Asbury are among some of Zoar's earliest Black leaders.[22]

In keeping with the tradition of choosing songs in line with African American spirituality and ideology, Zoar's members sang hymns like "A Charge to Keep I Have," "Oh! For a Heart to Praise My God,"[23] "How Firm a Foundation," and "All Hail the Power of Jesus' Name."[24] These were familiar hymns to all Methodists, but for Zoar's members, they were expressions of the religious life they and their forebears deliberately chose in America. The sound of Zoar's singing and worship has not been preserved, but several accounts give insight into its emotive quality and clarify why these African Americans were eager to worship separately from white people. At least until 1820, Black churchgoers in Philadelphia were incorporating improvisational singing, bodily movement, moaning, and shouting in their services. Even in 1888, J. C. Smith, the secretary of Zoar's official board, recounted how the "steering" emotion of the most recent worship service affected those present "like the precious ointment upon the head that ran down upon the beard, even Aaron's beard that went down to the skirts of his garment to our souls."[25]

Many of the hymns favored by Black Methodists provided kinship and unity language to a race shaping a collective identity. On September 17, 1888, in a special service devoted to Zoar's history, "Are We Yet Alive and See Each Other's Face," and "God Be with Us Till We Meet Again" were sung. "Are We Yet Alive," written by Charles Wesley, was a favorite hymn at Zoar:

> And are we yet alive,
> and see each other's face?
> Glory and thanks to Jesus give
> for his almighty grace!
>
> What troubles have we seen,
> what mighty conflicts past,
> fightings without, and fears within,
> since we assembled last!

> Yet out of all the Lord
> hath brought us by his love;
> and still he doth his help afford,
> and hides our life above.

In "God Be with Us," the singers sang to each other:

> God be with you till we meet again;
> Neath his wings securely hide you,
> Daily manna still provide you:
> God be with you till we meet again.
>
> Refrain:
> Till we meet, till we meet,
> Till we meet at Jesus' feet;
> Till we meet, till we meet,
> God be with you till we meet again.
>
> God be with you till we meet again;
> When life's perils thick confound you,
> Put his arms unfailing round you:
> God be with you till we meet again.
>
> God be with you till we meet again;
> Keep love's banner floating o'er you,
> Smite death's threatening wave before you:
> God be with you till we meet again.[26]

These hymns gave voice to the practical realities of African Americans living in Philadelphia, especially through the 1870s and 1880s; threatened by racism and violence in civil and social affairs, words like "Are we yet alive?" were vivid and real. Faced with unjust work conditions, meager living conditions, and fears related to daily survival and the quest for "daily manna," Zoar's members found strength in the communal emphasis of hymns that reinforced that they were not alone but part of a larger body.

To accompany congregational singing, Zoar had an organ and choir at least by the late 1860s, and it is known that instrumental music, probably for a small orchestra, was purchased for Christmas services in 1887.[27] An organ was a badge of honor, and like most established Black churches of the era, Zoar made regular payments to cover the cost of acquiring this instrument of function and prestige. Little record survives of the choir's activities; however, it participated regularly in Zoar's Sunday morning services throughout the second half of the nineteenth century and occasionally led in worship at the Delaware Annual Conference of Colored Churches (MEC) as in 1886, when "Anniversary services were opened with singing hymn 930, by Zoar M. E. Choir."[28] Sometime around 1890 members of Zoar formed the Allen Chapel Choir, most assuredly in honor of Richard Allen.[29]

In time, the Black MEC congregations of the area, including Zoar, organized separately as the Delaware Conference, still under the umbrella of the MEC.[30] Their records provide insight into conversations some Black ministers had on the expressive and spontaneous style of worship practiced by many African Americans. In the 1850s the conference began attempts to reshape music and worship practices they saw as "disgraceful to themselves, the race, and the Christian name."[31] Bethel AME was by then a strong model in Philadelphia for free Black church worship, whose ministers promoted hymnals for each singer or family, singing strictly by note, choral and instrumental leadership, choral anthems and other "sacred solos," and the elimination of extemporaneous bodily movement, singing, and shouting.

Still, broad generalizations about pastoral control and middle-class agendas cloud the fact that each church took a unique stance and developed its own "worship personality" depending on the interpretations of its leaders and the agency of its people. Even Payne had to admit, "I have been strongly censured because of my efforts to change the mode of worship or modify the extravagances indulged in by the people."[32] Though he was probably successful in influencing the development of a more "orderly" and structured style of worship as the norm for mainline Black churches in Philadelphia in the 1860s, it is clear that the emotive and demonstrative singing style many African Americans preferred was never eradicated.

When migrants began moving North during the 1870s and joined Zoar's congregation, latent tendencies resurfaced. The Delaware Conference complained of "excesses and extravagances." These were perhaps kept out of the sanctuary before emancipation, but they nonetheless survived in private meetings or fringe churches. Even in 1899 Du Bois could write, "There are . . . continually springing up and dying a host of little noisy missions which represent the older and more demonstrative worship."[33] In 1878, somewhere near Philadelphia, Payne attended a "bush meeting," where he "went to please the pastor" whose circuit he was visiting. According to Payne, "After the sermon they formed a ring, and with coats off sung, clapped their hands and stamped their feet in a most ridiculous and heathenish way."[34] Notably, this event was sanctioned and encouraged by a pastor.

In 1875, the Delaware Conference Committee on Public Worship gave an address on congregational singing and the "Mode of Worship" in their churches. The committee stated:

> Whereas, an occasional remark has been thrown out in the proceedings of this conference, intimating the importance of improving our mode of worship, and Whereas, This thought is one which may not be passed over lightly, as singing is a part of divine worship, therefore, to guard against formality in singing we offer for your adoption the following resolutions:
> Resolved 1st, That every minister having a charge, shall read the form of the discipline on the spirit and truth of singing on page 44 section 11
> Resolved 2nd that each minister shall preach sermons on the proper mode of worship
> Resolved 3rd That each Presiding Elder shall inquire in the Quarterly Conference whether the preacher has faithfully discharged this part of his duty.[35]

The committee's use of the term "mode of worship" makes plain they were addressing an Africanized worship style. During this period some white church leaders also complained about changes in worship, but their protests centered on the shift from freer worship forms to more structured forms.[36] African American leaders, however, often used the term "mode of worship" to refer to African sensibilities in religious music; this use may have been initiated by Payne, who often referred to the "ignorant mode of worship" practiced by the "masses" when describing ring shouts and other forms of slave-style worship, but it was repeated over and over by various Black church leaders.[37]

"Formality in singing" was a phrase used by John Wesley, who was "greatly disgusted at the manner of singing" while visiting a parish in Neath. The people singing "repeated the same words, contrary to all sense or reason, six, or eight or ten times over," and "different persons sung different words at one and the same moment."[38] Holding to their Methodist heritage as an interpretive tool, the Delaware Conference leaders used Wesley's term found in the MEC Discipline to discuss how to teach members to sing in "spirit and truth," particularly in light of southern influences in congregational singing as migrants filled their churches in the 1870s. At the Delaware Annual Conference in 1880, a "Report of the Special Committee on the State of the Church" was given to address this issue: "In accordance with the intellectual growth of our people, we advocate the giving of judicious instruction by precept and example, as to the mode of worship among our people, discountenancing the many extravagances and exces[s]es that have crept in within the past ten years."[39] This comment demonstrates the position many Black ministers took linking education with reserved expression in worship, yet historical record shows this belief was held with ambivalence.

Zoar was a place where various attitudes and ideas about race and racial needs coexisted and commingled; exploring Zoar's worship life makes it clear that conclusions drawn strictly from what the Delaware Conference discussed should be done cautiously. The tension between structured worship and a freer, more expressive worship style implicit in the religious life of Zoar's people gives a taste of the "double consciousness" African American Methodists in nineteenth-century Philadelphia experienced—the "two-ness," Du Bois spoke of when he claimed, "two souls, two thoughts, two unreconciled strivings; two warring ideals in one dark body."[40] Zoar's members were Methodists and part of the white-led MEC connection. Further, they were Black Philadelphians who were part of an urban, northern Black tradition rooted in the teaching of key African American leaders like Daniel Payne and influenced by their close Bethel peers, who believed racial uplift was dependent upon acceptance of the dominant culture's standards of "respectability."[41] But Zoar's heritage was built on Black freedom of expression and the choice to adhere to a religion they found authentic as African Americans. Zoar's people were neither passive members of their denomination nor mere imitators of white churches. They saw their position as a negotiated one—one they chose.

GOSPEL SONGS—THE KEY TO MUTUALITY

In the 1870s and '80s, when tension over musical preference and, ultimately, community identity was mounting, "gospel praise songs" entered the scene and served to align the interests of both those who wanted to "uplift" the race and those who wanted to worship in a genuine and enthusiastic way. When the Delaware Conference ministers tried to reform congregational singing in the late 1870s and early 1880s, member participation waned. Sunday services lacked vitality until the mid-1880s, when gospel hymnody began to enter the Sunday school and eventually Sunday services. This type of music popularized by the Moody and Sankey revivals of the period was emotional, evangelistic, and easy to sing and remember. Gospel songs met the approval of the Black MEC ministers, and in 1885, H. A. Monroe, the pastor of Zion ME Church in Wilmington, Delaware, told the Delaware Conference, "Gospel Praise meetings have been held monthly. The result has been increased attendance at all the other meetings a swell great improvement in the singing, the joining of Church and Sabbath School is in closer union and a deeper spiritual power upon the congregation."[42]

As gospel songs gained in popularity, they began being used for Sunday morning services. In 1889 J. H. Johnson, presiding elder for the Dover District, enthusiastically spoke of the usefulness of gospel songs, saying, "The songs of the Sunday School have found their way into the Sabbath Sanctuary, and have given new life and vigor to the songs of worship in the church." Advocating the evangelistic power of such songs, Johnson stated:

> The songs of the Sabbath School are a power in the conversion of souls. The sweet strains of the "Ninety and nine," have called back so many lost souls wandering afar off in the desert wilderness of sin. The lips of our little ones ringing out the bold strains of "Hold the Fort," have given fresh courage to many a doubting, despairing child of God, while the sweeter melody, "What a Friend We Have in Jesus" has been a God given message of comfort to many a sad, weary friendless heart.[43]

On September 17 the same year, evidently encouraged by the prospect of invigorating their Sunday worship, Zoar paid $2.50 "for Gospel Songs."[44]

Formerly enslaved Charlotte Brooks was greatly affected by a gospel song she heard called "All the Way My Savior Leads Me," written by Fanny Crosby in 1875.[45] Charlotte reported:

> Ever since I came to town I never miss going to church; and the other Sunday morning I went into the Sunday-school before church began, and I heard the children sing something like this: "All the way my Saviour leads me." And when them children sang that it filled my eyes with tears, for I just thought how good the Lord had been to me. He had brought me through so much hardship, and I said, "Here I am, Lord, blest to sit down and hear singing and preaching." It was the first time I had ever heard that hymn, and I thought it was so sweet to my soul.[46]

She heard the lyrics:

> All the way my Saviour leads me;
> What have I to ask beside?
> Can I doubt his tender mercy,
> Who through life has been my guide?

> Heavenly peace, divinest comfort,
> Here by faith in him I dwell!
> For I know whate'er befall me,
> Jesus doeth all things well.
>
> All the way my Saviour leads me;
> Cheers each winding path I tread;
> Gives me grace for every trial;
> Feeds me with the living bread;
> Though my weary steps may falter,
> And my soul athirst may be,
> Gushing from the Rock before me,
> Lo! a spring of joy I see.

Charlotte explained the meaning this song spoke into her everyday life:

> O, bless the Lord for the chance of hearing those words! They suit my case. I want to sing that very hymn in glory. Yes, "Jesus led me all the way." Sometimes I don't know where I'll get a piece of bread when I get up in the morning, but still I'm living and praising God. We poor old colored people were turned off the plantations without any thing in this world to go on—turned out like in the woods. Mrs. B.—promised me last week if I'd come around and wash dishes for her every day she would give me the scraps she had left always at meals. I thank the Lord for that much. I don't need much in this world, no how—just enough to keep soul and body together. I know I can't stay here much longer, I don't want nothing in this world. If I can just get a little coffee every morning and a piece of bread I am satisfied.[47]

Gospel songs were appealing because they could easily be personalized; very often they were written in first-person language, as in "for I know whate'er befall me, Jesus doeth all things well." Although Zoar incorporated gospel songs into their worship that were often written by white people, its crucial to understand, as James Cone taught, "Black people did not unquestioningly adopt the white interpretation of scriptural language. Rather, they invested scriptural language with the meaning that was consistent with their struggle to affirm themselves as people, their identity, and their freedom."[48] African Americans found gospel praise songs a means for voicing their experience as they entered urban life in the Reconstruction era. For them, these songs had a personal message with liberating power.

Gospel praise songs had the same effect in white churches as they did African American churches: they invigorated Sunday morning worship. But on a deeper plane, at least at Zoar, they united Black church leaders with their people and served as a sort of compromise. The rousing, singable gospel song, with its simple repeated chorus and hopeful message, was a musical form the pastors and various members of Black MEC churches like Zoar agreed on. It was structured, printed, and theologically sanctioned, but it was also rhythmic, repetitive, and emotional. Wyatt Walker called the gospel praise song "a transitional form that bridged the slavery and Reconstruction periods."[49] This agreement over music and worship style had a unifying effect that allowed the Zoar community to move past differences and strengthen its collective identity.

THE MEANING BEHIND THE SABBATH SCHOOL SERVICE

To understand the emotional power and practical significance of the Sabbath School Anniversary Celebration service described at the opening of this chapter, it is necessary to unpack some of how the Sabbath school operated, was seen, and was valued by members of Zoar and how Zoar's members filtered MEC Sabbath school resources through a race-conscious sieve, reappropriating them to service the needs of the African American community. Through its accessible music and graduated system of learning tailored to meet each student at his or her own level of progress, the Sunday school drew Zoar's people together, regardless of class, literary skill, or cultural background. Songs and musical training were an integral part of both their educational process and their cultural negotiation.

When Zoar set up its Sunday school in 1842, only five years after they became a fully independent church, they established what they saw as the primary agency for teaching their children skills needed for their "elevation." This included reading skills but also "decency, honesty and industry and above all the great and all important duty of the salvation of the[ir] souls."[50] For this purpose, they were "convinced of the importance of the Sunday School as a great reforming and Christianizing agency, and an indispensable auxiliary to the Church."[51] Certainly white churches of the era placed great value on the Sunday school; however, unlike their African American peers, white children were not denied access to public schools. From the time they were organized, Black churches run by free Black people always saw the church, the center of Black community life, as the place to educate their members. In his social study *The Philadelphia Negro*, Du Bois explained,

"The Negro churches were the birthplaces of Negro schools and of all agencies which seek to promote the intelligence of the masses."[52] One of their primary concerns was teaching people, and especially children, to read. The Committee on Education told the Delaware Conference in 1866, "We regard the higher attainments of literature to be of such paramount importance to our youths and the disciples of the Gospel, that we will do all in our power to aid this cause, for without it our race, must forever remain in ignorance and go to destruction.... The instruction and elevation of the youth depends on their education in a great measure."[53] Combining their evangelical heritage with "uplift" ideology, Black leaders at churches like Zoar believed that to increase moral capital, their members needed to be able to read the Bible independently. Ideas about moral and intellectual development were tightly entwined, so church leaders put great stock in literacy.

Undergirding this postemancipation impulse toward education was the powerful motivation to read inherited from an African value system "established in Islamic Africa and in areas touched by Christianity," where literacy was prized "as a means of acquiring the knowledge stored in books."[54] Thomas L. Johnson, a slave who became a Baptist minister after slavery, remembered his mother "would talk of Africa" and the freedom Black people had there before they were stolen and sold into slavery. He reminisced, "My mother's heartfelt desire seems to have been that I should be taught to read and write; and no opportunity was lost in trying to inspire me to look forward to freedom and an education."[55] Most African Americans were eager to read; during slavery many were forbidden from reading and writing, so understandably, these skills were esteemed as a privilege of freedom. As Mary James, an ex-slave from Virginia put it, "No one was taught to read or write. There was no church on the farm. No one was allowed to read the Bible or anything else."[56]

The Delaware Conference, including Zoar's leaders, held to the conviction they were directly responsible for "the great and important worth of evangelizing and instructing millions of fellow beings, a majority of whom have here to fore been deprived of an intelligent knowledge of the revelation of the Gospel of the Savior." They felt "the duty of ministry" was "not only the spiritual but also the temporal well-being of our People to recognize, sustain, and extend the principals of a liberal and practical education among the masses."[57] In the years that followed the Civil War, they would unequivocally state, "Education is of the most essential entity for the elevation and salvation of our people, both in this world and in that which is to come."[58] At Zoar, like most nineteenth-century Black churches, the Sunday school was the primary means for educating members of their community.

As the 1870s progressed into the 1880s, education was increasingly connected with the national good of African people and the continuation of freedom. In 1880, Zoar's presiding elder told the conference, a "persistent effort is being made in some churches to awaken a more national taste for useful knowledge.... Our people are grasping after education."[59] A year earlier, the Committee on Education stated plainly, "The education of our people is absolutely essential to the maintenance of our national freedom."[60] Freedom was to be enjoyed, but it came with great responsibility. J. H. Johnson explained:

> Education prepares a citizen to appreciate the rights and privileges of a free government and also qualifies them to perform the duties, responsibilities and obligations resting upon them. Intelligence and morality are towers of strength while ignorance is a source of weakness and danger and tends to idleness and viciousness. In an important sense the future of our republican institution is to be largely determined by the colored race numbering over seven million.[61]

Clearly describing a race-conscious objective, Zoar's ministers and church educators encouraged members to press on in their "efforts to educate themselves and children, striving to rise in the scale of being so as to be useful in Their day and to leave their work as monuments for future generations."[62] So, then, the Sunday school was more than a place for learning Bible stories; it was the most likely place an African American child, and even adult, would learn to read. It was the supreme device for molding moral character, and it was a powerful tool for promoting racial identity and a collective purpose.

Zoar's Sunday school was well established by the time it held its celebration in 1870. At the Colored Annual Conference of the MEC in 1863, Zoar's Sabbath school boasted it had "14 teachers, 84 Scholars, [and] 400 Volumes."[63] Books were an important acquisition for Sunday schools. Mifflin Wistar Gibbs— a "fatherless boy," "carpenter and contractor," "railroad builder," "attorney-at-law," "municipal judge," "consul to Madagascar," and Black Methodist— recorded, "It has been said that the true university of our days is a collection of books."[64] According to Isaiah Broughton, Zoar's pastor and a local preacher, Zoar was "in a very flourishing condition" at this time, with "173 members and 12 probationers."[65] As southerners made their way to Philadelphia in the 1870s and 1880s, Zoar's membership grew at a significant rate, increasing the size of the Sabbath school as well. By 1870, the year of the twenty-eighth Sabbath school celebration, they had grown to "195 members and 28 probationers," with "16 Officers and Teachers" and "128 Scholars" in the Sunday school.[66] These numbers continued to climb over the next fifteen years.

To organize such an entity, particularly one with such high aims, the proper materials, tools, and training were needed. Despite being created by their white-led denomination, Zoar found MEC Sunday school materials beneficial to their purpose. Church records indicate that by the 1870s Zoar was using a uniform lesson system developed by John Heyl Vincent for the Methodists called Berean Lessons.[67] These lessons "were predicated on the assumption that students would remain in school for many years, that they would grow gradually in religious knowledge, and that conversion would be a minor aspect of the overall experience."[68] This type of lesson ushered in a new style of teaching to Sunday schools in the 1870s, leading to what has been called the "second birth" of the Sunday school movement.[69]

Perfectly timed for Black churches like Zoar, whose classrooms now included recent migrants from the South, these lessons utilized the techniques of Johann Heinrich Pestalozzi, who advocated a teaching style that was nurturing, required students to participate actively and learn through the senses, and began with the simple elements of a subject before progressing to abstract concepts. His method has been called, "the education of the people as people, an education reaching all classes."[70] Pestalozzi emphasized early childhood learning and believed women, with their thoughtful insight and ability to nurture, were natural educators. This idea coincided well with an Africanized Christianity descended from traditional African religion, which Frey and Wood stress, "accorded greater recognition to the mystical power of women" and maintained that women's "special inspiration qualified them for various leadership positions."[71] African American educator and poet Olivia A. Davidson, later Olivia Davidson Washington, who founded Tuskegee Institute with her husband Booker T. Washington, called the schoolroom the site of "intellectual emancipation." She echoed Pestalozzi's convictions in a speech titled, "How Shall We Make the Women of Our Race Stronger?" Davidson urged teachers to especially single out girls in their classrooms, ascertain their individual capacities for learning, and then "train their mental powers." If a teacher was not equipped to do this, Davidson told them, "Pestalozzi and many others have in their writings made the way so plain that no earnest seeker can greatly err in finding it."[72]

For an oral culture, a teaching method founded on sensory experience was ideal. Learning through singing was an important aspect of Pestalozzi's method, one that Vincent readily incorporated into the Berean Lessons. In Sunday school, music was used to engage students and balance out the literary and cognitive aspects of learning. Lowell Mason, the well-known musicologist and hymnist, explained the merits of Pestalozzi's use of music and how it changed the face of education:

Our systems of education generally proceed too much on the principle, that we are merely intellectual beings, not susceptible of emotions, or capable of happiness. The feelings may and ought to be cultivated in connection with the intellect. Before our race can be much improved, the principle that the human soul is all mind and no heart, must be discarded; and human beings must be treated as possessing feelings as well as intellects. The feelings are as much the subject of training as the mind; and our happiness depends more on the cultivation of the former than of the latter.[73]

This was nothing new to African Americans who believed a person's intellect, feelings, and experiences were inseparable. But to a people long treated as mere bodies without souls, the popularity of Pestalozzi's holistic method and its incorporation into the church's teaching was an affirmation of Black humanity. Music was used as a means for uniting Black feeling with learning. Practically speaking, Sunday school lessons alternated singing with other learning activities to both reinforce lessons and refresh the pupils. As one songbook put it, "Singing, when it can be properly introduced, forms an interesting addition to the other exercises, in whatever form they may be conducted."[74] Song lyrics were carefully written to emphasize "some important Scripture lesson or practical truth, which the Sabbath-school is designed to teach."[75] Often they were put to melodies "more or less familiar" so they could be "sung almost at sight, thus not losing the present *effect* of the song in *learning* the tune."[76] With Pestalozzi's method, teachers were never to "permit *dull, lifeless* singing," and students were urged to clap or make some other percussive movement with their body to internalize the beat of the music.[77] These musical practices in the Sunday school were in keeping with West African communal practices that carried religious beliefs into action through ritual and the use of sacred rhythm.

When uniform lessons were introduced, they set up a comprehensive educational program replete with resources to make learning attractive and enjoyable. The lessons and manner of teaching were flexible and allowed Zoar's Sunday school teachers to adapt them to the needs of their students. Students could develop reading skills through responsive readings of the lesson and recitations of the subject, topic, and text of the lesson. Another aspect of Vincent's lessons for the MEC were tools available to help teachers master the Pestalozzi technique, develop their teaching skills, and learn to use "blackboards, illustrations, objects, and music in teaching."[78] He developed a teacher-training course to be taught during the Sunday school hour and granted diplomas to those who completed it. Teachers could attend conventions to hone their skills and bolster their enthusiasm, could subscribe to magazines that "offered detailed instructions on how to teach Sunday school classes using the techniques borrowed from the new state teachers' colleges," and could access teaching guides, advice books, and newspapers.[79] In addition, students received leaflets with each week's lesson, which was published weekly in secular newspapers.[80]

The superintendent or director of the Sunday school was a position of honor generally reserved for a man known for his administrative skills in the business world. In 1870, William H. Thomas, Zoar's Sabbath school superintendent, served alongside some of the most well-known superintendents of the period: "Lewis Miller, the inventor and industrialist, John D. Rockefeller, the oil magnate, and John Wanamaker, the Philadelphia department store tycoon."[81] The MEC Sunday school movement of the 1870s offered a fountain of educational resources for aspiring African Americans developing skills as teachers and administrators in addition to learning to read. Further, it provided nearly endless opportunities for success, achievement, personal growth, and the development of self-confidence.

When Zoar held its Sabbath school celebration in 1870, it followed a popular program format provided in *The Sunday School Speaker* by J. Kennaday, published in Philadelphia by Perkinpine & Higgins, the same publishing house that published the minutes of the MEC Colored Annual Conferences.[82] The structure of the service, which alternated music with addresses, recitations, prayer, and reports, prioritized the role of singing at anniversaries and celebrations. Zoar's Sabbath school program followed Kennaday's suggestions nearly perfectly, except that it reduced the number of recitations to be given and eliminated the examination of the Bible class. The service was primarily musical, emphasizing the performance of Sunday school songs by various children's groups coupled with congregational singing from the hymnal. The decision to emphasize singing over the erudite aspects of the school's training demonstrates the teachers' sensitivity to those in attendance at the celebration. Singing was the best method for reinforcing the church's teachings and cultural values in a mixed crowd of readers and nonreaders who held African oral sensibilities within; Zoar's Sabbath school celebration, centered on children and the unifying power of music, was a magnificent means for growing a society of sharing and mutual respect.

From the 1820s and into the 1870s, the body of music later termed "gospel hymnody" began to appear in "collections designed for America's rapidly growing Sunday schools."[83] These songs were simple musically and textually and generally included a refrain that repeated a central idea to be easily learned.[84] Most often they were rousing, cheerful, and upbeat. By the 1870s, thousands

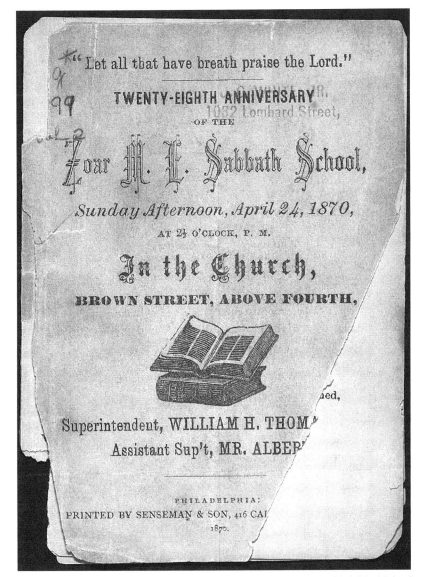

Cover of a rare, surviving Order of Worship. Twenty-Eighth Anniversary of the Zoar ME Sabbath School Order of Service, April 24, 1870. Collection of the Historical Society of Pennsylvania.

of Sunday school songs in various collections were available, and many times a gospel hymn was included in the weekly lesson leaflet. Pamela Helen Goodwin, a graduate of Oberlin College in 1868 and soon after a MEC Sunday school teacher, described "A Modern Sunday School in Session" in 1875.[85] According to her report, after roll call, "singing books are taken from desks without

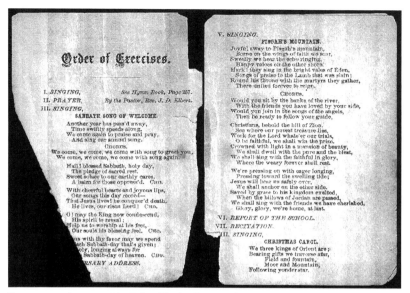

First two pages of a rare, surviving Order of Worship. Twenty-Eighth Anniversary of the Zoar ME Sabbath School Order of Service, April 24, 1870. Collection of the Historical Society of Pennsylvania.

confusion," and the students would sing for fifteen minutes before breaking into age-appropriate classes. Later, while the older groups were studying, the "Infant Department," made up of children from three to eight years, were "entertained and rested by singing, in which they [could] engage without disturbing the rest of the school."[86] All evidence indicates that at Zoar, this type of music was used as the primary means of attracting members of the community to the Sabbath school and engaging them in the educational process. The songs were easy to learn and could be sung by all, even those who could not read. Sunday school songs were well liked by the people who attended Black ME churches, so much so that the Delaware Conference believed "it desirable to bring the School and the Congregation into close sympathy by arranging for frequent attractive demonstrations in the School and by assigning to the children a part in the public worship of the church."[87]

A SIGNIFICANT CELEBRATION

The celebration program from Zoar's twenty-eighth anniversary of the Sabbath school gives concrete insight into how Zoar nurtured a culture of inclusion through singing. The songs of the service were new and mostly of the gospel song tradition, created for the full participation of student performers and congregation. Those who came were there to celebrate something of great meaning to them. The students welcomed the congregation by singing:

> We come, we come, we come with song to greet you,
> We come, we come, we come with song again.
> Hail! blessed Sabbath, holy day,
> The pledge of sacred rest.
> Sweet solace to our earthly cares,
> A balm for those oppress'd.

After an anniversary address, they continued by singing "Pisgah's Mountain" celebrating the place where God revealed the promised land.[88] Its second verse encouraged:

> Christians, behold the hill of Zion,
> See where our purest treasure lies,
> Work for the Lord whate'er our trials,
> O be faithful, we shall win the prize.
> Crowned with light in a mansion of beauty,
> We shall dwell with the pure and the blest,
> We shall sing with the faithful in glory,
> Where the weary forever shall rest.

It requires very little imagination to understand that nineteenth-century African Americans listened to and sang these lyrics with more than casual celebration in mind. By claiming a "balm for the oppress'd," agreeing to "work for the Lord whate'er our trials," and declaring a hopeful place where the "weary forever shall rest," these religious songs evoked and channeled real emotions around a shared Black existence. Zoar's community sang into a distinctively African American social space that upheld psychic resilience and defied greater society's dehumanizing strains.

This was more than singing for catharsis. A musical service such as this contained the power and location to help Zoar's members collectively negotiate what constituted Black accomplishment based on Black values and feeling. Borrowing from aesthetic theory, it is meaningful to note how art and music convey symbolic meaning and allow participants to act out great concepts through ritual events. As Susanne Langer explains, music "lacks one of the basic characteristics of language—fixed association. . . . We are always free to fill its subtle articulate forms with any meaning that fits them."[89] While church and

Sunday school leaders may have selected songs with lyrical content promoting certain ideals, the music held space for a variety of feelings and beliefs. Through musical creation, participation, and performance, these feelings and meanings melded and were encoded in song through the ritual of a worship service.

On the day of Zoar's celebration, various ideas, hopes, realizations, pressures, and changes mingled as a people united by color and African origin sought to decide what existence as free Americans would look like. They held varying ideas about education and religious space; all who found themselves within the walls of Zoar that April afternoon came with emotions and thoughts about these things. Through the interplay of music and song, participants expressed and exchanged feelings about life and ideas during what was a fluid period in African American history. Music gave them the means to explore these many undefined outlooks and sensations through community and with a collective purpose in mind.

After a report of the school, recitation, singing of "We Three Kings of Orient Are" (a popular contemporary song with a Resurrection ending), and another address, they sang "Our Mission Song," easily adapted to a call-and-response style of singing:

> Our hearts are very joyful in our Sunday-school today,
> Singing our mission song together;
> We'll never be discouraged but we'll labor while we may;
> Singing our mission song together.
> His gracious ear will listen while before his throne we bend
> Singing our mission song together.

The service included two more Sunday school songs, "Lord, Is It I?" and "O We Are Volunteers," a recitation, and a collection before continuing with

> Haste! Haste! Dearest mother, the school-bell is ringing,
> My teachers are waiting, and I should be there:
> To join, with my classmates in joyously singing,
> The praise of the Savior, to join in the prayer.

"The Children's Hosanna" was the next song and was probably sung by the youngest children:

> We are taught to love the Lord,
> We are taught to read his word,

> We are taught the way to heaven,
> Praise to God for all be given.

Here the discussion of music and symbol goes further when considering the ways education and religion are combined in these songs. In choosing these songs, Zoar's teachers and leaders put forth the connection between moral and cultural capital: if we can read, we can understand God and the Bible and, indeed, our lives as part of a grand cosmic scheme. The ideas are presented discursively through lyrics but were heard through music, notably, the voices of children. At most these songs were accompanied by simple organ accompaniment or, more likely, were delivered a cappella in the unison high notes of a child. The purity of sound no doubt had a poignant and lingering effect that easily facilitated the attachment of African American meanings and interpretations to these new symbolic forms.

Up to this point the service was standard MEC fare, including typical Sunday school songs.[90] At the end of the program, however, a shift in content is noticeable. As if to acknowledge to their guests the seriousness of life and its contrast to the happy hour just passed, the Sunday school teachers chose "Far beyond This World of Sorrow," a camp meeting and revival song "such as not to be found in the Church Hymn Book" published in Philadelphia just three years earlier.[91] Here the congregation sang into the deeply layered meanings of their complex existence:

> Far beyond this world of sorrow,
> Where the ransom'd millions rest,
> There's a glorious endless morrow,
> In the mansions of the blest.
>
> Shall we know them there,
> In that land, far away,
> They the same smile wear,
> In that land, far away,
> Shall we meet and know each other,
> In that happy land, far away.
>
> There 'neath bow'rs of deathless glory,
> Every heart with peace possess'd,
> Sweetly chant redemption's story,
> In the mansions of the blest.

> There are those we've loved and cherished
> Leaning on the Saviour's breast;
> They're at home—not dead or perished;
> In the mansions of the blest.
>
> Shall we love them still,
> In that land, far away,
> Where no partings chill,
> In that land, far away,
> Shall we meet and love each other,
> In that happy land, far away.
>
> Shall reunion's chain,
> In that land, far away,
> Hold our hearts again,
> In that land, far away,
> Shall we meet and love each other,
> In that happy land, far away!
>
> There the morn shall wake in gladness,
> There the night no fears infest,
> Neither sickness, pain nor sadness,
> In the mansions of the blest.
>
> Shall we meet thee there,
> In that land, far away,
> And its glories share,
> In that land, far away,
> Yes! Thro' [grace] we'll meet each other,
> In that happy land, far away.

Amid their swaying and murmur, Zoar's community conjured memory and connected to hope as they sang this song together. Lines like "Shall we know them there in that land far away?" and "They're at home—not dead or perished" were layered with meaning for Zoar's participants. The imagery of "shall reunion's chain hold our hearts again in that land far away?" must have had a powerful impact on a people only recently emancipated from the chains of slavery.

The hymn reflects two strongly African American priorities: an emphasis on eschatological language and the accentuation of ancestral ties. In West

African religion the spirits of ancestors are believed to hold significant power in the lives of their descendants and serve as what Albert Raboteau calls, the "watchful guardians of the customs of the people."[92] As he and others have established, early African American Christians may have continued a form of ancestral veneration, which they filtered through the lens of Christianity. The placement of "Far beyond This World of Sorrow" at the end of the Sabbath school program, then, takes on added significance when considering the importance ancestral ties held for members of the Zoar community. As they reached forward to form new familial ties with one another, they also reached behind to connect with loved ones no longer physically present. Sung in Black communities, the heavenly language of songs like this spoke transcendence into Black people's present existence.[93]

In an era of disjointed families and a shifting demography, Zoar's Sabbath school enabled community members to share the responsibility of socializing children and providing their education. Slavery shattered familial ties, and most nineteenth-century African Americans struggled against a racist society to establish family structure and cohesive bonds. In Philadelphia, members of Zoar assumed kinship roles with one another—a process that took time. Through the ritualized process of celebrating its twenty-eighth anniversary, the Zoar Sabbath school reinforced its abiding presence in the Black neighborhood. Long-standing members of Zoar welcomed southern migrants to their "family" and used the inviting songs of the Sunday school to promote race goals and speak of possibility.

Zoar's Sunday worship and its twenty-eighth Sabbath school anniversary celebration provide a rich look into Black religious life in border cities during the Reconstruction era. Analyzing how music and ritual were used to imbed values, race consciousness, and meaning into an evolving community identity makes it possible to trace a line of Black resistance and authentic Black expression further back into African American history and into a social space that at times is overlooked or dismissed as too influenced by white values or racialized identities.

The power behind this significant celebration is in the creativity and tenacity Zoar ME Church used to hold on to its very American Methodist identity, infused with true African cultural memory and values, while simultaneously developing new collective meanings. Zoar's members adjusted to their real-world situations, laden with racism and struggle, and resisted these by embracing the tools available for their own pleasure and purpose. Above all, this included an advantageous teaching method well fitted to an oral culture and an ever-growing body of songs they could select from and meld into symbols representing distinctly African American meanings.

Through singing, Zoar's members negotiated values, nurtured kinship, expressed various types of resistance, and channeled distinctive African cultural traits into an American religious space as they ritualized Black achievement. In this process, they confirmed their shared values of education and community. This very self-conscious process took place through the art of music.

Chapter Four

FINDING FREEDOM AND PERFORMING POWER

The Case of St. Luke's Protestant Episcopal Church, Washington, DC

On Monday evening, December 10, 1894, a reception was given for the Reverend Dr. Alexander Crummell at St. Luke's PE Church in Washington, DC, to celebrate the fiftieth anniversary of his ordination to the priesthood. Friends and parishioners crammed the pews of the gothic-style chapel, with its barrel arches reaching toward the sky, to hail "the oldest Negro Priest in America" by giving speeches, providing a "sumptuous" entertainment, and presenting gifts. The dim winter's eve downplayed the stained glass above Mrs. Annie J. Cooper[1] as she delivered an artful presentation address before the congregation and minister emphasizing the significance of Crummell's life and, even more, the "golden" character he demonstrated after years of frequent hardship and adversity. Candles flickered on the carved altarpiece behind her while she lamented to her audience and pastor, "As St. Luke's congregation accompanies you to the fiftieth milestone on your historic path, the feeling, I am sure in each heart today, as is in my own, is, would that we had loved you more! Would that we had lent more constantly the reinforcement of our sympathy and support during the struggle!"[2] Mrs. Cooper's words were addressed to a general audience, but they likely stirred poignant memories for members of the congregation well acquainted with

St. Luke's PE Church, built 1879. Courtesy St. Luke's PE Church, Washington, DC.

the bitter conflict Crummell had with the church's vestry and choir some twelve years earlier—a conflict that simmered for at least three years and lingered long after. The mounting conflict erupted when Crummell refused to let the choir sing the Magnificat at an Easter service in 1880 and culminated in the vestry's resolution to terminate their rector in 1882. After a long paper trail and subsequent trial, Bishop William Pinkney and the Standing Committee of the Diocese of Maryland upheld Crummell's position, which he retained until his retirement in 1894. In her address, Mrs. Cooper alluded to the difficult relationship between Crummell and the vestry when she suggested, "Few men can appreciate an altitude above their own plane of activity, or comprehend a depth beyond their own soundings."[3] It seems the vestrymen were some of the capital city's social climbers who, as Crummell put it, were part of "a clique . . . [of] clerks and messengers in [government] Departments" who "got themselves elected" in order "to rush in . . . and make St. Luke's the fashionable Church of the city."[4] Crummell was no respecter of these men's personal ambitions and rigidly held to what he deemed "the maintenance of righteousness . . . [and] to upholding the lame of Christ's Church."[5] Highly accomplished and fairly influential by the time he reached St. Luke's, Crummell consistently stood for the poor and marginalized and especially devoted himself to the training of African American leaders and the development of women. Apparently, Mrs. Cooper felt the faction against Crummell simply could not comprehend Crummell's aspirations for the race.

According to Mrs. Cooper, Crummell knew "that here are loyal hearts and true in this little band of St. Luke's, who will always love and cherish your character and example."[6] Some of these loyal band members signed a petition, some with only their mark, an X, sent to the bishop in 1882 protesting the vestry's actions against Crummell. Eventually, their support for Crummell overshadowed the vestry's power and influence. The conflict subsided at St. Luke's as pastor and people resolved their issues of self-conscious identity. At his retirement, St. Luke's was ready to give Crummell "relief from the engrossments of one congregation . . . [for] the larger work of the country."[7]

The events that transpired around music and worship at St. Luke's PE Church in Washington, DC, in the 1870s and 1880s are intriguing; they unfold much like a play, with several leading characters, a thickening plot, a theatrical climax, and perhaps even a bit of irony. In fact, St. Luke's interactions over music and worship played out so much like a dramatic piece it may be useful to turn to anthropologist Victor Turner's social drama model for meaningful analysis. Turner's model applies when an individual or members of a developing group create conflict either "deliberately or by inward compulsion, in a public setting." Turner explains that after this occurs:

> Conflicts between individuals, sections, and factions follow the original breach, revealing hidden clashes of character, interest, and ambition. These mount toward a crisis of the group's unity and continuity unless rapidly sealed off by redressive public action, consensually undertaken by the group's leaders, elders, or guardians. . . . If a social drama runs its full course, the outcome . . . may be either the restoration of peace and 'normalcy' among the participants or social recognition of irremediable breach or schism.[8]

This model not only fits the 1880s' crisis and its upshot at St. Luke's, but it also gives deep insight into how those events were part of one Black community's need to define who they were in a period of instability and disintegrating optimism. As Turner explains, "Social dramas can be definitional, meaning the group creates an identity by telling a story about itself" in which the community marries "present problems to a rich ethnic past."[9] The social drama model depends on a concept called "liminality," a sort of threshold, described as a "no-man's-land betwixt and between the structural past and the structural future." Turner describes the "liminal phase" as "being dominantly in the subjunctive mood of culture, the mood of maybe, might be, as if, hypothesis, fantasy, conjecture, desire. . . . Liminality can perhaps be described as a fructile chaos, a storehouse of possibilities, not a random assemblage but a striving after new forms and structures, a gestation ... of modes appropriate to postliminal existence."[10] As the Reconstruction era neared its close, the African American congregation that was to become St. Luke's PE Church was in a state of liminality.

In 1879, just before Crummell's dispute with the choir, the congregation moved into a magnificent new building. Passing from a white church mission to an independent, richly endowed, and self-sustaining African American institution was nothing short of a rite of passage for those involved. Imaginations ran wild over the possibilities a new, stately building could bring. A superb musical offering and an eloquent African American pastor in the pulpit would represent the "best of the race" each Sunday in the new edifice. And for Black Washingtonians, this celebration of dignity, self-activity, achievement, and acquisition of wealth and property was a powerful form of resistance. While strengthening civic organizations like St. Luke's, the Black community championed political influence and the civil rights they felt slipping away under the shadow of Jim Crow.

BEGINNINGS

St. Luke's descended from St. Mary's Chapel which began in June 1867, when "a few color[e]d Episcopalians who were anxious to establish a church of that faith and order in the District" spoke with the rectors of their parish about a mission for African Americans. Prompted by postwar migration to Washington, DC, they claimed they were eager to form their own congregation, "especially with the fact patent to us that a large number of our Race had been by the changes of the War located in Washington who had been raised in the states of Maryland and Virginia in that church, and faith, by their former Masters, who had no church to worship in and were being led astray to either the Methodist, Baptist, Catholic, and other churches."[11] A simple wooden building used as a chapel during the Civil War was given to the group, where they shortly began holding public services.[12] Various white clergymen led St. Mary's congregation of "about 25 persons" for nearly six years; however, the congregation desired a Black leader.[13] John W. Cromwell,[14] founder and editor of *The People's Advocate* and a regular attendee at St. Luke's, recorded:

> Among the clergymen considered were William H. Josephus, a talented West Indian, and William J. Alston, who had been rector of St. Phillip's in New York and of St. Thomas in Philadelphia. John Thomas

Photograph of the Reverend Alexander Crummell, age fifty-eight, 1877. Courtesy of the Archives of the Episcopal Church, Austin, Texas.

Johnson, a progressive Negro citizen who in the reconstruction times was Treasurer of the District Government, began on behalf of a number of interested people a correspondence with Dr. Alexander Crummell with a view to securing him as the spiritual leader of these Episcopalians. This effort resulted in bringing Dr. Crummell to Washington in June, 1873.[15]

Initially, because Crummell planned to return to Liberia, where he had worked as a priest for the previous twenty years, he agreed to serve St. Luke's for a term of only six months.[16]

Not much is known about the first members of St. Mary's mission, though in a letter to Bishop Whittingham in 1871 their sense of dignity and self-advocacy is evident. They wrote, "We are poor, yet we are anxious to promote the best interests of the Church. We are ignorant and require instruction[,] but we are not abject slaves."[17] When Crummell arrived in Washington in 1873, St. Mary's "was in a state of absolute poverty"[18] though its membership included at least two government clerks, John Thomas Johnson and Jerome A. Johnson, who worked in the Treasury Department of the Internal Revenue Office.[19] J. T. Johnson, Black councilman for Ward III in 1869 and delegate for the District of Columbia at the National Convention of the Colored Men of America the same year, lent significant leadership to the small congregation.[20] In one instance, less than a year after the Compromise of 1877 that led to disenfranchisement and the loss of public office for Black men, the vestry of St. Mary's fiercely contested the (white) deacon in charge for reversing their appointment as vestrymen. Johnson wrote to the bishop with unequivocal passion saying, although McKee (the deacon) stated from the pulpit "those who were dissatisfied could leave and go elsewhere," the assembly at St. Mary's determined:

> God being our helper, not to l[o]se one. St. Mary's is our pride. Some of our Mothers lived and died in that faith and some of us have given our children to God right there before Mr. McKee knew of such a place.... We want a church and we want to feel at least that it is Our church and that we are at home in it.[21]

J. T. Johnson corresponded with Crummell, persuading him to fill the position of rector and later attended the Episcopal convention with Crummell as St. Mary's delegate.[22] St. Mary's 1871 petition to Bishop Whittingham lists both Johnsons as vestrymen and includes thirty-three members' names, fifteen men and eighteen women, all in J. T. Johnson's hand. St. Mary's congregation, made of women and men, formerly enslaved and recently free, literate or not, worked together to achieve autonomy and a private community dedicated to the Black agenda.

St. Mary's entire congregation was enthused when Crummell came to be their rector. In 1874, one year after Crummell's arrival, St. Mary's reported seventy-five communicants and had begun taking subscriptions for a new building.[23] By 1876, it was estimated there were three hundred individuals in the cure, and according to Bishop Whittingham, their spirit of devotion was "not equaled by any other church in the diocese."[24] The white Episcopal clergy of the district appointed St. Mary's a "nucleus of a concerted work" and saw Crummell as the perfect solution to their felt obligations among the African American population of Washington, DC.[25] Despite the obvious racial distancing this arrangement promoted, Crummell took the opportunity to create a weblike ministry within St. Mary's community that reflected his ideals and the needs of African American people. The result was a flourishing church body that supported Sunday schools and Sunday services in various parts of the city, including Howard University and a very poor neighborhood known as "The Island."[26] Crummell invested himself in mentoring African American leaders, both laity and those preparing for professional Episcopal ministry, and freely handed off various aspects of religious and community efforts to them. Crummell praised his communicants for their commitment to church work:

> I feel that I have very great reason for gratitude for the zeal, devotedness, liberality, and harmony wh[ich] characterizes the people of St. Mary's Ch[urch]. Their attendance at Divine Service is most admissible, the Ch[urch] is always full; and they show the greatest willingness to engage in all good works.... The Sunday School I have referred to n[ea]r Howard University has an attendance of 70 odd children [and] is carried on entirely by the young ... members of St. Mary's; albeit at a remote distance from their homes.[27]

St. Mary's members were unified in their purpose of upbuilding the Black community.

MUSIC AND WORSHIP AT ST. MARY'S CHAPEL

St. Mary's service structure closely followed a typical Episcopal format with the priest, or visiting priests, and lay readers reading or chanting prayers and reading the lessons and various service elements, such as the offertory sentence, collections, and blessings.[28] Hymns were used for congregational singing, probably from the PE hymnal, and generally chosen by the rector, as Crummell mentions, "I gave Fleetwood the Hymns for Easter."[29] Following Episcopal as well as African American tradition, the congregation also sang from the Psalter, with a leader "lining out" each phrase and the congregation following. Crummell indicates that for a time, the choir sang "after the Psalter in the Morning Service," indicating its continued use.[30] One of St. Mary's extended evening services also had the children from "the Island" singing from the Psalter as well as chanting.[31] B. F. DeCosta's history of St. Philip's Church of New York City, where Crummell first felt "a strong desire for the work of the sacred ministry,"[32] reveals "for the benefit of those who never enjoyed literary privileges, it was the custom, as in many churches . . . to line off the psalms and hymns, in order that all might join in the praise of the Almighty God."[33] Since many of St. Mary's communicants were very recent migrants from the southern states and were barred from learning to read chants and psalms while enslaved, the congregation continued the oral tradition of lining out hymns. The first members of St. Mary's made it clear their church was to be one representing their faith and traditions; the oral singing style was both practical and a reflection of their African cultural heritage.

If St. Mary's had an organ, it would be neither surprising nor uncommon. In this era, PE churches viewed the organ as standard equipment. DeCosta noted that organs were introduced into African American PE congregations as early as 1820 and that these congregations viewed the organ as central to worship, "so much so that at St. Philip's-St. Luke's (New Orleans) . . . a pipe organ was purchased in 1880 for a congregation of three men and ten women."[34] Since St. Mary's was the special project of the parish and a mission of wealthy white St. John's Church, it is probable that at least a simple reed organ was provided when the chapel was donated to the congregation.

St. Mary's had a choir from its earliest days. Crummell recorded, "In the year 1877 I was absent in the East soliciting funds. During my absence Mr. C. A. Fleetwood left the choir of the 15th St. Presbyterian Church, came to St. Mary's Chapel, and took the position of Choir Master."[35] John Wesley Cromwell, "a gentleman . . . so very unassuming and retiring in his disposition and manners that no one would judge, when in his presence, that there was a man with a head full of grammars, arithmetics, geographies, spellers, dictionaries, histories and other books, before him," sang bass in St. Mary's choir as early as 1875.[36] The choir rehearsed regularly on Saturday evenings at the church and while Crummell was rector, according to his "invariable rule," he always joined them during their time of practice.[37] St. Luke's records tell more of the choir's unusual activities than their liturgical role, as when Fleetwood had them regularly singing the "Gloria in Excelsis" after the Psalter. Thankfully, records from St. Mary the Virgin, an African American PE mission in Baltimore, give some insight into how the choir was generally used in liturgy.[38] Calbraith Perry (who was white) began work at St. Mary's, Baltimore in 1873 about the same time Crummell started at St. Mary's in Washington,[39] and the two priests assisted at each other's churches with some regularity, making it possible to draw some conclusions about the congregation's similarities in worship.[40] In a typical funeral service at St. Mary's, Baltimore, for instance, the choir processed into the church "chanting a solemn Miserere" with the clergy at the start. It then processed before the body and congregants all the way from the church to a remote burial ground afterward. The sound and appearance of these St. Mary's choirs set ritual events apart from daily existence, aesthetically dignifying Black life and death. When members of the Baltimore congregation came to church, they saw a white-robed choir with red cassocks process in and sing from the front. Later the cassocks offended "some over-tender consciences" so were sent to the dyehouse, where they "became a more sober blue."[41] St. Mary's choir in Washington probably did have bright cassocks, at least under Crummell, who believed his parishioners were of a "tropical race" and that "tropical warmth could be found in Black songs and in Black people's love of color."[42]

According to Bishop Whittingham, "The Chapel was densely crowded during all the Service" when he attended St. Mary's, Baltimore, in March 1877. That evening fifty-one people were confirmed, many who were friends and relatives of St. Mary's, Washington, DC, communicants. "The Rev. Dr. Crummell was present" as were several of his parishioners, who participated in the service, which was "choral throughout."[43] The event is significant because within a matter of months, Christian A. Fleetwood was induced to leave the Presbyterian Church and come to St. Mary's, Washington, as choir director. Evidently the event in Baltimore excited some of the Washington communicants, who then wanted to ramp up the musical offerings in their own church. As mentioned previously, Fleetwood's move took place while Crummell was out of the city; Crummell clearly stated that placing Fleetwood in the position of choirmaster "was done without my knowledge, my solicitation or my assent."[44]

St. Mary's choir sang chants and led congregational song supplemented with perhaps an occasional anthem until Fleetwood came in 1877. Under his direction the choir began the regular preparation of classical European works, and in 1878 a "grand vocal and orchestral concert" given to raise funds for the new building was devoted exclusively to the works of Haydn. The choirs of "all the principal colored Protestant churches in the city" gave the performance at Lincoln Hall, which was "crowded to overflowing." *The Washington Post* gave details of the program and critiqued the performance saying:

> The first [piece], "Thanks be to God" from Elijah was rendered poorly. The next one, the Inflammatus from the "Stabat Mater," the chorus being full, was much better sung, and the third, "The Heavens are Telling," from the Creation was a still greater improvement, though

the effect was much injured by singing the part written as a quartette, in a full chorus, thus loosing the beautiful effect of contrast intended by Haydn. The last, the "Hallelujah Chorus," though exhibiting a slight falling off, chiefly from a weakness and apparent want of confidence in the tenor and bass, was very creditably rendered.[45]

An orchestra accompanied the chorus, and Miss Emma Smith "presided at the piano, with marked ability." It was Christian Fleetwood who "wielded the baton" over the entire company.[46]

There is no historical record telling of Fleetwood's musical training, but his Civil War journal indicates singing and music were a regular part of his daily activities.[47] He was born to free Black parents in 1840 and received his early education from a wealthy white family. Later he served as secretary for the Maryland Colonization Society, spent a brief stint in Liberia and Sierra Leone, and graduated from Ashmun Institute, now Lincoln University, in Pennsylvania. He was a sergeant major in the United States Colored Volunteer Infantry, where he was responsible for the army's colors and for training and overseeing the color guard. Fleetwood received a Congressional Medal of Honor "for meritorious action in saving the colors at Chapin Farm, September 29, 1864, where he seized them after two color-bearers had been shot down, and bore them throughout the fight."[48] In the 1880s Fleetwood organized an African American high school cadet corps called the Washington Cadets, which marched and performed in a multitude of civil parades and celebrations.[49] Even at 5 feet 4 inches, as a choir director Fleetwood was commanding and regimented and, in a modest congregation like St. Mary's, probably a bit formidable.

Crummell never cared for Fleetwood, believing he lacked any spiritual inclination or purpose. Fleetwood recorded more musical activities than religious activities in his journal but did say on Sunday, September 11, 1864, that he "rode out to Church alone." With characteristic drollery, Fleetwood felt obliged to add he was "more amused than profited thereby."[50] Crummell endured Fleetwood's presence and tried to work with him, as Crummell said, "in order to avoid difficulty."[51] Fleetwood seems to have had some of his own prejudices against the enslaved or formerly enslaved; in his journal he refers to them as "Africans" and "n-----s," saying in one instance that he "let in on Africans like bricks."[52] Fleetwood volunteered for the infantry on August 11, 1863, and on August 19, only eight days later, was promoted to sergeant major. When not in battle, he spent his days drilling the regiment and writing reports and correspondence. Accustomed to a position of authority and command over other African Americans,

Photograph of Christian Abraham Fleetwood, age forty-four, ca. 1884. Manuscript Division, Library of Congress, Washington, DC.

Fleetwood carried with him a form of paternalism that affected his openness to the humbler communicants of St. Mary's. Nevertheless, Fleetwood's strong musical leadership combined with Crummell's abilities and the excitement of an impending move to a new building drew members of the

African American community. When Bishop Pinkney visited St. Mary's on April 7, 1878, to preach and confirm "twenty-four persons," he recorded, "The congregation was closely packed, and yet many had to go away." He enthusiastically added, "The service was exceedingly spirited. The signs of growth are most heart-cheering."[53]

THE TRANSITION TO ST. LUKE'S CHURCH

The year 1879 was a tipping point for St. Mary's, and music was the stimulant that aroused boiling hot issues of ownership and identity as the congregation prepared to move into a new church and change its name to St. Luke's Protestant Episcopal Church.[54] The growth of St. Mary's congregation after Crummell's arrival prompted plans to erect a stately "solid stone structure, modeled after the English church at Stratford-upon-Avon."[55] For almost four years, Crummell "went out and spoke in the cities in all the States of the North and East except Maine and New Hampshire," raising $13,000 for the building project.[56] The congregation chose twenty-two-year-old Black architect and builder Calvin Brent from Washington to design the building.[57] The process the St. Mary's group went through as they waited for St. Luke's to be built and then adjusted to worshipping in the new space can be thought of as a transitional progression or rite of passage, which explains why music, a ritual form, was so significant during the change.[58] As fully free people recently enfranchised, the physical building project was equivalent to an identity building project.

The five-year span from the time the congregation started raising money for their building to the day they entered it was a period of turbulent political change for all Black Americans and was especially poignant for St. Mary's congregants, rooted in the nation's capital. Though they started the project as optimistic American citizens embarking on a new journey of community building, they were fiercely disheartened and schooled in the fragility of their civic freedoms when Reconstruction ended not long before their move to the new church. Eddie Glaude Jr. stresses how crucial this point is when he says, the "social and political context in the United States, one animated by the value gap, shapes and informs . . . African American religion and its social place and function."[59] There is no way to understand St. Mary's transition or the power and dignity they summoned to move forward without looking at the political events overlapping the timeline of their move.

In the recent light of the Fifteenth Amendment's ratification, St. Mary's members imagined the permanent acquisition of civil rights, only to see it swept away in a meeting held at one of their very own church member's establishments: Wormley's Hotel, owned by James Wormley, a well-known Black business owner, caterer, and member of St. Mary's. The Wormley Compromise, or the Compromise of 1877, took place at the hotel on February 27, 1877, and gave Rutherford B. Hayes the presidency in exchange for the removal of troops in the South, which ended Reconstruction, brought about disenfranchisement, and ushered in the era of Jim Crow. Members like Johnson, Cromwell, and Fleetwood, who served in government positions, fought with the Union Army, were part of the National Convention of 1869 that sent a committee on suffrage to speak before Congress, and worked nonstop for Black schools, their church, and their community organizations—to say nothing of the women and men they sang with in the pews—felt sucker punched. In the words of historian Kidada E. Williams, it was "the rejection of Black people's right to have rights. Not just their legal equality, the vote, or their service in elected office, but life, security, family, home, property, education, religion, and community. All the freedoms formerly enslaved people cherished and had achieved."[60] Despite this damaging setback and all the ways it played out, St. Mary's pressed to see fulfillment.

They shared common characteristics with all liminal persons or groups who either "(1) fall in the interstices of social structure, (2) are on its margins, or (3) occupy its lowest rungs."[61] The St. Mary's congregation was in a process of separating from white control to develop into autonomous, free-acting Black Episcopalians; much more was at stake than church membership. When St. Mary's congregation resolved to build a new house of worship, they made a symbolic commitment to separate from "an earlier fixed point in the social structure, from a set of cultural conditions (a "state"), or from both." Reconstruction ended during the second, liminal phase, which had "few or none of the attributes of the past or coming state." Finally, when they moved into St. Luke's, they evoked a "social drama," and eventually the "passage" was "consummated." Turner explains that at the end of the rite of passage, "the ritual subject, individual or corporate, is in a relatively stable state once more, and by virtue of this, has rights and obligations vis-à-vis others of a clearly defined and 'structural' type."[62]

The congregation's separation from St. Mary's, as well as the humble state and white control it represented, symbolically began when Crummell took charge. As members of the PE Church, they would not completely escape white control and attitudes of superiority; however, with the bishop's support and a Black priest at the helm, they were much freer to steer their own course. St. Mary's members worked to find an African American rector for some time, and when he came, it was a fulfillment of their hopes. Crummell did not disappoint; his presence attracted many new members and soon he cast the vision for a new building and tirelessly worked to make it a reality. At this point, St. Mary's began to alternate between what Turner has called "fixed" and "floating" worlds.[63] The new church's style of worship and place in the community was yet undetermined. As the congregation moved into an increasingly liminal state, members experienced a freedom they had perhaps not experienced before: freedom to imagine a community that fully reflected their values. When members of the vestry and congregation persuaded Fleetwood to come as choir director while Crummell was away and without his knowledge, they were trying out their ability to shape the course of the congregation and challenge the leadership status quo. Turner argues, "If liminality is regarded as a time and place of withdrawal from normal modes of social action, it can be seen as potentially a period of scrutinization of the central values and axioms of the culture in which it occurs."[64] Significantly, these leaders believed music was the most essential factor for setting the tone of their new status and identity. They pulled in Fleetwood because they were convinced he possessed the skill to take them where they wanted to go. What would follow was a dramatic conflict between members of the church who wanted to shape it into an elegant social institution and those who were in line with Crummell and his vision of a church that ministered to all members of the Black community regardless of stature.

The "new Temple of worship" was "pronounced to be singularly beautiful," and many of St. Mary's communicants prepared for the move to the new building, which was set for Thanksgiving Day, 1879. Fleetwood, who "although present in the city, did not attend St. Mary's" for several months, promised Crummell he would prepare for the occasion by rehearsing and drilling the choir, which "had fallen into sad decline" during Fleetwood's absence. In a clear power play, moments after the first service ended, Fleetwood sent Crummell his formal resignation, leaving the church with no choral leadership, and essentially no choir, for its first Sunday service two days later. Fleetwood's stated reason for giving up the leadership of the choir was that "he did not like the location of the Choir at the Chancel" at the front of the church facing the congregation.[65] Crummell reported, this was "the second time, when, without any cause, and without any notice, this self-appointed Leader had thus coolly dropt me."[66]

Why Fleetwood resigned immediately after this significant long-anticipated Thanksgiving service is interesting to ponder. Obviously, he hoped to put Crummell in a dither before Sunday morning and prove his importance to the new church. Whether his actions stemmed simply from a narcissistic need for admiration or deeper fears related to control and power is difficult to say. But it is apparent that other members of the vestry found something shocking and a bit unsettling in the reality of moving to St. Luke's. The events of the day, both positive and negative, were monumental. Wilhelm Dilthey, a German philosopher, would have called them "*an* experience."[67] Separate from simple daily experiences, *an* experience is one that "stands out from the evenness of passing hours and years." It is one that is "formative and transformative."[68] The vestry and others at St. Luke's that day in 1879 entered a "new lifeway," like going to school, joining the army, or getting married.[69] When they entered the building they brought with them a host of aspirations, memories, and fears. Turner contends:

> These experiences that erupt from or disrupt routinized, repetitive behavior begin with shocks of pain or pleasure. . . . They summon up precedents and likenesses from the conscious or unconscious past. . . . Then the emotions of past experiences color the images and outlines revived by present shock. What happens next is the anxious need to find meaning in what has disconcerted us, whether by pain or pleasure, and converted mere experience into *an* experience. All this when we try to put past and present together.[70]

One can only imagine the emotions the congregation felt as they entered the large ornate building and realized they would be worshipping there each week. A far cry from the "Invisible Institution," the move to St. Luke's was another step in the structuring of African American religion in Washington, DC. It was most assuredly overwhelming for a great number who attended that day, but for those who believed they belonged to a higher class, it was the fruition of their aspirations. The clash between Crummell and his vestry after Fleetwood's resignation can be seen as the natural stirrings of deep-seated fears and desires as the new church struggled to agree on characteristics that would identify them as a community. The move to St. Luke's acted similarly to what anthropologists call a "ritual of status elevation" in which "the ritual subject or novice is being conveyed irreversibly from a lower to a higher position in an institutionalized system of such positions."[71] Those who saw their move to St. Luke's as a move up the social ladder naturally turned to the ritual form of music to symbolically express their transformation. Drawing on the work of Dilthey, Turner says, "Experience urges toward expression, or communication with others. . . . The arts depend on this urge to confession or declamation. The hard-won meanings should be said, painted, danced, dramatized, put into circulation. Here the peacock's urge to display is indistinguishable from the ritualized need to communicate."[72] The vestry was composed of Fleetwood's cohorts, and his resignation put them into a tailspin. For them, Fleetwood was the man of the hour; it was his skill and leadership that produced the "elevated," glorious musical sounds that resonated through the sanctuary. Through his discipline and rigorous training, the choir performed in a manner sure to attract the most dignified members of society—white and Black. Their hopes rested on him. Musical accomplishment would be the banner for African American sophistication in the coming years.

Once Crummell accepted Fleetwood's resignation, he hoped St. Luke's internal strivings would cease, but the vestry was committed to their musical plan. Crummell recalled, "Fleetwood's friends, members of the Vestry, repeatedly called upon me and insisted that I should invite him back to the choir." To this incitement, Crummell tersely responded, "I have never appointed Mr. Fleetwood Leader of my Choir and certainly after this treatment I never shall." After a while, the vestry, bent on their agenda of reinstating Fleetwood, attempted to persuade Crummell to allow them to organize another choir under Fleetwood's direction if he would not. Separating himself from the prospect, Crummell replied, "I will have no responsibility in this matter" but conceded to let them attempt it.[73] An intense and growing discordance between Crummell and the vestry, which included Fleetwood, stemmed from this event. The matter over who should direct the choir divided the congregation into two factions: those driving to make the church the pinnacle of Black identity and accomplishment and those who stood with the rector to keep the church as a center of service to all members of the Black community, including the needy and uneducated.

The problem with the choir and Fleetwood reached Bishop Pinkney, who wrote the vestry in December 1879, saying he was "sorry to hear of the disquietude in your midst. It is the result of a total misconception of the duties of vestries and rectors." He clarified that they had control of the property and finances and were responsible for electing the rector. "The music," he continued, "is placed wholly in the hands of the Rector and he must be recognized in his rights."[74] Later that year, in part of his speech at the Diocese Convention of Maryland, the bishop spoke of Black activity in the District of Columbia, saying Crummell was "in the vanguard." Among those present at the convention was Henry Johnson,[75] another of St. Luke's vestry members. With words probably intended for Johnson, the bishop alluded to the developing contention at St. Luke's when he went on to say Crummell

> brings to the work a ripe learning, great intellectual power and a life in all respects beautifully ordered. If harmony prevail, and there be

a sweet blending of will with will, there can be no assignable limit to the spread of the Gospel in the Church in this portion of our vineyard. But harmony is essential, for where there are division and strife, there must be an end to all work of the Spirit. He is a God of love and love is ever gentle, easy to be entreated, long suffering and patient. The rule of love is the golden law; and submission to that rule is the chief of virtues.[76]

But the seeds of discord were sown. The words intended by the bishop to mend and define the relationship between rector and vestry served only to inform the vestry of the tools they had for gaining control of the church. With music out of their hands, the vestry turned to the power of money, property, and, eventually, control over the rector's position.

MOUNTING CONFLICT

It was Crummell's dream to build a new, beautiful building for the St. Mary's congregation, and it was due to his efforts speaking and making appeals for funds that the dream became a possibility. In his biography of Crummell, Wilson Moses claims, "A stately edifice had always meant a great deal" to Crummell, who once wrote, "We must build a church that will hold a thousand or more persons; or otherwise the work will be perpetually a feeble, unhelpful, begging and beggarly scheme; unable to stand by itself, or to help others. Build us a large church, and then with God's blessing we shall sustain ourselves; and also become an arm of strength to the Diocese."[77] However, the excitement of this tremendous undertaking attracted members of African American society who, not necessarily interested in spiritual edification or community benevolence, saw the possibility of developing the new St. Luke's into a grand social center for the highest class. This was certainly not Crummell's nor the diocese's intent when they chose to locate St. Luke's "at 1514 Fifteenth Street, N. W., which placed it within a few blocks of the White House and also in proximity to some of Washington's most dismal alley life."[78] It was a few of these elite who used their influence and finances to take control of St. Luke's. Crummell recorded that the vestry "put the registration fee at $2.00 a year; and the years of 80 and 81, it has been held there; thus, excluding several of my poorer members from voting." With voting power in the hands of a few, "they brought in a number of men from the departments, members of no church, but nominally Baptists and Methodists; and so got themselves elected."[79]

In Crummell's mind, the primary instigators of conflict were Henry Johnson, J. William Cole,[80] Solomon Johnson, and Fleetwood, who in 1879 joined with a small unnamed "troublesome element" already at St. Mary's, most likely Jerome Johnson and Walker Lewis.[81] Henry Johnson, a "trustee of the Public Schools," and Cole, like Fleetwood, had been "attendants" at the Presbyterian Church, Johnson being the "great disturber of its peace." He was there "until unable longer to endure him the people rose up in disgust and indignation and thrust him out." Solomon Johnson, the exception, "went to no Church, was a rum-seller, and spent his time chiefly on Sundays, in hunting." All four men were well known to visit houses of prostitution; Solomon Johnson's wife sent for Crummell to tell him "about the absence of her husband with a harlot, 2 or 3 days at a time, from his home" and Cole "debauched the daughter of Worml[e]y the Hotel-keeper, taking her for a long time to a house of infamy in 15th St. At last, at point of the Pistol, he was forced to marry her." Later he was caught in a "house of ill-fame" with a schoolteacher, and the two were carried to the police court, where they were charged. Fleetwood was "in the same house at the same time" but denied it. Drunkenness was apparently another characteristic of this gang. It was these men, along with Spencer Murray, whom Crummell caustically referred to as "another of my precious vestry members," who got themselves voted into power.[82]

Though the vestry gained control of St. Luke's money and property, they were still eager for full control of the musical offerings and program of the church, undoubtedly under the powerful influence of Christian Fleetwood. One for pomp and pageantry, Fleetwood saw St. Luke's as a platform for increasingly greater musical display. In January 1880 Fleetwood was back at the baton, and J. W. Cromwell advertised in *The People's Advocate* that he sang bass with J. William Cole in the church's "recently organized choir."[83] They began preparation of contemporary composer Harrison Millard's "Magnificat," a showy, Christmas anthem considered by St. Luke's organist to be "unfit for a Church; more like a dance than a sacred anthem."[84] Fleetwood's intention was to have the choir sing the "Magnificat" at Easter services, and in an apparently underhanded move, he refrained from rehearsing it with the choir at church when Crummell was present; instead "the rehearsal of this piece was carried on at Mr. Fleetwood's private residence in 12th St."[85] When a few days before Easter Crummell became aware that a "Magnificat" was to be sung, he informed Fleetwood that it was inappropriate for the season and suggested instead that "there were a number of appropriate Anthems, such as 'Christ is Risen,' etc." Fleetwood obstinately responded, "He had prepared [the "Magnificat"] and could have no other 'Sing.'"[86] Equally indomitable in his stance, Crummell would not allow the anthem and shortly received a note in response:

Reverend Sir.

I am directed by the choir to state—that in consequence of their inability in the time remaining to substitute other creditable music for the Magnificat, arbitrarily excluded by you from the Easter services, they have unanimously Resolved that under existing circumstances they will take no part whatever in the services Easter Sunday.

Very respectfully,
C. A. Fleetwood

More than ready to be rid of Fleetwood as a "musical martinet," Crummell "immediately sent the following reply":

Dear Sir.

I have just received your favor of last evening which informs me that the choir of St. Luke's have resolved not to take any part in the services of Easter day. I am obliged to you for thus early informing me, and beg to say that I shall henceforth look elsewhere for musical assistance.

Your Obdt. Servt.
Alex Crummell[87]

The battle was on. Fleetwood and his comrades were in an uproar and began a campaign of public slander against Crummell in what Crummell called "newspaper warfare" that extended from Washington, DC, all the way to Louisiana. The vestry went to *The Washington Post*, which consequently ran an article titled "St. Luke's Choir Disbanded" on March 24, 1880. Refuting Crummell's assertion that he had not informed Crummell of his intention to perform the "Magnificat," Fleetwood told the papers Crummell had been informed six weeks earlier and "made no objections." The article included an interview with Miss Mattie Lawrence, "the leading soprano" of St. Luke's choir, "a very handsome and accomplished young lady, whose success as *Josephine* in the church choir 'Pinafore'[88] at Lincoln hall last fall attracted so much attention." Miss Lawrence told the *Post*, "It is gratifying to us of the choir to know that the people are very sorry to think we shall leave, and that they wish the doctor would yield in the matter. But I think that as he desires to control the choir, he will not give in." Miss Lawrence added that she heard Crummell wanted to establish an all boys' choir to which the reporter quipped, "Going to Rome, eh?" Picking up on the insinuation, Miss Lawrence admitted a boys' choir would be rather "ritualistic."[89] Over the next few days the *Post* ran several more articles claiming to "present both sides of the difficulty," including an interview with Crummell in which he stated again that he knew nothing of the "Magnificat" and never asked Fleetwood to be the choir leader. It was followed the next day by letters printed in the paper from Fleetwood, Henry Johnson, and Frances Upshur contending that Crummell's memory on the point was "defective" and that these two assertions were "not the only instances of Dr. Crummell's proven untruthfulness."[90] Crummell scraped together a small choir composed of "several white gentlemen and ladies, with a few of [his] own people" in time for Easter. Jerome Hopkins, an experienced organist, educator, and founder of the American Musical Association and the Orpheon Free Music Schools, was visiting the city when he read of St. Luke's trouble in the *Post* and told Crummell he would play the organ for Easter "as a favor" and would "drill" the choir too. Crummell told the bishop later that under Hopkins, "never before or since have we had such Easter music."[91]

The articles in the *Post* set up a sharp line between those who believed the rector and those who did not. The *Post* surmised, "No event in the colored church history of the city has for years created so much feeling as this unfortunate difference of opinion between the rector and the choir of St. Luke's." This was an accurate portrayal of the confusing situation manifested at St. Luke's, intriguingly just in time for vestry elections, which as always were scheduled for Easter Monday evening. The *Post* predicted the meeting would be "a stormy and interesting one," and "as the feeling is very bitter, both parties will put forth their strongest efforts."[92] The vestry managed to secure their position and began an intense race for complete control of St. Luke's. After the Easter 1880 scuffle and election, they passed the following resolutions:

1. To suspend the payment of Rector's salary.
2. To abolish the office of collector of subscriptions.
3. To pay no organist.
4. To close the Organ . . . forbidding its use at Divine service.
5. Instructing Fleetwood to write to Rev. Mr. Mansfield, the owner of the Organ to take down his organ and to remove it at once from the Church.[93]

Through their control of finances and church property, the vestry strong-armed Crummell and attempted to sabotage what was left of the music program. With still more to come, this deliberate action revved up the battle between parties as the vestry members explored their power and influence. When activating a social drama like the one at St. Luke's, "groups take stock of their current situation: the nature and strength of their social ties, the power of their symbols, the effectiveness of their legal and moral controls, the sacredness of their religious traditions and so forth."[94]

St. Luke's vestrymen were stymied in political and civic life and struggled to rise in the Black community. Sick of subordination, they no longer desired Crummell's leadership so tried to force him out by refusing to pay him. Relationships are restructured during rites of passage, and leadership once guiding and comforting "seems threatening and even mendacious, perhaps even reviving unconscious fears of physical mutilation and other punishments for behavior not in accordance" with authority.[95] The vestrymen were not unclear about their need to lead, as can be seen in Fleetwood's army resignation letter, which states:

> I see no good that will result to our people by continuing to serve, on the contrary it seems to me that our continuing to Act in a subordinate capacity, with no hope of advancement or promotion is an absolute injury to our cause. It is a tacit but telling acknowledgement on our part that we are not fit for promotion, [and] that we are satisfied to remain in a state of marked and acknowledged subserviency.[96]

Struggle for control was all part of the social drama playing out at St. Luke's.

Crummell was not without allies. Reverend Mansfield, "the owner of the Organ," "hearing from others the conduct of the Vestry," gave control of the organ to Crummell and forbade the vestry from moving it. Some "faithful members" established a rector's aid society that paid Crummell from five dollars to eight dollars a month in absence of his regular salary of twenty dollars per month but were not given credit by the vestry "for their subscriptions."[97] And so the congregation struggled forward, but now with an ever-growing financial handicap and increasing bitterness between members.

With Fleetwood gone and the church in financial need, the choir of St. Luke's began preparations for another production to raise funds. *The Washington Post* reported, "It is asserted that the proposed entertainment has been originated somewhat secretly, by Dr. Crummell and his choir, without consulting his vestry as to the propriety of using the body of the church for secular entertainments. Members of the vestry assert that they had not the least knowledge of such an entertainment, until the tickets made their appearance."[98] The vestry responded by sending a resolution to the bishop:

> Whereas: This Vestry having understood that a public concert, at which an admission fee will be charged, will, by consent of the Rector, Rev. Alexander Crummell, be given in this St. Luke's Church

on a certain day in November next, and Whereas, the Canons of the General Convention of Maryland provide against using the Church for any "unhallowed, worldly or common use," Canon xxi, title 1, Sec. 3, therefore, Be it resolved, that this Vestry, being a body corporate with the Protestant Episcopal Church of the United States, and acknowledging the authority of the Church laws of Maryland, do hereby enter our protest against the innovation of the above law, by Rev. Alexander Crummell, Rector of said Church, and declare it to be our conviction, that the Church should be used only for strictly religious purposes.[99]

The bishop, grasping the relational dynamic at St. Luke's, told the vestry how glad he was "to learn that you have so warm a zeal for the honorable house of God" but assured them he was "quite satisfied" Crummell would not "desecrate the building nor succumb it to others."[100] Crummell responded, "I beg to assure you that the charge of 'secularity,' in those resolutions is absolutely false" and to invite the bishop to review the concert program "and so get the certainty that nothing [except] what is sacred [and] religious, is sung." He told the bishop that the concert, as well as a series of lectures, "are immediate necessities for our monetary relief. I must use every legitimate means to get rid of pressing obligations and I have no one to help me."[101] A week later he addressed another letter to the bishop informing him of his struggle with St. Luke's vestry:

> The difficulty with my Vestry is that they have set out with the principle [and] determination [that] the Rector is, [and] shall be under the control of the Vestry, and hence interference with me concerning my Sunday School, Music, [and] even calling me to account for not preaching Funeral sermons. . . . Under the guidance of one man, constitutionally an "agitator," a majority of them, not all, give themselves up to strife; utterly neglect the monetary responsibilities of the Ch[urch]; leave me to bear *all* the burdens; [and] at the same time vote to "suspend the payment" of the small sum they are bound to give me.[102]

The conditions at St. Luke's were rising to a troublesome level, so the bishop met all parties in January 1881 "by request." Besides the bishop, Montgomery Blair, former US postmaster general under President Lincoln, defense council for Dred Scott, and "learned layman," was there to arbitrate, as well as the Reverends Thomas Addison and John S. Lindsay, who "rendered most signal service."[103] Fleetwood told the congregation that no one was there when he told Crummell the "Magnificat" was to be sung and that it was a matter of truthfulness between the rector and him.[104] Evidently Crummell left the issue alone, since the bishop was "charmed with the spirit displayed by both Rector and people." The vestry too laid aside arguments, and according to the bishop, "acted very nobly."[105] Later, the vestry claimed they were agreeable during the meeting because it was their understanding "all things should be restored as they had been prior to the controversy," including reinstatement of the choir under Fleetwood. Crummell did not reinstate Fleetwood and the choir, and although "all the vestrymen voluntarily retired at Easter of 1881," they were back in the saddle in March 1882 and immediately called for Crummell to be removed from St. Luke's.[106]

THE MOMENT OF CRISIS

The vestry submitted a lengthy petition to Bishop Pinkney on March 28, 1882, to "demand the termination of the present pastoral relations therewith of Rev'd Alexander Crummell, D. D. Rector." According to their appeal, an irreconcilable "rupture of relations" between pastor and people was so compelling as to render Crummell useless to the congregation. The vestry's letter of resolutions does paint a dire picture: Crummell "preserved a cold and forbidding manner," "visited but few of the people," "has not administered to them even in sickness," and "made charges so gross and unbecoming against those who are obnoxious to him, that the hearts of the people have been closed to him and they are no longer impressed by his preaching." The stated rupture between Crummell and the congregation "originated in an order of the Rector forbidding the singing at Easter 1880, of a piece of music composed for such an occasion." That they pin all their grievances against Crummell on this one seemingly trivial moment indicates there was more at stake than a piece of music.

The vestry's petition makes it seem the entire congregation was discontent with Crummell; yet there was a surprising countermove on the part of the laypeople, one that calls into question the accuracy of the charges. On April 3, 1882, two petitions signed by over one hundred members of St. Luke's were delivered to the bishop, with cover letters reading:

Dear Sir:
    We the undersigned Communicant Members of St. Luke's P. E. Church, do earnestly protest against the action of those men claiming to represent "The Vestry and Congregation" of the above named church; Such is *not* the case, for they only represent a part of the

Signatures of St. Luke's members in support of Alexander Crummell from letter to Bishop Pickney, April 2, 1872. Courtesy of the Maryland Diocesan Archives, Baltimore.

former, and a part of the latter, as will be seen by the names attached to this paper. We sincerely pray that before taking final action in the matter, you will give it a careful consideration, for we all stand loyal to our Rector, and very respectfully ask to be heard in his defence.[107]

Crummell told the bishop, "The Congregation, by a large majority, comprising fully two thirds of my communicants, at the least, are true and loyal to their Rector. A more faithful pious, devoted set of men and women cannot be found in this city. True they are poor, many of them servants; but they are sober, not drunkards, not debauchees; and they are generous and ardent in their Christian life and devotion."[108] By the petitions and names sent to the bishop on Crummell's behalf, it appears Crummell was right: many of St. Luke's members were loyal to him.[109]

Seemingly the bishop weighed the facts to the best of his ability. All the petitions and letters from St. Luke's in 1882 have been carefully preserved in the bishop's records along with a twenty-six-page statement from Crummell and several written opinions of St. Luke's situation from the Episcopal Convocation Committee on Colored Work in Washington, DC, solicited by the bishop. On May 3, 1882, the bishop handed down his decision:

In the case of the controversy in St. Luke's Church in the city of Washington, DC I summoned the Standing Committee as Council of Advice, who, having considered the evidence laid before them by me, which was all the evidence in my possession, unanimously reached the conclusion that said evidence has not convinced them that the interests of religion and the prosperity of St. Luke's Ch[urch] would be promoted by the dissolution of the pastoral relation between the Rector and St. Luke's congregation. I adopt their conclusion as my judgment in this case.[110]

Thwarted for a time in their attempt to eject Crummell from St. Luke's, the vestry still had control of the business aspects of church life, which financially continued to worsen. In 1882, the vestry interrupted the church financial program put in place by Crummell and, according to Crummell, misused funds. Crummell described the situation to the bishop:

Subscriptions amounting to about $80 per month, were made to me by the members of the Church, in '80, to be collected monthly. The collector used to get between $40 and $50 per month; and about as much more used to be deposited in the Church, in collecting basins.

The Vestry broke up the whole system. It is owing to these systematic plans of the Vestry that the revenue of the Church has declined. Many members declaring that while these men hold power they will put no monies in their hands, while others, aware of their misuse of funds I have collected, will give their subscriptions to the "Convocational Committee," only.[111]

Backing Crummell's statement that separate funds were collected outside the vestry's control to pay the rector, St. Luke's 1882 parochial report to the Diocese of Maryland indicates that $60.14 was collected through Communion alms with "all other Contributions (exclusive of Clergyman's salary)" amounting to $1,400.69. In 1883, after the bishop's decision to uphold Crummell as rector, contributions dropped to $385.12.[112] Practically in a stalemate, neither side would use their finances to support the other. With the vestry in control, communicants like Dr. A. T. Augusta, "one of the finest colored Physicians in the U.S.," told Crummell he would "not have anything to do with St. Luke's Church, while these wretched men are at the head of it." The vestry's ring, on the other hand, unwilling to sustain the church under Crummell, also refrained from supporting St. Luke's.

The vestry had their eyes open for evidence to support the rector's faultiness. A few months after the spring troubles of 1882, they sent a resolution to the bishop "in order that you may be cognizant of the manner in which said body are and have been treated by their Rector Rev. Alex Crummell" in which, grasping at straws, they condemned Crummell for "tearing down partitions, and making material alterations in the basement of St. Luke's P. E. Church without advising with or consulting the vestry of said church."[113] With the bishop's verdict behind him, as well as the support of over half his congregation, Crummell evidently began operating around the vestry.

RESOLUTION

When it came time for vestry elections on Easter Monday, March 26, 1883, Crummell and his supporters, "acting under the advice of 'two church lawyers,'" instigated a plan for change. Outwitting the vestry, they took control of the election through a surprise move described in *The Washington Post* the following day:

Easter Monday is the legal day for the election of a new vestry in the Episcopal church, and the time fixed is "immediately after the morning service." Convenience has created a custom very generally observed, of having an adjourned meeting take place in the evening, at which an election is held. Yesterday a larger congregation than usual was observed, and the then vestrymen, who were by then nearly all anti-Crummell men, were notified and attended in a body before the service closed. A stormy scene ensued upon Dr. Crummell taking his seat as chairman of the church meeting, which succeeded the service and, instead of adjourning until 7:30 p.m., as had been the custom, proceeded to hold an election. The methods adopted to defeat this action included the whole category of dilatory parliamentary motions, but all in vain. The vestrymen, register and treasurer thereupon left in a body.[114]

Obviously prepared for the action, Crummell's followers quickly replaced the troublesome vestry members with some of their own. The *Post* reported, "The subsequent proceedings resulted in the dropping of the names of Henry Johnson, C. A. Fleetwood, William Washington and J. W. Cole from the vestry, and the election of R. Nugent,[115] D. Syphax,[116] Daniel Murray,[117] and Langston Allen[118] to their places." An ambassador, a businessman, a librarian, and a doorman now joined St. Luke's leadership team, each bringing with them unique contributions for a consciously Black-focused civic organization—one that leaned away from class stratification as it leaned into full freedom for all members of the Black community. Never inclined to give up easily, the old vestry decided to go forward with an evening election in which they managed to elect themselves back into office. At 7:30 that evening "Walker Lewis, the senior warden, called the meeting to order." The treasurer began the meeting by reading a financial report showing "a total debt of $8,175.05 with a revenue for the year of $318.80[,] a falling off of one-half from" the previous year. He informed those gathered that if "Mr. S.E. Middleton, the banker," did not receive his payments on the tenth and twenty-seventh of the month "he would advertise the church building for sale the first Monday in April, under the mortgage which he holds." The payment amounts far exceeded the church's holdings; the only plausible plan was to elect a vestry with means and power. Consequently, elections were held, and "Spencer Murray, Jr., William Washington, C. A. Fleetwood and Charles Murray, of the old vestry, were then dropped and re-elected by a vote of forty, the vestrymen holding over being Henry Johnson, J. W. Cole, Solomon Johnson and Jerome A. Johnson." The *Post* reported two protests to this action, one by Daniel Murray, who argued, "The [voter] registration books were closed on February 16, seven days before the regular time," and one by F. G. Barbadoes, who dissented "because non-members had voted." According to the paper, both objections "were tabled."[119]

Finally prepared for their antics, Crummell and the Men's Guild, "an organization formed to wrest the control of the church from the malcontent members," had collected "from their own and the white Episcopal congregations in the city" $1,000 "in cash" for the payment on the building. Combined with the new vestrymen's "individual notes for the other $500 due," this action solved the church's financial problems, and "Mr. Middleton had withdrawn the notice of sale." Many of St. Luke's women backed Crummell and the new leadership and donated $120 "to the cause" through the Women's Aid Society.[120] If financial giving is an indication of whom the laypeople favored, then in 1884 the Diocese of Maryland parochial report for St. Luke's shows they wanted Crummell: contributions amounted to over $3,200.00.[121]

Now after a five-year struggle, St. Luke's was back in the hands of Alexander Crummell and the people who kept him in leadership. They moved forward shaping a particular identity for St. Luke's—one centered on meeting practical needs in the Black community of Washington, DC. Believing African Americans had "suffered the demoralization of heathendom, of the slave trade, and of two hundred years of bondage, and the large expectations about them are unreasonable,"[122] Crummell was known "to instruct and advise, in plain heart-to-heart talks"[123] and encouraged African Americans to pursue useful skills and live balanced lives free from excess. St. Luke's would become a hub for education and spiritual training that focused on the realistic improvement of conditions for Black people in Washington. Women were a priority at St. Luke's, and Crummell, who once said, "The education of girls was of more importance than that of boys," joined with them to fight white supremacy and establish the first Black "Girls' Friendly Society" at St. Luke's.[124] In an era of pew rents, St. Luke's kept their pews free and open to all, choosing to maintain an egalitarian social system over a hierarchical one.[125]

The social drama that played out at St. Luke's in the early 1880s was a secondary effect of the structuring process St. Mary's congregation went through as its members assimilated more and more into urban life in the nation's capital. Most of St. Mary's early members were raised as Episcopalians in their masters' homes, but the pending move to St. Luke's attracted members of various denominational backgrounds. Many from Baptist, Methodist, and

Presbyterian backgrounds had memories of private gatherings for prayer and worship in their quarters or deep in the woods, even Episcopalian's who had not been allowed to participate fully in the worship of their masters' churches. Though church buildings represented freedom, achievement, and autonomy to those who built them, they affected the nature of Black worship. Inevitably, the "Invisible Institution" emerged visible and changed as property was acquired and churches were constructed. Turner's societal model differentiating "offices, statuses, and roles" explains the actions of St. Luke's vestry and their followers who accepted the ideals of mainstream society with its class differentiations. Turner's other societal model, one in which society is "a communitas of concrete idiosyncratic individuals, who, though differing in physical and mental endowment, are nevertheless regarded as equal in terms of shared humanity," better fits the group that stayed at St. Luke's. Crummell's, and ultimately most of the congregation's, resistance to the vestry's power and agenda demonstrates their ambivalence toward mainstream society's structural ideals. Though they accepted ecclesiastical authority and organized themselves into various roles, ultimately, they rejected structures that restricted community formation and continued to prioritize community over individual.

Music performance was key to the transitional process because it signified cultural achievement and even cultural superiority. Conversely, religious music contained powerful memories, held symbolic meanings, and was a mode for talking about shared experiences. When Fleetwood and his band of followers attempted to turn St. Luke's into something more of a concert hall than a church, they asserted the type of rituals Samuel A. Floyd Jr. says are "complete with procedures and codes of conduct that make up the ceremonies that carry and celebrate the myths of high culture."[126] More than a mere musical preference, St. Luke's vestrymen bought into the myth that concert music was the most "elevating" type of music and that performing it held power to literally change their status and acceptance in mainstream culture. For Fleetwood and the vestrymen, musical performance at St. Luke's held little if any religious meaning. Their issues were wound up in social stratification and a deep need to be valued according to their accomplishments. It is also possible these male soldiers, masons, civic leaders, and federal workers wanted to emotionally detach from the sounds of slavery. They sought to ritualize their rite of passage into upper levels of society through concert music; the Black church was the only social space where they had freedom to muster such ambitions.

The most compelling discovery in the study of St. Luke's is how ultimately Crummell and the congregation rejected this form of music as ritual. They insisted music as a religious and cultural symbol had meaning. It was more than an emblem of "high culture" and status achievement. Instead, they continued following an African American tradition that made no "distinction between high and low music."[127] Rejecting the notion they should come to church each week to passively sit and listen while others skillfully delivered "high" musical works of art, they clung to a distinctly Black cultural value that maintained that community participation was vital to any musical expression voiced within the walls of the church.

A hard battle, seemingly fought over omitting a musical selection at Easter services, altered the course of St. Luke's PE Church. The battle served to refine the character of the church; though it wearied those involved, it sharpened their sense of purpose and solidified their sense of direction in the Black community. When he retired from St. Luke's in 1894, Crummell could look back and say:

> All along the lines of my personal life I have seen the gracious intrusions of a most merciful providence. . . . It is not merely a personal experience. It is a wider truth. It is a fact and a principle which pertains to the large and struggling race to which we belong. There is a Divine, an infinite, an all-powerful hand which moves in all our history; and it moves for good![128]

AFTERWORD

Even as a young girl I felt a powerful longing to know more of the beautiful burned-out buildings and hollow boulevards of downtown Detroit when our suburban family made a trip to the city. My grandparents never spoke of their families' flight from their birth home in the fifties and sixties, yet even without words I could see the stark contrast—spray-painted bridges and manicured gardens, boarded up Tudors and sprawling ranches, the Black fist and Centennial Park. How could the world be so divergent and so oddly separated in such a small distance? We were "from Detroit," but we didn't live "in Detroit." It didn't make sense. But we're white, so it was our prerogative to claim both Motors and Motown if we felt like it (or so we thought).

Most of the time we white people don't know what we don't know. I think of William Matthews, an AME pastor from Baltimore who described Black existence before emancipation saying:

> A free colored man could not walk the street after ten o'clock at night, even in a case of mercy or dire necessity, without a permit from a mayor. But as most of the policemen, or watchmen, as they were called, could neither read nor write, I remember, with a malicious delight, how those of us who could read, got around them by either writing our own passes, or showing them, on demand, scraps of letters or receipts or any odd bits of paper we happened to have, which the Hibernian guardian of the peace and dignity of the State would take,—and us with it,—to the nearest lamp-post, hold it, in many cases, upside down, and, after duly inspecting it, tell us in the authoritative and official tone, "All right, pass on." What quiet chuckles we would have![1]

They laughed at the white watchmen, but only a small victory laugh reverberating in a world of oppression—more like a "you may as well laugh as cry" kind of laugh. Black people hold many such knowings, such streams of consciousness white people miss out on.

That event and so many like it are absurd. Not only did Pastor Matthews and his friends have skills the watchman did not, they also had the kind of education and knowledge few of us can fathom today. Their poise and dignity, too, were exquisite. Many nineteenth-century Black Americans were near tireless in their rigorous and intentional pursuits of learning, community building, civic responsibility, business pursuits, church life, and more. A self-evident theme in Black history is that Black people had (have) to work twice as hard to get (not even) half as much. I don't need anyone to point this out to me—it's obvious to anyone who reads and listens to Black people's stories.

I want to tell the stories of these forgotten leaders and everyday people—brilliant and resilient men and women who made lives for themselves and their families outside of oppressive, degraded, and dangerous constraints—to shine a light on them so the roads they carved out of rock can be paved and driven on. I write from the perspective of deep admiration for the stunning, hardworking, inspiring people who were never recognized as equal or significant in the American landscape of their day. Their message of creativity and passion exceeds my understanding. I know I can't do them justice, but I will try.

This is more than a fashionable area of research for me; this is my act of solidarity. By bringing forgotten voices forward, I hope to uphold historic Black institutions with their transformative power and legacy of telling Black truth. I seek to remind the Black church of its earned civic position as a space for all community members to fight, frolic, assert, argue, rest, reason, and sing. Black church resistance is more than the first Black churchgoers who walked out to worship elsewhere or the space where they sang, "We Shall Overcome." There is a continuous stream of profound sacrifice and bravery from the days of Allen through the ministry of Martin Luther King Jr. and beyond.

Nor is there a gap in authentic Black religious and musical expression between slavery and the Great Migration. In the Reconstruction era, many Black church people displayed unthinkable courage and self-sacrifice in fighting for civil rights; the contours of their worship life reflect this. The same people who came to church singing and celebrating freedom came back with songs of lament when their shoulders were heavy under the weight of lynchings and church burnings as well as the loss of employment, public office, voting rights, and so much more. Laborers and laundresses used up the extent of their physical strength each day, and more educated types taught, recorded history, tutored, conducted letter campaigns, and traveled in support of numerous networks for change at great cost. Every Sunday they collectively lifted their heads and gathered at church to sing.

A foremost aim of this book is to highlight Black people's agency and creativity in resisting cultural oppression from without and from within the Black church by insisting on music making that was authentic and purposeful to their existence. It also suggests the ways Black people used worship life to work out power relations and establish organizational values during an intense era of identity building and citizenship formation. By exploring how Black people struggled through singing in the postemancipation Black church, we get a closer look at their hearts as they turned the never-going-back corner of freedom and embarked on the long road of rights realization.

This study invites scholars to consider the intersection of art, theology, and religion as an essential space for unpacking the combinations of feeling and belief that propelled so many throughout Black history. By looking at symbolic assignments and the ways meaning is attached and reattached to song, we can discover more about past people's motivations, ideals, and needs. We can also explore how these driving forces are passed on generationally in a form of musical storytelling. When P. Diddy released "I'll Be Missing You" in 1997, it included a one-line quotation from the gospel song "I'll Fly Away," written by (white) sharecropper Albert E. Brumley in 1929. For those who recognize the melody and lyrics, it calls up associations of death, future glory, the living dead, religious belief, and more. P. Diddy's song captured hip-hop's essential characteristics and themes while infusing it with religious and historical meaning in a way only song can do. In this way, Black church music is representational, helping people make sense of an ever-changing world while continually mixing sacred and profane to explore new realities and express self-conscious identity.

Singing through Struggle suggests that both structuration and agency were elements in building the Black church and its civic role during Reconstruction. Building and growing Black institutions gave an energizing stability and strength to its community as it created space for members to express themselves freely in ongoing group and individual self-discovery. Exploring how the church's music and worship life stimulated the exchange of beliefs and ideas through cultural expression shows how other deep studies of church life may further uncover invaluable aspects of Black resistance in the nineteenth century. These churches imagined themselves part of a growing, national community fighting for full freedom; their song can still be heard.

Today, vibrant grassroots efforts are emerging to address racial injustice and the kind of disparities I saw growing up in Detroit. These developing "people power" groups are creative, purposeful, and effective. Many of them are young people. In *Black Democracy*, Glaude emphasizes that Occupy movements like these need "safe and creative spaces to combat racism" and warns of the danger the "collapse of Black institutional life" presents.[2] Rather than relying on one voice or personality, protests that represent many voices, not one, are on the rise. This trend is in step with the heart of Black religious history, which, as *Singing through Struggle* shows, has contained forests or forums large enough for all Black voices for most of its life. Institutionalization may have facilitated top-down leadership styles, but the Black church today stands on a rich foundation of collective purpose. Singing together may be the key. As I see it, the only way to talk about today's realities is through history, and the only way to touch on how it feels is through song.

ACKNOWLEDGMENTS

Gratitude is so powerful when it comes to living a resilient life and weathering storms. I would never have made it through my maelstrom of struggles without stepping outside of them (sometimes more, sometimes less) to acknowledge the hand of God in directing my path by providing so many wise and kind people to help me along the way. The death of my first son stopped this work in its tracks. In the long period that has followed, the people who walked with me, sorrowed with me, and continued to see my light are the ones I owe the most thanks to as I complete this book. Thank you for the many ways you sing for me and with me.

To David Hempton, my exceptional, inspiring adviser and friend, for telling me it was time to bring this work out again. I hold in awe the combination of magnanimous mind, warm heart, and real person you are. You taught me to be a historian in the most subtle and painless manner. It felt like conversation, but it was really craft you taught this musician girl. Even as you raised your eyebrows and asked me what I imagined I would actually do with this area of expertise, you encouraged me and let me run my course. Thank you for believing in me and for giving me the strength and skills to see it through.

I feel deep gratitude for two women music and worship scholars who paved the way for me. First, Karen Westerfield Tucker for her wise training in history and liturgy and for standing as an authentic example of what it is to be a woman walking the academic path. Thank you for your genuine investment and care—it means the world. Also to Linda Clark, who literally fought for me as a musician entering the doctoral program in history at Boston University. Thank you for caring so deeply, and for investing so much, to broaden my understanding of art and aesthetic in congregational life.

ACKNOWLEDGMENTS

Many imaginative and generous scholars invested their time and creativity in helping to shape this work. I am especially grateful to Robert Orsi, who made me think of history in new ways and who set this journey in motion by encouraging my ideas with enthusiasm when I was in his course at Harvard. *Singing through Struggle* certainly would not exist were it not for the many honest questions and conversations I exchanged with the late Dale Andrews. His capacity to challenge and teach from a space of invested leadership and vision was rare. There are not enough words to express how his enduring impact runs through these pages. Special thanks to Bryan Stone for guiding me through the land of liberation and Wesleyan theology at Boston University. Your good humor and insight made these serious inquiries human and obtainable. I hope the legacy of your mentorship comes through. Dana Robert and Christopher Brown also provided feedback and shared wisdom and opportunity with me during my time at Boston University. My friend and fellow worship theologian Stephen Martin is ever a source of encouragement and new thoughts. I learn so much from the way you teach and bring out others' talent, and I admire the deep thoughtfulness you bring to both classroom and friendly conversation. Thank you for sharing your large mind and heart with me and so many others. Peniel Joseph listened to an excerpt of this book and asked one centering question that helped me articulate what the history was telling me all along. It changed everything. Thank you for bringing me into the conversation. You are the kind of historian I hope to be—we rest on the shoulders of scholars before, with a keen passion for why it matters today. Thank you for inspiring me. I am immensely grateful to the University Press of Mississippi for valuing this scholarship and the anonymous scholars who read deeply and offered so much to help me move it from the shadows into the light. Thank you for honoring me with your valuable insight.

Thank you to the welcoming, incredible congregations featured in this book! I owe everything to Bethel AME, St. Luke's PE, and Zoar United Methodist Church for holding on to their history and for partnering with me in bringing to focus new stories from their past. I pray this work warms your hearts and invigorates your ministry. I celebrate the "great cloud of witnesses" that went before and you, as witnesses for today. Thank you for your sacrifice and faithfulness. The late Saleem Wooden of Bethel AME was a kind, generous, and astute lay historian. His warmth and assistance were very significant to this project—may his memory be honored in the stories we unfolded together. I am grateful to Rectors Virginia Brown-Nolan and Kim Turner Baker for their deep understanding of St. Luke's historical legacy and the gift of time they shared with me as partners in the work. Thanks to Christian Savage, pastor of St. John's AME in Norfolk, Virginia, for his cocuriosity in learning more about the Reverend George Watkins and AME history and for his help in tracking down records and confirming some essential points.

Documenting the American South, the digital archive at the University of North Carolina at Chapel Hill is the greatest resource in Black church history I have encountered. Were it not for this collection, I am doubtful this work could be done. Thank you for your generosity and for making so many incredible African American stories available to the world. I am also grateful to the archivists at the Schomburg Center in Harlem for their assistance finding resources, especially church records. Thanks to the Maryland State Archives for their church record holdings, their numerous and carefully cataloged items related to Maryland history, and the well-researched items the archivists there have created to make the historian's job easier. Thank you to Drew University and the Methodist Archives and to the Boston University and Boston University School of Theology Libraries for the bounty of resources they contain related to AME and music history. Many other archives and digital collections were vital for my research, including Harvard Divinity School, Radcliffe Institute for Advanced Study, the Library Company of Philadelphia, the Historical Society of Pennsylvania, the Enoch Pratt Library in Baltimore, the Rhode Island Black Heritage Society, Brown University, the Boston Public Library, and the Library of Congress.

A warm thank you to Kate Nolan and Donna Miller, archivists at the United Methodist Historical Society of the Eastern Pennsylvania Conference, for their genuine interest and enthusiasm as research partners and to St. George's United Methodist Church, Philadelphia for acknowledging their past with humility and making their records available and open to all. The wonderful Mary Klein, archivist for the Episcopal Archives in Baltimore, holds many keys to unlock doors of forgotten history and is a gifted historian. Thank you, Mary, for the years of research and conversation that shaped the chapter on St. Luke's PE.

Several kind and sacrificing people read portions of my book and gave of their time to discuss it with me. Dale Rosenberger deserves millions of dollars, groceries for life, a bounty of fast and pretty cars, never ending vacation days in the sun, and whatever other boon he would like for his genuine and steadfast investment in my book. Always with an eye to scholarship and clarity, he kept me focused on the beauty and prophetic nature of these stories. Dale, you are kind beyond words, and I'm eternally grateful for our friendship and how it came about. Nicole L. Johnson, my faithful, fellow graduate student and forever friend, from the nine-hour days we spent studying by the fire at Panera during Boston autumns and winters to the CVs, papers, and book sections you read—thank you for walking the walk with me and for leading the way. At every step you graciously share your learning and experience, and all the while bless me with your example and friendship. Antipas Harris, I am grateful for our long friendship and ability to easily share ideas and feelings about life, faith, and music. Thank you for talking through things with me in the process of forming essential ideas for this book and for the support you continually give this fellow sojourner. Thanks to John Hewett, who read with a critical eye and yet found my work "stellar." It's so good to have a relentless cheerleader, someone who thinks you are gold no matter what. Thanks for nothing and everything at the same time. Don Katz, my neuroscience buddy and bandmate, humbled himself to discuss bad science and metaphorical possibilities with me as I explored interpretive ideas in chapter 2. Knowing enough to be dangerous is, well, dangerous, and I'm grateful you veered me away from sinking sand.

Thank you to two very special students turned teachers, pastor-scholars Kenneth Young and Bernard Smith. Kenneth, your words are few but always powerful and poignant. You are a careful, deeply intelligent thinker, and I am profoundly thankful for your willingness to let me ask and say freely and for the truth you tell. You call me out, and you encourage me too. I have a watchful eye on you, knowing your developing work plays a significant role in the fight for justice. Bernard, you have the biggest heart of anyone I know. You always make time for my questions, and you talk to me like a true friend. The kind of freedom and openness you share makes me grow and learn. Thank you for your deep thoughtfulness and sacrifice. Thanks to my former student and mentee John Jones, who in so many ways is my superior. What I love most about our friendship, John, is the time we spent getting to that place where we can talk Black and white in the raw. Thank you for trusting me and helping me create learning spaces where others feel safe to say what is real.

I'll never forget the significance of my interview with Mark Harden at the Center for Urban Ministerial Education at Gordon-Conwell and the indelible mark it left on me when he acknowledged the value of my work, saying, you "can't talk about the Black church without talking about music." Because he grew up a member of C. L. Franklin's New Bethel Baptist in Detroit, I consider him an authority on the subject. Thank you, Mark, for the vision you cast on my teaching career that day. I cherish it and live by it still.

I'm forever grateful to Geoffrey Dana Hicks for his beautiful compositions and the musical light he shines everywhere. Thank you for finding me and making me a singer. To Doug Leaffer, my soulmate musician, for those wordless moments when our souls shine best. And to my own funk brothers,

Rich, Jack, Alessandro, Mike, Don, and John, because I made it through the struggle singing with you.

This book would not exist were it not for the strength and support of two exceptionally treasured friends, Katherine Lee Melton and Jennifer Lynne Holcomb. For listening, praying, knowing, believing, and being witnesses to my life—thank you from the deepest part of my heart.

To my sister, Stephanie, and to Aunt Cheryl for believing in me through it all. To Mom and Dad and Jon for supporting me in the California Dream that has taken me this far. With loving memories, I thank my grandparents who engulfed me with love. My grandma's scrapbook of Grandpa's dance band days captivated my musical imagination and made me believe I was destined to follow. The Bill Hitter Orchestra broke up when the band members went off to war, but they left a deep imprint on me and ultimately this work. When my grandparents took me dancing with them, I learned instinctively that music is essential for life.

To my children, whose ear infections and stomach bugs make me ever so much prouder of completing this work: You are my little jewels and always my top priority. You are my song.

To the women and men whose stories fill these pages. As I stand in the shadow of their towering forms, I am moved beyond words. The extraordinary resilience and determination these churchgoers demonstrated in the face of trauma, the base depravity of white supremacy, and discouragement upon discouragement sings of an internal confidence and power few can comprehend. May their songs rise and give hope to the weary.

NOTES

INTRODUCTION

1. Booker T. Washington, *Up from Slavery: An Autobiography* (New York: Doubleday, Page, 1904), 113–14.

2. Marc Brackett, *Permission to Feel: The Power of Emotional Intelligence to Achieve Well-Being and Success* (New York: Celadon Books, 2019), 27.

3. James Cone, *The Spirituals and the Blues, with a New Introduction by Cheryl Townsend Gilkes*, 50th anniversary ed. (Maryknoll: Orbis Books, 2022), xxiv.

4. J. Miller M'Kim, *The Freedmen of South Carolina. An Address Delivered by J. Miller M'Kim, in Sansom Hall, July 9th, 1862. Together with a Letter from the Same to Stephen Colwell, Esq., Chairman of the Port Royal Relief Committee, to Stephen Colwell, Esq., Chairman of the Port Royal Relief Committee* (Philadelphia: Willis P. Hazard, 1862), 11, Historical Society of Pennsylvania, Philadelphia.

5. For more on ritual practices and their meaning, see Catherine Bell, *Ritual Theory, Ritual Practice* (New York: Oxford University Press, 1992) or Dimitris Xygalatas, *Ritual: How Seemingly Senseless Acts Make Life Worth Living* (New York: Little, Brown Spark, 2022). Additionally, I draw on Susanne Langer's philosophical and aesthetic theories in *Philosophy in a New Key*, 3rd ed. (Cambridge: Harvard University Press, 1957) and *Feeling and Form: A Theory of Art Developed from Philosophy in a New Key* (New York: Charles Scribner's Sons, 1953).

6. Cornel West, "Prophetic Religion and the Future of Capitalist Civilization," in Jürgen Butler et al., *The Power of Religion in the Public Sphere* (New York: Columbia University Press, 2011), 97.

7. In this study, "border cities" refer to eastern cities in the United States that are close to the Mason-Dixon line.

8. Data compiled from US Bureau of the Census, *Population of the United States in 1860; Compiled from the Original Returns of the Eighth Census, under the Direction of the Secretary of the Interior by Joseph C. G. Kennedy, Superintendent of Census* (Washington, DC: Government Printing Office, 1864); US Bureau of the Census, *The Statistics of the Population of the United States, Embracing the Tables of Race, Nationality, Sex, Selected Ages, and Occupations to Which Are Added the Statistics of School Attendance and*

Illiteracy, of Schools, Libraries, News-Papers and Periodicals, Churches, Pauperism and Crime, and of Areas, Families and Dwellings. Compiled from the Original Returns of the Ninth Census, (June 1, 1870) under the Direction of the Secretary of the Interior, by Francis A. Walker, Superintendent of Census (Washington, DC: Government Printing Office, 1872); and US Bureau of the Census, *Report on Population of the United States at the Eleventh Census: 1890 by Robert P. Porter, Superintendent of Census* (Washington, DC: Government Printing Office, 1895). Accessed September 30, 2023. http://www.census.gov/history/www/through_the_decades/overview/index.html.

9. US Bureau of the Census, *Population of the United States in 1860*.

10. Thomas W. Henry, *From Slavery to Salvation: The Autobiography of Rev. Thomas W. Henry of the A. M. E. Church* (Baltimore, 1872; repr., Jackson: University Press of Mississippi, 1994), 55.

11. Elizabeth Keckley, *Behind the Scenes, or, Thirty Years a Slave, and Four Years in the White House* (New York: G. W. Carleton, 1868), 111–13. Documenting the American South, University Library, University of North Carolina at Chapel Hill, 1999, http://docsouth.unc.edu/neh/keckley/keckley.html.

12. Hallie Q. Brown, *Homespun Heroines and Other Women of Distinction* (Xenia, OH: The Aldine Publishing Company, 1926; repr., New York: Oxford University Press, 1988), 22.

13. Steven Hahn, *A Nation under Our Feet: Black Political Struggles in the Rural South from Slavery to the Great Migration* (Cambridge, MA: Belknap Press of Harvard University Press, 2003), 3.

14. "History of Shiloh Baptist Church," ca. 1973, *Shiloh Baptist Church Records, 1863–1992*, Schomburg Center for Research in Black Culture, New York Public Library, New York, microfilm.

15. From a collection of oral histories taken by Elizabeth Clark-Lewis and found in *Living In, Living Out: African American Domestics and the Great Migration* (New York: Kodansha International, 1994), 36.

16. Judith Butler et al., *The Power of Religion in the Public Sphere* (New York: Columbia University Press, 2011).

17. "Official Board Minutes, 1870–1875," December 11, 1874, March 5, 1875, and July 9, 1875, *Bethel African Methodist Episcopal Church Collection, 1825–1936*. Maryland State Archives, Annapolis, MD. Microfilm.

18. Phyllis Weliver, *Women Musicians in Victorian Fiction, 1860–1900* (Burlington: Ashgate, 2000).

19. Evelyn Brooks Higginbotham, *Righteous Discontent: The Women's Movement in the Black Baptist Church, 1880–1920* (Cambridge, MA: Harvard University Press, 2003).

20. Weliver, *Women Musicians*, 32.

21. Pierre Bourdieu, *Distinction: A Social Critique of the Judgement of Taste* (London: Harvard University Press and Routledge, 1984, repr., 2010), 396.

22. Josephine Delphine Henderson Heard, *Morning Glories* (Philadelphia, 1890), 67, Schomburg Center for Research in Black Culture, New York Public Library, New York.

23. The phrase "politics of respectability" is attributed to Evelyn Brooks Higginbotham. My findings support her description of the Black church as a "dialogic model rather than dialectical," which recognizes "dynamic tension" in a multiplicity of protean and concurrent

meanings and intentions more so than in a series of discrete polarities." Higginbotham, *Righteous Discontent*, 16.

24. Alex Ross, "Black Scholars Confront White Supremacy in Classical Music," *The New Yorker*, September 14, 2020, https://www.newyorker.com/magazine/2020/09/21/black-scholars-confront-white-supremacy-in-classical-music.

25. "Report of the Special Committee on the State of the Church," 1882, 198, *Minutes of the Delaware Annual Conference, 1864–1888*. The Schomburg Center for Research in Black Culture, New York Public Library. Microfilm.

26. I agree with Lawrence Schenbeck, who argues that a "component of uplift was its search for ways to construct and represent a positive black identity" and cautions against "simplistic dismissals of the strategy." See Schenbeck, *Racial Uplift and American Music: 1878–1943* (Jackson: University Press of Mississippi, 2012), 6. See also Kevin K. Gaines, *Uplifting the Race: Black Leadership, Politics, and Culture in the Twentieth Century*. Chapel Hill: University of North Carolina Press, 1996 for essential work on uplift ideology in nineteenth-century Black cultural expression.

27. For a selective history and set of perspectives on Black authenticity, see Martin Japtok and Jerry Rafiki Jenkins, eds., *Authentic Blackness/Real Blackness: Essays on the Meaning of Blackness in Literature and Culture* (New York: Peter Lang, 2011).

28. Octavia V. Rogers Albert, *The House of Bondage, or, Charlotte Brooks and Other Slaves, Original and Life Like, as They Appeared in Their Old Plantation and City Slave Life; Together with Pen-Pictures of the Peculiar Institution, with Sights and Insights into Their New Relations as Freedmen, Freemen, and Citizens* (New York: Hunt & Eaton, 1890), 77–78. Documenting the American South, University Library, University of North Carolina at Chapel Hill, 2000, http://docsouth.unc.edu/neh/albert/menu.html.

29. *Federal Writers' Project: Slave Narrative Project, Vol. 9, Mississippi, Allen-Young*. 1936. Library of Congress, Manuscript/Mixed Material. www.loc.gov/item/mesn090/.

30. Lawrence Levine, *High Brow/Low Brow* (Cambridge, MA: Harvard University Press, 1990), 9.

31. Peniel Joseph, *The Third Reconstruction: America's Struggle for Racial Justice in the Twenty-First Century* (New York: Basic Books, 2022).

CHAPTER ONE: REMEMBERING, REMAKING, RETELLING: BLACK RELIGIOUS MUSIC AND RECONSTRUCTION

1. Perry A. Hall, *In the Vineyard* (Knoxville: University of Tennessee Press, 2004), 146.

2. William Francis Allen, Charles Pickard Ware, and Lucy McKim Garrison, *Slave Songs of the United States* (New York: A. Simpson, 1867), xx. Author's personal collection.

3. Quoted in Andrew Ward, *Dark Midnight When I Rise: The Story of the Jubilee Singers Who Introduced the World to the Music of Black America* (New York: Farrar, Straus, and Giroux, 2000), 157.

4. Olly Wilson, "The Heterogeneous Sound Ideal in African American Music," in *Signifyin(g), Sanctifyin,' & Slam Dunking: A Reader in African American Expressive Culture*, ed. Gena Dagel Caponi (Amherst: University of Massachusetts Press, 1999).

5. See, for instance "Colored People's Demonstration at Laurel Hill," *The Baltimore Sun*, June 1, 1875, 1; "The Independent Order of Seen Wise Men," *The Baltimore Sun*, May 8, 1877, 4; and "The Lincoln Statue at Washington," *The Baltimore Sun*, April 15, 1876, 4.

6. Charles E. Jackson, "History of the Asbury M. E. Church" ca. 1916, 6, *Asbury United Methodist Church Records, 1836–1986*, Schomburg Center for Research in Black Culture, New York Public Library, New York. Microfilm.

7. Mohamad El Haj, Pascal Antoine, Jean Louis Nandrino, Marie-Christine Gély-Nargeot, and Stéphane Raffard, "Self-Defining Memories during Exposure to Music in Alzheimer's disease," Cambridge University Press, May 28, 2015. https://www.cambridge.org/core/journals/international-psychogeriatrics/article/abs/selfdefining-memories-during-exposure-to-music-in-alzheimers-disease/81C594D467755ECB81A96D1D5C175CDC.

8. Genevieve Fabré, "African-American Commemorative Celebrations in the Nineteenth Century," in *History & Memory in African-American Culture*, ed. Genevieve Fabré and Robert O'Meally (New York: Oxford University Press, 1994), 75. See also, Nicole Myers Turner, *Soul Liberty: The Evolution of Black Religious Politics in Postemancipation Virginia* (Chapel Hill: University of North Carolina Press, 2020), 50 for more on "how the religious and political intersected in theology and in practice."

9. African Methodist Episcopal Zion Church, *Centennial Souvenir, 1796–1896*, 8, United Methodist Archives, Drew University, Madison, NJ.

10. "Hold the Fort (2)," Digital Tradition Folk Music Database, accessed October 1, 2023, http://sniff.numachi.com/pages/tiHOLDFRT2;ttHOLDFORT.html.

11. "Hold the Fort," history and lyrics available on the Digital Tradition Folk Music Database, accessed October 1, 2023, http://sniff.numachi.com/pages/tiHOLDFORT;ttHOLDFORT.html.

12. African Methodist Episcopal Zion Church, *Centennial Souvenir*, 34.

13. Courtney Brown, *Politics in Music: Music and Political Transformation from Beethoven to Hip-Hop* (Atlanta: Farsight Press, 2008), 4.

14. Samuel A. Floyd Jr., *The Power of Black Music* (New York: Oxford University Press, 1995), 9.

15. Susanne Langer, *Feeling and Form: A Theory of Art* (New York: Scribner, 1953), 28.

16. Langer, *Feeling and Form*, 27.

17. Floyd, *Power of Black Music*, 114. Floyd develops the "musical trait and practice 'call and response'" into an interpretive framework he calls "Call/Response" in Samuel A. Floyd Jr. with Melanie L. Zeck and Guthrie Ramsey, *The Transformation of Black Music: The Rhythms, the Songs, and the Ships of the African Diaspora* (New York: Oxford University Press, 2017), xxiv, defining "the Call" as "African musics (and musical traits) on the continent" and "the Response," as "the Diaspora's transformation of these musics and musical traits into new entities."

18. Henry McNeal Turner, ed., *The African Methodist Episcopal Church Hymn Book: Being a Collection of Hymns Designed to Supersede All Others Hitherto Made Use of in That Church. Selected from Various Authors.* Lyrics by Charles Wesley (Philadelphia: Jas. B. Rogers, Printer, 1872), 5, United Methodist Archives, Drew University.

19. *African Methodist Episcopal Church Hymn Book*, 289.

20. *African Methodist Episcopal Church Hymn Book*, 195.

21. "The Year of Jubilee," 1874, *Union Congregational Church File*, The Rhode Island Black Heritage Society, Providence.

22. Hymns 649, 650, and 972 from *African Methodist Episcopal Church Hymn Book*.

23. Richard R. Wright Jr., *Centennial Encyclopaedia of the African Methodist Episcopal Church Containing Principally the Biographies of the Men and Women, Both Ministers and Laymen, Whose Labors during a Hundred Years, Helped Make the A. M. E. Church What It Is; Also Short Historical Sketches of Annual Conferences, Educational Institutions, General Departments, Missionary Societies of the A. M. E. Church, and General Information about African Methodism and the Christian Church in General; Being a Literary Contribution to the Celebration of the One Hundredth Anniversary of the Formation of the African Methodist Episcopal Church Denomination by Richard Allen and others, at Philadelphia, Penna., in 1816* (Philadelphia: Book Concern of the A. M. E. Church, 1916), 223. Documenting the American South, University Library, University of North Carolina at Chapel Hill, 2001, https://docsouth.unc.edu/church/wright/wright.html.

24. Hymn 1029, *Hymnbook of the African Methodist Episcopal Church*, 841.

25. Hymns 1016 and 894, *Hymnbook of the African Methodist Episcopal Church*, 829, 734.

26. *New Hymn and Tune Book of the African Methodist Episcopal Zion Church* (Charlotte: A. M. E. Zion Publication House, 1892), 446. Schomburg Center for Research in Black Culture, the New York Public Library.

27. Frederick Douglass, *Narrative of the Life of Frederick Douglass, An American Slave, Written by Himself*, ed. Benjamin Quarles (Cambridge: Belknap Press of Harvard University Press, 1960), 36.

28. Hymn 545, McNeal Turner, *The Hymnbook of the AME Church, 1877*, 455.

29. Jon Michael Spencer, *Theological Music: Introduction to Theomusicology* (New York, Westport, Connecticut and London: Greenwood Press, 1991), xi.

30. *Minutes of the Delaware Annual Conference, 1864–1888*, 42.

31. Leroi Jones, *Blues People* (New York: W. Morrow, 1963), 41.

32. "Seventy-six are Baptized: Ingathering at the Mt. Olivet African Baptist Church," *The Sun* (New York, NY), November 12, 1899, 3, accessed October 1, 2023, Library of Congress, https://www.loc.gov/item/sn83030272.

33. *Afro-American* (Baltimore), April 29, 1893, 1, accessed October 1, 2023. Maryland State Archives, https://msa.maryland.gov/megafile/msa/speccol/sc4900/sc4968/pdf/18930429.pdf.

34. *Afro-American* (Baltimore), April 29, 1893, 4, accessed October 1, 2023. Maryland State Archives, https://msa.maryland.gov/megafile/msa/speccol/sc4900/sc4968/pdf/18930429.pdf.

35. Turner, ed., *The Hymn Book of the African Methodist Episcopal Church*, 9th ed., Table of Contents.

36. An excellent analysis of primary sources, legalities, and the practical and emotional realities of marrying after emancipation can be found in Tera W. Hunter, "Reconstructing Intimacies," in *Slave and Free Black Marriage in the Nineteenth Century* (Cambridge: The Belknap Press of Harvard, 2017).

37. Jackson, "History of the Asbury M. E. Church," 7.

38. *Minutes of the Delaware Annual Conference, 1864–1888*, May 10, 1886, 13.

39. "Board of Trustees Minutes, 1878–1902," 265, *Bethel African Methodist Episcopal Church Collection, 1825–1936*. Maryland State Archives, Annapolis, MD. Microfilm.

40. James Watkins, *Struggles for Freedom; or The Life of James Watkins, Formerly a Slave in Maryland, U.S.; in Which is Detailed a Graphic Account of His Extraordinary Escape from Slavery, Notices of the Fugitive Slave Law, the Sentiments of American Divines on the Subject of Slavery, etc., etc.*, 19th ed. (Manchester: Printed for James Watkins, 1860), 44. Documenting the American South, University Library, University of North Carolina at Chapel Hill, 2000. https://docsouth.unc.edu/neh/watkins/watkins.html.

41. Vaughn A. Booker, *Lift Every Voice and Swing: Black Musicians and Religious Culture in the Jazz Century* (New York: New York University Press, 2020), 27.

42. "Our Sunday Schools," in *The Christian Recorder* (Philadelphia), March 6, 1869, African American Newspapers, Accessible Archives, 2021, https://www.accessible.com/accessible/preLog.

43. Michael Eric Dyson, *Entertaining Race: Performing Blackness in America* (New York: St. Martin's Press, 2021), 5.

44. Hollis Robbins and Henry Louis Gates, Jr., eds., *The Portable Nineteenth-Century African American Women Writers* (New York: Penguin Books, 2017), 230.

45. Turner, *Soul Liberty*, 9.

46. From a collection of oral histories taken by Elizabeth Clark-Lewis and found in, *Living in, Living Out: African American Domestics and the Great Migration* (New York, Tokyo and London: Kodansha International, 1994), 36.

47. Frank Burch Brown, *Religious Aesthetics: A Theological Study of Making and Meaning* (Princeton: Princeton University Press, 1989), 74–75.

48. Calbraith B. Perry, *Twelve Years Among the Colored People: A Record of the Work of Mount Calvary Chapel of S. Mary the Virgin, Baltimore* (New York: James Pott & Co., 1884), 21–22, Internet Archive, August 25, 2008, https://ia804607.us.archive.org/5/items/twelveyearsamongooperr/twelveyearsamongooperr.pdf.

49. *The Weekly Anglo-African* (New York), June 2, 1860, 2, Library of Congress, accessed October 1, 2023. https://www.loc.gov/resource/sn83030179/1860-06-02/ed-1/?st=gallery.

50. Turner, ed., *The Hymn Book of the African Methodist Episcopal Church*, 9th ed., preface.

51. "Board of Trustees Minutes, 1878–1902," August 3, 1881, 51, and August 6, 1900, 372, *Bethel African Methodist Episcopal Church Collection*, reel 1384. Maryland State Archives.

52. Theophilus Gould Steward, *Fifty Years in the Gospel Ministry from 1864 to 1914. Twenty-seven Years in the Pastorate; Sixteen Years' Active Service as Chaplain in the U. S. Army; Seven Years Professor in Wilberforce University; Two Trips to Europe; A Trip in Mexico* (Philadelphia: A. M. E. Book Concern, ca. 1921), 143–44. Documenting the American South, University Library, University of North Carolina at Chapel Hill, 2000, https://docsouth.unc.edu/church/steward/steward.html#:~:text=It%20is%20biographical%2C%20covering%20a,political%20history%20of%20the%20times. Steward references the "Seven Sleepers of Ephesus," a sixth-century Christian legend about seven men who fell asleep in a cave and woke up two hundred years later—meaning there were numerous headstones in the walls of the building!

53. Henry N. Jeter, *Pastor Henry N. Jeter's Twenty-five Years Experience with the Shiloh Baptist Church and Her History. Corner School and Mary Streets, Newport, R. I.* (Providence: Remington Printing Company, 1901), 17. Documenting the American South, University Library, University of North Carolina at Chapel Hill, 2001, https://docsouth.unc.edu/neh/jeter/jeter.html.

54. Henry Russell, *Cheer! Boys, Cheer!: Memories of Men & Music* (London: J. Macqueen, 1895), 84–85, Eastman School of Music, November 21, 2005, http://hdl.handle.net/1802/2222.

55. Daniel A. Payne, *History of the AME Church* (Nashville: Publishing House of the A.M.E. Sunday School Union, 1891), 452. Documenting the American South, University Library, University of North Carolina at Chapel Hill, 2001, https://docsouth.unc.edu/church/payne/payne.html.

56. Quoted in Eileen Southern, *The Music of Black Americans: A History*, Second Edition (New York and London: W. W. Norton & Company, 1983), 131.

57. John Wesley, "Minutes of Several Conversations between the Rev. Mr. Wesley and Others; from the Year 1744 to the Year 1789" in vol. 7 of *The Works of the Reverend John Wesley, A.M.*, ed. John Emory (New York: T. Mason and G. Lane, 1839), 224.

58. Eileen Southern, "Musical Practices in Black Churches of Philadelphia and New York, Ca. 1800–1844," *Journal of the American Musicological Society* 30, no. 2 (Summer, 1977): 302–3.

59. Karen B. Westerfield Tucker, *American Methodist Worship* (Oxford and New York: Oxford University Press, 2001), 159.

60. Robert Moten Williams, "Brief Historical Sketch of Asbury Methodist Episcopal Church" in "Centennial Souvenir and Program, 1836–1936," 12, *Asbury United Methodist Church Records, 1836–1986*.

61. Payne, *History of the AME Church,* 456. Payne is using Wesleyan language found in the AME Discipline and drawn from I Corinthians 14:15.

62. "Loose Pages Found in Volume," "Proceedings of the monthly meeting of the board of Trustees of Bethel Church held March 5th, 1834," *Bethel African Methodist Episcopal Church Collection, 1825–1936*, reel 1390, no. 61.

63. W. D. Wright, *Black Intellectuals, Black Cognition, and a Black Aesthetic* (Westport and London: Praeger, 1997), 156–57.

64. Williams, "Brief Historical Sketch."

65. "History of Shiloh Baptist Church."

66. Perry, *Twelve Years among the Colored People*, 78.

67. "History of the Choirs," 1938, *Ebenezer United Methodist Church Records, 1865–1980*.

68. Daniel A. Payne, *Recollections of Seventy Years* (Nashville: Publishing House of the A.M.E. Sunday School Union, 1888), 290. Documenting the American South, University Library, University of North Carolina at Chapel Hill, 2001. https://docsouth.unc.edu/church/payne70/payne.html.

69. Payne, *Recollections of Seventy Years*, 293.

70. A. J. Abbey and M. J. Munger, *White Robes for the Sunday-School. A Choice New Collection of Songs Quartets, and Choruses for Sunday-Schools, Devotional Meetings, and the Home Circle* (Boston: Oliver Ditson & Co., and New York: C. H. Ditson & Co., 1879), Boston University, Theology Library, Boston.

71. *Afro-American* (Baltimore), November 30, 1895, 1.

72. *Afro-American* (Baltimore), August 31, 1895, 3.

73. "Board of Trustees Minutes, 1846–1867," 24, 70, *Bethel African Methodist Episcopal Church Collection, 1825–1936*, reel 1384.

74. *New Hymn and Tune Book of the African Methodist Episcopal Zion Church* (Charlotte: A.M.E. Zion Publication House, 1892), iii. Schomburg Center for Research in Black Culture, New York Public Library.

75. *New Hymn and Tune Book of the African Methodist Episcopal Zion Church*, iv.

76. George F. Bragg, *The First Negro Priest on Southern Soil* (Baltimore: Church Advocate Print, 1909), 30. Documenting the American South, University Library, University of North Carolina at Chapel Hill, 2000, https://docsouth.unc.edu/church/bragg/bragg.html.

77. "Chronology," ca. 1988, *Sharp Street Memorial United Methodist Church Records, 1873–1993*. Schomburg Center for Research in Black Culture, New York Public Library, microfilm.

78. Jackson, "History of the Asbury M. E. Church," 8.

79. Robert F. Gellerman, *The American Reed Organ and the Harmonium* (Vestal: Vestal Press, 1996), 8.

80. Gellerman, *American Reed Organ*, 88.

81. Gellerman, *American Reed Organ*, 88.

82. Gellerman, *American Reed Organ*, 111.

83. Tanya Y. Price, "Rhythms of Culture: Djembe and African Memory in African-American Cultural Traditions," *Black Music Research Journal* 33, no. 2 (2013: 227–47, https://doi.org/10.5406/blacmusiresej.33.2.0227.

84. "History of Shiloh Baptist Church."

85. Irene V. Jackson, "Music among Blacks in the Episcopal Church: Some Preliminary Considerations," *Historical Magazine of the Protestant Episcopal Church* 48 (1979): 28.

86. *A Short History of the African Union Meeting and School-House, Erected in Providence (R.I.) in the Years 1819, '20, '21; With Rules for Its Future Government* (Providence: Brown & Danforth, 1821), 31–32, Hay Drowne Collection, Brown University Library, Providence.

87. *Short History of the African Union*, 6.

88. Jackson, "History of the Asbury M. E. Church," 6–7.

89. *New Hymn and Tune Book of the African Methodist Episcopal Zion Church*, iii.

90. Andrew Waters, ed., *Prayin' to Be Set Free: Personal Accounts of Slavery in Mississippi* (Winston-Salem: John F. Blair, 2002), 14.

91. Jon Michael Spencer, *Black Hymnody: A Hymnological History of the African-American Church* (Knoxville: University of Tennessee, 1992), 4. A second edition of Allen's hymnal was published later the same year (1801) and added ten hymns to the original fifty-four.

92. "Daughters of the Conference Minutes," April 30, 1887, 210, *Minutes of the Delaware Annual Conference, 1864–1888*.

93. See Spencer, *Black Hymnody* for a study on Black hymnals.

94. *The Weekly Anglo-African* (New York), September 24, 1859.

95. Harry Eskew and Hugh T. McElrath, *Sing with Understanding: An Introduction to Christian Hymnology* (Nashville: Broadman Press, 1980), 42.

96. Walter F. Pitts, *Old Ship of Zion: The Afro-Baptist Ritual in the African Diaspora* (New York: Oxford University Press, 1993), 83.

97. Floyd et al., *Transformation of Black Music*, 155.
98. *New Hymn and Tune Book of the African Methodist Episcopal Zion Church*, iv.
99. Williams, "Brief Historical Sketch," 12.
100. Jackson, "History of the Asbury M. E. Church," 6.
101. "History of the Church."
102. Calvin S. Morris, *Reverdy C. Ransom: Black Advocate of the Social Gospel* (Lanham: University Press of America, 1990), 113.
103. Brown, *Homespun Heroines*, 162.
104. "Board of Trustees Minutes," March 27, 1893, *Plymouth Congregational United Church of Christ Records, 1896–1982*. Schomburg Center for Research on Black Culture, New York Public Library, microfilm.
105. "Board of Stewards Account Book, 1850–1866," 25A, *Bethel African Methodist Episcopal Church Collection, 1825–1936*, reel 1387.
106. *Order of Service in the A.M.E. Church, Revised and Enlarged* (Philadelphia: A.M.E. Book Rooms, 1887), 4, United Methodist Archives, Drew University, Madison, NJ.
107. *Weekly Anglo African* (New York), September 24, 1859.
108. *Afro-American* (Baltimore), April 29, 1893.
109. Southern, "Musical Practices in Black Churches," 306–7.
110. W. E. B. Du Bois, *The Philadelphia Negro: A Social Study. With a New Introduction by Elijah Anderson, Together with a Special Report on Domestic Service by Isabel Eaton.* (Philadelphia: University of Pennsylvania Press, 1899, repr., Philadelphia: University of Pennsylvania Press, 1996), 204.
111. Henry N. Jeter, *Pastor Henry N. Jeter's Twenty-five Years Experience with the Shiloh Baptist Church and Her History. Corner School and Mary Streets, Newport, R.I.* (Providence: Remington Printing, 1901), 48, 89. Documenting the American South, University Library, University of North Carolina at Chapel Hill, 2001, http://docsouth.unc.edu/neh/jeter/jeter.html.
112. Joseph Morgan, *Morgan's History of the New Jersey Conference of the A.M.E. Church, from 1872 to 1887, and of the Several Churches, as far as Possible from Date of Organization, with Biographical Sketches of Members of the Conference* (Camden: S. Chew, Printer, 1887), 150–51. United Methodist Archives, Drew University, Madison, NJ.
113. *The American Citizen* (Baltimore), April 19, 1879, Library of Congress, Washington, DC, 2011, https://www.loc.gov/collections/chronicling-america/?dl=page&fa=number_page:0000000001%7Cnumber_lccn:sn83027092&sb=date&st=gallery.
114. Thomas Wentworth Higginson, *Army Life in a Black Regiment*, 1869, American Antiquarian Society Online Exhibition, 2006, https://www.americanantiquarian.org/Manuscripts/higginson.html.
115. Hymn 1028, *Hymn Book of the African Methodist Episcopal Church*, 839.
116. Eric Lott, *Love and Theft: Blackface Minstrelsy & the American Working Class* (New York: Oxford University Press, 2013), 244.
117. *The New York Herald*, August 11, 1873, 9, Newspaper Archive, https://newspaperarchive.com/new-york-herald-aug-11-1873-p-2/.
118. *The New York Herald*, September 7, 1874, 5. Newspaper Archive, https://newspaperarchive.com/new-york-herald-sep-07-1874-p-1/.

119. *Hymn Book of the African Methodist Episcopal Church*, iv.

120. *Hymn Book of the African Methodist Episcopal Church*, 858.

121. Thomas W. Henry, *Autobiography of Rev. Thomas W. Henry, of the A.M.E. Church*. Documenting the American South, University Library, University of North Carolina at Chapel Hill, 2003, https://docsouth.unc.edu/neh/henry/henry.html, 23.

122. James M. Wright, *The Free Negro in Maryland: 1634–1860* (New York: Columbia University, 1921), 234. Some irony exists in this story as chapter 2 on Bethel AME Church will show. Apparently, the Bethel congregation ousted Stokes using Daniel Payne's very own tactics—discharging him because of his "heathenish" worship practices. In Payne's *History*, he tells how he and others defended Stokes as "one of the best of their members" and writes a lengthy section on the inappropriateness of a local governing board expelling a preacher. Payne declared, "All who understand the science of government, both civil and ecclesiastical" would know they had no power to do so, and together with other leaders of the Conference, reinstated Stokes. Payne, *History of the AME*, 244–49.

CHAPTER TWO: STABILIZING STRUCTURES AND SPONTANEOUS SONG: THE CASE OF BETHEL AFRICAN METHODIST EPISCOPAL CHURCH, BALTIMORE

1. "Official Board Minutes, 1871–1875," September 27, 1872, *Bethel African Methodist Episcopal Church Collection, 1825–1936*. Maryland State Archives, Annapolis, MD, reel 1385, no. 5.

2. Payne, *History of the AME Church*, 93.

3. Payne, *Recollections of Seventy Years*, iv.

4. For instance, Fannie Jackson Coppin, who "rose from the depths of slavery and became one of the most eminent educators of this country" after Daniel Payne awarded her nine dollars a year upon entering Oberlin." Brown, *Homespun Heroines*, 119–21.

5. Watkins served as pastor at St. John's AME Church in Norfolk, VA from 1866–1869 and from 1880–1884. Records from that period consist of minutes from St. John's Official Board, the Quarterly Conference, and the Virginia Annual Conference Minutes. They are held at St. John's AME, Norfolk, VA.

6. Israel L. Butt, *History of African Methodism in Virginia OR Four Decades in the Old Dominion* (Hampton: Hampton Institute Press, 1908), 34. Documenting the American South, University Library, University of North Carolina at Chapel Hill, 2000, https://docsouth.unc.edu/church/butt/butt.html.

7. Butt, *History*, 34.

8. William J. Simmons, *Men of Mark: Eminent, Progressive, and Rising* (Cleveland: Geo. M. Rewell, 1887), 810. Documenting the American South, University Library, University of North Carolina at Chapel Hill, 2000, https://docsouth.unc.edu/neh/simmons/simmons.html#p588.

9. "William Watkins (b. circa 1803–d. circa 1858), Educator and Minister, Baltimore City, Maryland." Biographical Series. Maryland State Archives, MSA SC 5496-002535, accessed October 3, 2023, https://msa.maryland.gov/megafile/msa/speccol/sc5400/sc5496/002500/002535/html/002535bio.html. Watkins's niece, Francis Ellen Watkins Harper, grew

up in his home after the death of her mother and attended his school. Later she became a teacher, poet, and antislavery lecturer. More about her and William Watkins can be found in George F. Bragg Jr., *Men of Maryland* (Baltimore: Church Advocate Press, 1914). Documenting the American South, University Library, University of North Carolina at Chapel Hill, 2001, https://docsouth.unc.edu/neh/bragg/bragg.html. See also Wright, *Centennial Encyclopaedia of the African Methodist Episcopal Church*.

10. William Watkins, "Address Delivered before the Moral Reform Society, in Philadelphia, August 8, 1836," in *Early Negro Writing: 1760–1837*, ed. Dorothy Porter (Baltimore: Black Classic Press, 1995), 155–66.

11. *Sunday School Report*, Bethel AME Church Records, December 1, 1899, 233.

12. Alexis Wells-Oghoghomeh, *The Souls of Womenfolk: The Religious Cultures of Enslaved Women in the Lower South* (Chapel Hill: University of North Carolina Press, 2021), 206.

13. Katie M. Hemphill, *Bawdy Houses: Commercial Sex and Regulation in Baltimore, 1790–1915* (Cambridge: Cambridge University Press, 2020), 209. See also Seth Rockman, *Scraping By: Wage Labor, Slavery, and Survival in Early Baltimore* (Baltimore: Johns Hopkins University Press, 2009), 168.

14. For more on how Black congregational members developed "legal acumen" by working "between the Constitution and the law of the church," see Martha S. Jones, "Making Congregants Citizens" in *Birthright Citizens: A History of Race and Rights in Antebellum America* (Cambridge: Cambridge University Press, 2018), 71–88. Dennis Patrick Halpin explores how Black pastors used the legal system to support early civil rights work in Baltimore in *A Brotherhood of Liberty: Black Reconstruction and Its Legacies in Baltimore, 1865–1920* (Philadelphia: University of Pennsylvania Press, 2019).

15. "Official Board Minutes, 1871–1875 and Financial Records for those Years," November 28, 1873, Bethel AME Church Records, reel 1385.

16. Tera W. Hunter, *Bound in Wedlock: Slave and Free Black Marriage in the Nineteenth Century* (Cambridge: Belknap Press of Harvard University, 2017), 204.

17. "Official Board Minutes, December 5, 1873." Bethel AME Church Records.

18. In *Men of Maryland*, Bragg records, "During the period immediately following the Civil War, Isaac and George Myers were the distinguished and effective leaders of racial interests. Isaac Myers was also most active in Bethel Sunday School and Church," 61. One wonders how Isaac Myers found the time to do all that he did; his name is found in countless surviving newspapers, convention records, histories, and books describing his varied roles as a labor leader and delegate for the National Labor Movement Convention, "Master of Ceremonies," Bethel Board Member, delegate for the National Convention of the Colored Men of America in 1869, founder of the Colored Men's Ship Yard in Baltimore, "Odd Fellow," and more. His precise and beautiful handwriting portrays a thoughtful, keen personality and leadership ability, as does the way others referred to him and deferred to him in accounts of his life. More can be learned of his legacy at the Frederick Douglass—Isaac Myers Maritime Park in Baltimore, as well as in historical records like the *Proceedings of the National Convention of the Colored Men of America: Held in Washington, D.C., on January 13, 14, 15, and 16, 1869*, Colored Conventions Project, accessed October 4, 2023, https://omeka.coloredconventions.org/items/show/452; *The American Citizen* (Baltimore), April 19, 1879, Library of Congress, Washington, DC, 2011, https://www.loc.gov/

collections/chronicling-america/?dl=page&fa=number_page:0000000001%7Cnumber_lc
cn:sn83027092&sb=date&st=gallery. To learn about Isaac Myer's influence in the Black
Labor Movement at the time of Reconstruction, see Benjamin T. Lynerd, "Republican
Ideology and the Black Labor Movement, 1869–1872." *Phylon (1960-)* 56, no. 2 (2019):
19–36. https://www.jstor.org/stable/26855822.

19. John H. Murphy was also a sergeant in the Union army from March 10, 1864 to December 18, 1865 and an elected alternative delegate from the fourth congressional district of Maryland for the National Republican Convention held in Chicago on June 3, 1884. His legacy is well known in Baltimore, particularly through his children and grandchildren, who have continuously maintained *The Afro-American* newspaper to today. See "History and Roster of Maryland Volunteers, War of 1861–6, Volume 2," Maryland State Archives, Annapolis, MD, https://msa.maryland.gov/megafile/msa/speccol/sc2900/sc2908/000001/000366/html/am366--252.html; *Statement of L. G. Martin, William C. Clay, Joseph Warren, and John H. Murphy, relative to their election as delegates to the Republican national convention from the fourth Congressional district of Maryland. Baltimore, Md. May 15* (Baltimore, 1884), Library of Congress, pdf, accessed October 4, 2023, https://www.loc.gov/item/2020778329/, Francesca Cohen, "The Office of John H. Murphy, Sr," *Explore Baltimore Heritage*, accessed October 11, 2023, https://explore.baltimoreheritage.org/items/show/723, and "'We Shall Overcome Someday:' The Equal Rights Movement in Baltimore, 1935–1942." Maryland Historical Magazine, 1994, Volume 89, No. 3, 261–73. https://msa.maryland.gov/megafile/msa/speccol/sc5800/sc5881/000001/000000/000356/pdf/msa_sc_5881_1_356.pdf.

20. "Stewards Records, January 6, 1871," *Bethel AME Records*. Maryland State Archives, Annapolis, MD, reel 1385, no. 5.

21. "Probationer Book and Membership Roll, 1815–1853," 34, *Bethel African Methodist Episcopal Church Collection, 1825–1936*. Maryland State Archives, Annapolis, MD, reel 1383, no 1. Original held at Bethel AME Church, Baltimore, MD

22. "Membership Roll, 1815–1853," 17. At Bethel Church, Baltimore.

23. "Board of Trustees Minutes, 1846–1867," 24, reel 1384, no. 1.

24. Martha S. Jones, *Birthright Citizens*, 71–88. See also, Archives of Maryland online, October 6, 2023, https://msa.maryland.gov/megafile/msa/speccol/sc2900/sc2908/000001/000200/html/am200b--143.html for court documents regarding the case.

25. Lawrence Mamiya, "A Social History of the Bethel African Methodist Episcopal Church in Baltimore: The House of God and the Struggle for Freedom," *American Congregations, Portraits of Twelve Religious Communities*, vol. 1, ed. James P. Wind and James W. Lewis (Chicago: University of Chicago Press, 1994), 230.

26. "Membership Roll, 1815–1853," 31.

27. Daniel Coker, "Sermon Delivered Extempore in the African Bethel Church in the City of Baltimore, on the 21st of January, 1816, to a Numerous Concourse of People, on Account of the Coloured People Gaining Their Church (Bethel) in the Supreme Court of the State of Pennsylvania" in *The Methodist Experience in America: A Sourcebook*, ed. Russell E. Richey, Kenneth E. Rowe, and Jean Miller Schmidt, 2 (Nashville: Abingdon Press, 2000), 197–98.

28. Payne, *Recollections of Seventy Years*, 93–94.

29. Albert Raboteau, *Slave Religion: The "Invisible Institution" in the Antebellum South* (Oxford: Oxford University Press, 1980).

30. John Dixon Long, *Pictures of Slavery in Church and State; Including Personal Reminiscences, Biographical Sketches, Anecdotes, etc., etc., with an Appendix Containing the Views of John Wesley and Richard Watson on Slavery* (Philadelphia, 1857), 383. Documenting the American South, University Library, University of North Carolina at Chapel Hill, 2000, http://docsouth.unc.edu/neh/long/long.html#long.

31. Payne, *Recollections of Seventy Years*, 255.

32. Of Wormley Hotel, Washington, DC. Wormley was a member of St. Luke's Protestant Episcopal Church; more of his story is discussed in chapter 4.

33. James M. Trotter, *Music and Some Highly Musical People: Containing Brief Chapters on I. A Description of Music, II. The Music of Nature, III. A Glance at the History of Music, IV. The Power, Beauty, and Uses of Music. Following Which Are Given Sketches of the Lives of Remarkable Musicians of the Colored Race. With Portraits, and an Appendix Containing Copies of Music Composed by Colored Men* (Boston: Lee and Shepard; New York: Charles T. Dillingham, 1881).

34. Payne, *History of the African Methodist Episcopal Church*, 456–57.

35. "Board of Trustees Minutes, 1846–1867," 14.

36. "Board of Trustees Minutes, 1846–1867," 24.

37. "Membership Roll, 1815–1853," n.p.

38. Fredrika Bremer, *America of the Fifties: Letter of Fredrika Bremer*, ed. Adolph B. Benson (New York: American-Scandinavian Foundation; London: Oxford University Press, 1924), 190–91.

39. Braxton D. Shelley, *Healing for the Soul: Richard Smallwood, the Vamp, and the Gospel Imagination* (New York: Oxford University Press, 2021), 56–57.

40. See, for instance, "Board of Trustees Minutes, 1846–1867, February 2, 1864," receipt from "Thomas Bradford fair."

41. George F. Bragg, *The First Negro Priest on Southern Soil* (Baltimore: Church Advocate Print, 1909), 30.

42. Payne, *History of the African Methodist Episcopal Church*, 457. Payne notes the organ was purchased in 1872, but Bethel's trustees' records confirm fundraising began in 1873, and the organ was installed in 1874. To learn more about Bethel's organ, see Michael Friesen, "Two Indiana Organbuilders in Baltimore," *The Tracker: Journal of the Organ Historical Society* 54, no. 2 (2010): 20.

43. James A. Handy, *Scraps of African Methodist Episcopal History* (Philadelphia: A.M.E. Book Concern, 1902), 231. Documenting the American South, University Library, University of North Carolina at Chapel Hill, 2000, https://docsouth.unc.edu/church/handy/handy.html.

44. "Visitors' Book, 1879–1936," 4, *Bethel African Methodist Episcopal Church Collection, 1825–1936*. Maryland State Archives, Annapolis, MD, reel 1388, no 4.

45. "Official Board Minutes, 1871–1875, July 1872."

46. Rodney Jantzi, email to Carolynne Hitter Brown, October 18, 2023. Mr. Jantzi of the Reed Organ Society explains, "There were many reed organ builders in the east of the USA by this time, the most expensive were by Mason & Hamlin that had a model in the early 1870s that sold for $750."

47. "Official Board Minutes, 1871–1875, September 26, 1873."
48. "Official Board Minutes, 1871–1875, September 26, 1873."
49. "Official Board Minutes, 1871–1875," n.p., spring 1873. It is obvious from Payne's *History of the African Methodist Episcopal* that Watkins did report the purchase of the new organ at the conference in 1874.
50. See, for example, "Official Board Minutes, 1871–1875, October 18, 1872, September 6, 1873."
51. "Official Board Minutes, 1871–1875, July 17, 1873."
52. Payne, *History of the African Methodist Episcopal Church*, 194.
53. Turner, *Hymn Book of the African Methodist Episcopal Church*.
54. Spencer, *Black Hymnody*, 11.
55. "Official Board Minutes, 1871–1875," 20, 26.
56. Trotter, *Highly Musical People*, 328–29.
57. William L. Andrews, ed., *Born in Slavery: Three Black Women's Autobiographies of the Nineteenth Century* (Bloomington: Indiana University Press, 1986), 66–67, 106–7.
58. "Official Board Minutes, 1871–1875, November 27, 1874" and "Official Board Minutes, 1876–1880, 247, December 9, 1883," *Bethel African Methodist Episcopal Church Collection, 1825–1936*, reel 1385, no. 6.
59. Payne, *Recollections of Seventy Years*, 254–55.
60. "Official Board Minutes, 1871–1875," December 1873.
61. "Minutes, Quarterly Conference, 1845–1856," January 7, 1848, 25, *Bethel African Methodist Episcopal Church Collection, 1825–1936*, Bethel African Methodist Episcopal Church Collection, 1825–1936, reel 1368, no. 1.
62. "Official Board Minutes, 1871–1875," 56.
63. "Official Board Minutes, 1871–1875, December 1873."
64. "Official Board Minutes, 1871–1875," "Mode of Expression, Expressive of the Services of the Rev. W. R. Revels, 1872."
65. "Official Board Minutes, 1871–1875, November 21, 1873."
66. "Official Board Minutes, 1871–1875, December 1873."
67. "Minutes, Quarterly Conference, 1845–1856, January 7, 1848," 25.
68. "Official Board Minutes, 1871–1875, December 1873."
69. "Official Board Minutes, 1871–1875," 6.
70. "Official Board Minutes, 1871–1875, August 2, 1872," 76.
71. "Official Board Minutes, November 27, 1874."
72. "Official Board Minutes, December 4, 1874."
73. "Official Board Minutes, December 4, 1874."
74. "Official Board Minutes, December 11, 1874."
75. "Official Board Minutes, March 5, 1875."
76. "Official Board Minutes, March 26, 1875."
77. "Official Board Minutes, 1876–1880, June 22, 1877."
78. Handy, *Scraps of African Methodist Episcopal History*, 344.
79. *Memoir of Old Elizabeth, a Colored Woman and Other Testimonies of Women Slaves* (Philadelphia: Collins, Printer to Jayne Street, 1863; repr., Oxford: Benediction Classics, 2010), 5.
80. *Memoir of Old Elizabeth*, 7.

81. "Board of Trustees Minutes, 1878–1899," *Bethel African Methodist Episcopal Church Collection, 1825–1936*, reel 1384, no. 11.

82. Phoebe Palmer, *The Way of Holiness, with Notes by the Way; Being a Narrative of Religious Experience Resulting from a Determination to be a Bible Christian* (New York, 1854), 201–2, author's personal collection.

83. Andrews, *Sisters of the Spirit*, 119.

84. Andrews, *Sisters of the Spirit*, 219 and 220. Payne asked Foote to come in late summer 1849 when his nine-month-old baby girl became ill and passed away; his wife died on the day of her birth. He was away from Bethel during these "severe domestic afflictions," and Foote came to minister for several months while he was gone. The congregation, free of Payne's restrictions and encouraged by the holiness influence and freedom they found under Foote's ministry, revolted when Payne returned, resulting in "the terrible Church trouble" of 1849 described earlier in this chapter. Payne, *Recollections of Seventy Years*, 92.

85. Andrews, *Sisters of the Spirit*, 192–93.

86. Andrews, *Sisters of the Spirit*, 188–89.

87. "Official Board Minutes, 1871–1875, January 30, 1874."

88. Clara Davis, ex-slave, interviewed by Francois Ludgere Diard, July 6, 1937, *Born in Slavery: Slave Narratives from the Federal Writers' Project, 1936–193*. Alabama Narratives, vol. I, 109, http://memory.loc.gov/ammem/snhtml/snhome.html.

89. Rogers Albert, *House of Bondage*, 66.

90. Andrews, *Sisters of the Spirit*, 212.

91. "Official Board Minutes, 1871–1875," n.p., 1872.

92. "Official Board Minutes, 1876–1880," 65.

93. Payne, *Recollections of Seventy Years*, 253–54.

94. "Board of Trustees Minutes, 1878–1899, July 18, 1881," 51.

95. "Board of Trustees Minutes, 1878–1899, January 6, 1891," 209.

96. "Board of Trustees Minutes, 1878–1899, February 16, 1897, March 22, 1897, April 6, 1897," 299–301.

97. "Board of Trustees Minutes, 1878–1899, January 7, 1901," 381.

98. "Board of Trustees Minutes, 1878–1899, January 14, 1901," 381.

99. "Board of Trustees Minutes, 1878–1899, February 20, 1901," 387–88.

100. "Board of Trustees Minutes, 1878–1899, February 4, 1902," 401–2.

101. See, for instance, "Board of Trustees Accounts, 1937–1941, November 7, 1938," 51, *Bethel African Methodist Episcopal Church Collection, 1825–1936*, reel 1385, no. 2.

CHAPTER THREE: EDUCATION, EMPOWERMENT, AND ESSENTIAL MUSIC IN THE FIRST FREEDOM SCHOOLS: THE CASE OF ZOAR METHODIST EPISCOPAL CHURCH, PHILADELPHIA

1. W. C. Dickerson, "History of Zoar Church, No. 7" in "Church Record Book, 1879–1885," reel 4, microfilm, *Zoar United Methodist Church Records, 1841–1981*. Schomburg Center for Research in Black Culture, New York Public Library, New York. Dickerson wrote with pride in 1879, "An Organ commensurate to the building stands at the South End of the whole Establishment is Extremely creditable to the Colored people."

2. Several significant dates stand out in the chronology of African American religious independence in Philadelphia, and variations in recorded dates make it difficult to identify a singularly decisive moment when the independent Black church there was formed. Richard Allen does not give the exact date he and the others walked out of St. George's in his account of the events leading up to the founding of the AME Church but simply discusses it in his explanation of how the Free African Society, a mutual aid society, was formed. My decision to use 1787 as the approximate date they left St. George's is based on both AME tradition and Black PE tradition and documentation, which place the event at this time. However, in her research on African Methodists in Philadelphia, Doris Andrews argues for 1792 as a possible date of departure based on financial records at St. George's and a comment in Asbury's journal. See Richard Allen, *The Life, Experience, and Gospel Labours of the Rt. Rev. Richard Allen. To Which Is Annexed the Rise and Progress of the African Methodist Episcopal Church in the United States of America. Containing a Narrative of the Yellow Fever in the Year of Our Lord 1793: With an Address to the People of Colour in the United States* (Philadelphia: Martin & Boden, 1833). Documenting the American South, University Library, University of North Carolina at Chapel Hill, 2000, https://docsouth.unc.edu/neh/allen/allen.html; George F. Bragg, Jr., *The First Negro Organization: The Free African Society Established on April 12th, 1787* (Baltimore: G.F. Bragg, 1924); Doris Andrews, "The African Methodists of Philadelphia, 1794–1802," in *Perspectives on American Methodism: Interpretive Essays*, ed. Russell E. Richey, Kenneth E. Rowe, and Jean Miller Schmidt (Nashville: Kingswood Books, 1993), 145–55.

3. Zoar separated from St. George's and assumed its own financial responsibilities under a gradual plan called the "Covenant of Assumption." This plan was finalized in 1836. Zoar wrote a constitution and was chartered in 1837. The constitution provides the first written documentation of Zoar's full title, including the description "African." For background on the "Covenant of Assumption," see Joshua E. Licorish, "History of Zoar United Methodist Church, Founded 1794, Campingtown, Pennsylvania," in *African Zoar United Methodist Church 175th Anniversary Program.* "Zoar File," St. George's United Methodist Church Archives, Philadelphia; *Constitution of the African Zoar Methodist Episcopal Church* (Philadelphia: Manly, Orr and Lippencott, 1842). United Methodist Archives, Drew University, Madison, NJ.

4. When Sodom and Gomorrah were destroyed because of their wickedness, God allowed Lot and his family, because of their righteousness and that of Abram's, to flee to the small nearby town of Zoar (Genesis 19:18–22).

5. In his book *A Will to Choose: The Origins of African American Methodists* (Lanham: Rowman & Littlefield, 2007), J. Gordon Melton provides a general description of Zoar's early history, which does not need to be repeated here. Melton primarily draws from secondary sources and the unpublished works of Joshua E. Licorish, Zoar's pastor from 1957–1981, and Janet Harrison Shannon, who in 1988 presented her paper, "Faith of Our Mothers and Fathers: Resurrecting the Histories of Early Black Churches," to the 11th Annual Conference on Black History at Wilkes Barre, PA. Melton filed copies of these papers at the Institute for Study of American Religion in Santa Barbara, CA, but they can also be found in "Zoar File," St. George's United Methodist Church Archives, Philadelphia. Licorish was an astute historian and civil rights activist. Some of his works

can be found at African Zoar United Methodist Church in Philadelphia, the Schomburg Center in Harlem and the United Methodist Archives at Drew University, Madison, NJ. A short description of Zoar's origins is included in J. H. Graham, *Black United Methodists: Retrospect and Prospect* (New York: Vantage Press, 1979), 57–58.

6. Graham, 57.

7. For more on Robert Green's complicated relationship and legal history with Bethel AME and St. George's ME, see Sarah Barringer Gordon, "The African Supplement: Religion, Race, and Corporate Law in Early National America," 2015, Faculty Scholarship at Penn Carey Law, 1575, https://scholarship.law.upenn.edu/faculty_scholarship/1575.

8. Green's letter was duplicated in *African Zoar United Methodist Church 175th Anniversary Program* found in "Zoar File," St. George's United Methodist Church Archives, Philadelphia.

9. Melton, 100, 121.

10. See, for instance, Zoar Methodist Episcopal Church "Stewards' Records," November 21, 1887, 24 and March 19, 1888, 46, *Zoar United Methodist Church Records, 1841–1981*. Schomburg Center for Research in Black Culture, New York Public Library, microfilm.

11. Zoar MEC, "Stewards' Records," December 12, 1887, 28.

12. Zoar MEC, "Stewards' Records."

13. Zoar MEC, "Stewards' Records," October 22, 1888, 85.

14. Zoar MEC, "Stewards' Records," November 19, 1888, 90.

15. Joshua E. Licorsish, *Harry Hosier, African Pioneer Preacher Including Brief History of African Zoar Methodist Church Founded 1794, Philadelphia, Pennsylvania* (Philadelphia: Afro-Methodist Associates, 1967). "Zoar file," St. George's United Methodist Church Archives, Philadelphia.

16. Charles Blockson, *The Underground Railroad in Pennsylvania* (Jacksonville: Flame International, 1981), 13.

17. Probably a reference to the tension between Abram's herdsmen and Lot's herdsmen that led to their parting near the plains of the Jordan River (Genesis 13:7–10).

18. Dickerson, "History of Zoar Church, No. 7." Dickerson was pastor of Zoar from 1876 to 1879. On April 27, 1875, Dickerson's wife Elmira died "in peace" at the age of thirty. On February 14, 1878, he married Martha "Mattie" Deborah Bryan, a member of the Zoar Congregation. Mattie died of "hemorrhages" on October 27, 1882, at the age of twenty-nine, just three years after she was married. In her obituary Dickerson wrote, "She did as much to build up the church as he did. . . . She always had a kind word for every body, and could always smile at the raging storm of afflictions and trials." Her obituary can be found in *The Journal of the Delaware Conference of the Methodist Episcopal Church*, 197, and Elmira's under "Memoirs" for 1875. Dickerson's naming of his history as "No. 7" leaves us to conclude there were six previous histories, none of which are extant.

19. *The Journal of Zoar Celebrating the Centennial of the Delaware Annual Conference the Methodist Church, 1864–1964 and the One Hundred and Seventieth Anniversary of Zoar Methodist Church, 1794–1964.* "Zoar File," St. George's United Methodist Church Archives, Philadelphia.

20. Allen, *Life, Experience, and Gospel Labours*, 17.

21. *Methodist Error, or, Friendly, Christian Advice to Those Methodists Who Indulge in Extravagant Emotions and Bodily Exercises, by a Wesleyan Methodist* (Trenton: D. & E. Fenton, 1819). Internet Archive, from the Music Library, University of North Carolina at Chapel Hill, June 11, 2014, https://archive.org/details/methodisterrororoowesl/page/n5/mode/2up.

22. G. A. Raybold, *Reminiscences of Methodism in West Jersey* (New York: Lane & Scott, 1849), 168. Drew University Library, Madison, NJ. This source also states that Harry Hoosier was buried in "the ground attached to Old Zoar."

23. "Stewards' Records," September 5, 1887 and January 2, 1888.

24. *Minutes of the Delaware Annual Conference, 1864–1888*, 1886, 19. The Schomburg Center for Research in Black Culture, New York Public Library, microfilm.

25. A reference to Psalm 133, which begins, "Behold, how good and how pleasant it is for brethren to dwell together in unity!"

26. Words and music by Jeremiah E. Rankin, 1880.

27. "Stewards' Records," November 21, 1887, 21.

28. *Minutes of the Delaware Annual Conference, 1864–1888*, 1886, 19. It is unclear what anniversary is being celebrated but likely a thirty-year celebration of the year 1856, when "the General Conference provided that a Bishop might call . . . a Conference once a year of our colored local preachers, within the bounds of any one or more of our districts, for the purpose of conferring with them with respect to the wants of the work among our colored people." *History of Zoar Methodist Church of Philadelphia, Pennsylvania, 1944.* African Zoar United Methodist Church, Philadelphia.

29. "Stewards' Records," December 8, 1890, 239.

30. A brief history of the Delaware Conference is important to understanding resistance among Black MEC churches, especially Zoar, whose leaders were crucial in founding this critical organization. In the 1850s African American Methodist local preachers began taking action to achieve greater responsibility for their churches. They formed the Colored Annual Conference of the MEC, and the first meeting was held at Zoar in 1857. At this meeting, "a call was made to ascertain the number of churches desirous of being served with colored preachers and willing to contribute to their support." *Colored Annual Conference of the Methodist Episcopal Church, Held at Zoar Church, Philadelphia, April 5th, 1857* (Philadelphia: Higgins & Perkinpine, 1857), 4, pdf file from St. George's Methodist Episcopal Church Archives, Philadelphia, PA. The Conference was not allowed to elect deacons or elders, so most of the control was still in the hands of the white-led annual conferences. Finally, in 1864, the General Conference of the MEC began to face its fractured identity and provided for the formation of two African American annual conferences: the Washington Conference and the Delaware Conference, which included Philadelphia. This was after receiving a decade's worth of petitions from African American preachers and churches stating their desire to be associated together in conference. Bishop Matthew Simpson told the General Conference the Black pastors had two reasons for wanting to meet separately. First, they felt they were not treated equally and, second, they wanted to be more intimately associated with one another and with the other Black churches. See Graham, *Black United Methodists: Retrospect and Prospect*, 35–36.

31. Payne, *Recollections of Seventy Years*, 254.

32. Payne, *Recollections of Seventy Years*, 254.

33. Du Bois, *Philadelphia Negro*, 220.

34. Payne, *Recollections of Seventy Years*, 253.

35. "Appendix," 1875, *Minutes of the Delaware Annual Conference, 1864–1888*.

36. James F. White, *Protestant Worship: Traditions in Transition* (Louisville: Westminster/John Knox Press), 1989, 164; Westerfield Tucker, *American Methodist Worship*, 278–79.

37. Payne, *Recollections of Seventy Years*, 256. Considering Payne's concern for the "civilization" of his race, it seems likely that some of his ideas about how African American Christians should worship were influenced by John Wesley's sermon "The Mystery of Iniquity," found in the second volume of Wesley's *Sermons for Several Occasions*, first published in 1748. In this sermon Wesley traces the "mystery of iniquity" throughout history, at one point highlighting how sin was at work in the "prosperity of Ham," from whom nineteenth-century African Americans often traced their lineage. When asserting how quickly sin entered the "primitive church," Wesley argued it was only the early Christians' "mode of worship" that separated them from the religious ways of the "heathen."

38. Luke Tyerman, *The Life and Times of the Rev. John Wesley, M.A., Founder of the Methodists*, vol. 3 (London: Hodder and Stoughton, 1871), 20.

39. "Report of the Special Committee on the State of the Church," *Minutes of the Delaware Annual Conference, 1864–1888*, 1880, 79.

40. Du Bois, *The Souls of Black Folk* (Chicago: A. C. McClurg, 1903, repr., New York: Penguin Books), 1996, 5.

41. Here I am referring to Bethel of the 1870s and 1880s, now under the strong influence of Payne and other AME leaders, not early Bethel, when Allen led it.

42. "A Report Made of the Pastor of Zion ME Church, Wilmington, Del.," May 28, 1885, H. A. Monroe, 511, *Minutes of the Delaware Annual Conference, 1864–1888*. Monroe was Zoar's pastor from 1899 to 1904.

43. "Report of the Presiding Elder, J.H. Johnson, Dover District," 1888, 373–74, *Minutes of the Delaware Annual Conference, 1864–1888*. Johnson was Zoar's pastor for two months in 1892. The lyrics of *The Ninety and Nine* were written by Elizabeth C. Clephane, 1868 and the music by Ira Sankey, 1874. *Hold the Fort* was written by Philip Bliss, 1870. The lyrics of *What a Friend We Have in Jesus* were written by Joseph Scriven, 1855, music by Charles Converse, 1868.

44. "Stewards' Records," September 17, 1888, 93.

45. First published in *Brightest and Best: A Choice Collection of New Songs, Duets, Choruses, Invocation and Benediction Hymns for the Sunday School and Meetings of Prayer and Praise* (New York: Biglow & Main, 1875), Benson Collection of Hymnals and Hymnology, Princeton Theological Seminary, available at Theological Commons, accessed April 19, 2023, https://commons.ptsem.edu/id/brighte00lowr.

46. Roberts Albert, *House of Bondage*, 43–45.

47. Roberts Albert, *House of Bondage*, 43–45.

48. Cone, *Spirituals and the Blues*, 61.

49. Wyatt T. Walker, *Somebody's Calling My Name: Black Sacred Music and Social Change* (Valley Forge: Judson, 1979), 75–78.

50. "Sunday School Report," 1866, 48, *Minutes of the Delaware Annual Conference, 1864–1888*.

51. "Sunday School Report," 1865, 27.

52. Du Bois, *Philadelphia Negro*, 207.

53. "Report of the Committee on Education," 1867, 80, *Minutes of the Delaware Annual Conference, 1864–1888*.

54. Sylvia R. Frey and Betty Wood, *Come Shouting to Zion: African American Protestantism in the American South and British Caribbean to 1830* (Chapel Hill: University of North Carolina Press, 1998), 85.

55. Thomas L. Johnson, *Twenty-Eight Years a Slave, or the Story of My Life in Three Continents* (Bournemouth: W. Mate & Sons, Limited; London: Christian Workers' Depot, 1909), 4. Documenting the American South, University Library, University of North Carolina at Chapel Hill, 1999, http://docsouth.unc.edu/neh/johnson1/johnson.html.

56. Interview with Mary Moriah Anne Susanna James, ex-slave, by Rogers at 618 Haw St., Baltimore, September 1937, *Born in Slavery: Slave Narratives from the Federal Writers' Project, 1936–1938*, Maryland Narratives, vol. VIII, 39, https://www.loc.gov/resource/mesn.080/?sp=40&st=text.

57. "Report on Education," 1876, 336, *Minutes of the Delaware Annual Conference, 1864–1888*.

58. "Report on Education," 1874, *Minutes of the Delaware Annual Conference, 1864–1888*, 288.

59. "Philadelphia District Report," 1880, *Minutes of the Delaware Annual Conference, 1864–1888*, 60.

60. "Report of the Committee on Education," 1879, *Minutes of the Delaware Annual Conference, 1864–1888*, 37.

61. "Presiding Elder Report, Dover District, J. H. Johnson," 1889, *Minutes of the Delaware Annual Conference, 1864–1888*, 372–73.

62. "Report of the Committee on Education," 1866, *Minutes of the Delaware Annual Conference, 1864–1888*, 49.

63. *Minutes of the Seventh Colored Annual Conference of the Methodist Episcopal Church, Held at Wilmington, August 6, 1863* (Philadelphia: Collins, 1863), 8, pdf file from St. George's United Methodist Church Archives, Philadelphia. Zoar's four hundred volumes were most likely used by the Sunday school and for a lending library. A catalog of the Zoar Sabbath School Library from 1844 and a circulation record are included in the *American Negro Historical Society Collection, 1790–1905* at the Historical Society of Pennsylvania. The Historical Society of Pennsylvania also contains an independent study done by Margaret Jerrido on April 27, 1981, titled "Sabbath Schools of the African Methodist Episcopal Church: History, Purpose, Accomplishments," which provides nineteenth-century library lists from several Black churches.

64. Mifflin W. Gibbs, *Shadow and Light: An Autobiography* (Washington, DC, 1902, repr., New York: Arno Press and the New York Times, 1968), 167.

65. *Minutes of the Seventh Colored Annual Conference*, 5.

66. *Minutes of the Seventh Colored Annual Conference*, "Statistical Table," 1870, 145.

67. *Minutes of the Seventh Colored Annual Conference*, "Presiding Elder Report, Philadelphia District," 1880, 60.

68. James E. Kirby, Russell E. Richey, Kenneth E. Rowe, *The Methodists* (Westport: Praeger, 1998), 211.

69. Kirby, *Methodists*, 211.

70. Roger De Guimps, *Pestalozzi: His Life and His Work*, trans. J. Russell (New York: D. Appleton, 1904), viii.

71. Frey and Wood, *Come Shouting to Zion*, 12.

72. Philip S. Foner and Robert J. Branham, eds., *Lift Every Voice: African American Oratory, 1787–1900* (Tuscaloosa: University of Alabama Press, 1998), 650.

73. Lowell Mason, *Manual of the Boston Academy of Music, for the Instruction in the Elements of Vocal Music, on the System of Pestalozzi*, 5th ed. (Boston: J. H. Wilkins & R. B. Carter, 1839), 24, accessed November 2, 2023, https://books.google.com/books/about/Manual_of_the_Boston_Academy_of_Music.html?id=zTQWAAAAYAAJ.

74. George W. Pratt and J. C. Johnson, *Pestalozzian School Song Book* (Boston: Geo. P. Reed, 1855), 6. School of Theology Archives, Boston University, Boston.

75. Philip Phillips, *Musical Leaves for Sabbath Schools, Composed of Musical Leaves Nos. 1, 2, 3, and 4, with an Addition of One Hundred Popular Hymns* (Cincinnati: Philip Phillips, c. 1865), 2. School of Theology Archives, Boston University, Boston.

76. T. C. O'Kane, *Every Sabbath: A New Collection of Music Adapted to the Wants and Capacities of Sunday-Schools, the Home Circle and Devotional Gatherings* (Cincinnati: John Church, 1874), preface. School of Theology Archives, Boston University, Boston.

77. Edward L. White and J. Edgar Gould, *The Wreath of School Songs; Consisting of Songs, Hymns and Chants, with Appropriate Music: Designed for the Use of Common Schools, Seminaries, &c. &c. to Which Are Added the Elements of Vocal Music. Arranged According to the Pestalozzian System of Instruction; with Numerous Exercises, Intended to Supersede (in Part) the Necessity of the Black-Board* (Boston: Benjamin B. Mussey, 1848), 74. School of Theology Archives, Boston University, Boston.

78. *Methodists*, 207.

79. *Methodists*, 208.

80. *Methodists*, 211.

81. Methodists.

82. J. Kennaday, *The Sunday School Speaker, or Exercises for Anniversaries and Celebrations Consisting of Addresses, Dialogues, Recitations, Bible Class Lessons, Hymns, Etc., Adapted to the Various Subjects to Which Sabbath School Efforts Are Directed*, 11th ed. (Philadelphia: Perkinpine & Higgins, 1860), accessed April 18, 2023, http://books.google.com/books?hl=en&id=seoPAAAAYAAJ&dq=The+Sunday+School+Speaker,+or+Exercises+for+Anniversaries+and+Celebrations+Consisting+of+Addresses,+Dialogues,+Recitations,+Bible+Class+Lessons,+Hymns,+Etc.,+Adapted+to+the+Various+Subjects+to+Which+Sabbath+School+Efforts+Are+Directed&printsec=frontcover&source=web&ots=z8eUL3BZWN&sig=h9WpxSYLZgCdNo4zY7PIbCz9oEk&sa=X&oi=book_result&resnum=1&ct=result.

83. Eskew and McElrath, *Sing with Understanding*, 176.

84. William J. Reynolds, Milburn Price, David W. Music, *A Survey of Christian Hymnody*, 4th ed. (Carol Stream: Hope, 1999), 121.

85. John William Leonard, ed., *Women's Who's Who of America* (New York: American Commonwealth Company, 1914), 681.

86. Pamela Helen Goodwin, "A Teacher Describes a Modern Sunday School in Session," 1875, in *The Methodist Experience in America: A Sourcebook*, vol. 2, ed. Russell E. Richey, Kenneth E. Rowe, and Jean Miller Schmidt (Nashville: Abingdon Press, 2000), 377.

87. "Report of the Sabbath School Committee," 1868, 100, *Minutes of the Delaware Annual Conference, 1864–1888*.

88. Deuteronomy 34:1.

89. Langer, *Feeling and Form*, 31.

90. No tunes are included in the anniversary pamphlet.

91. *Revival and Camp Minstrel, Containing the Best Hymns and Spiritual Songs, Original and Selected* (Philadelphia: Perkinpine & Higgins, 1867), accessed April 18, 2023, https://www.google.com/books/edition/Revival_and_Camp_Meeting_Minstrel/mTkPAAAAIAAJ?hl=en&gbpv=1.

92. Raboteau, *Slave Religion*, 13.

93. Cone, *Spirituals and the Blues*, 83.

CHAPTER FOUR: FINDING FREEDOM AND PERFORMING POWER: THE CASE OF ST. LUKE'S PROTESTANT EPISCOPAL CHURCH, WASHINGTON, DC

1. Annie J. Cooper, more commonly known as Anna J. Cooper, was a visionary Black feminist orator, writer, and educator who completed her PhD at the University of Paris in France in 1925 at age sixty-seven. A collection of her essays is found in *A Voice from the South: By a Black Woman of the South* (Xenia: The Aldine Printing House, 1892), available at the University of North Carolina at Chapel Hill: *Documenting the American South*, https://docsouth.unc.edu/church/cooper/cooper.html. I am grateful to Debbie Jackson, "a cradle Episcopalian of St. Luke's" for helping me make the connection between Annie and Anna Cooper and for bringing her fortitude to my attention. Cooper named Part One of her book "Soprano Obligato," which strongly suggests she was a choir member at St. Luke's during the years of this story.

2. *The Shades and the Lights of a Fifty Years' Ministry. 1844 to 1894. Jubilate. A Sermon by Alex. Crummell, Rector, and a Presentation Address by Mrs. A. J. Cooper, St. Luke's Church, Washington, DC, December 9th, 1894* (Washington, DC: R. L. Pendleton, Printer, 1894), 29. Maryland Diocesan Archives, Baltimore (hereafter cited as MDA).

3. *Shades and the Lights*, 29.

4. Alexander Crummell to Bishop William Pinkney, April 22, 1882, 12, 19–20, MDA.

5. Crummell to Pinkney, April 22, 1882, 26.

6. *Shades and the Lights*, 29.

7. *Shades and the Lights*, 30.

8. Victor Turner, *The Anthropology of Experience* (Urbana: University of Illinois Press, 1986), 39.

9. Turner, *Anthropology of Experience*, 40.

10. Turner, *Anthropology of Experience*, 40.

11. St. Mary's congregation to Bishop William Whittingham, May 22, 1871, 1, MDA.

12. *Inventory of Diocese of Maryland Archives*, 1940, 249, MDA.

13. George F. Bragg, *Afro-American Church Work. Historical Addresses* (Baltimore: G. F. Bragg, 1918), 4.

14. A detailed biography of Cromwell's life with letters and numerous accounts of those in his sphere was recently compiled and written by Cromwell's granddaughter. See Adelaide M. Cromwell, *Unveiled Voices, Unvarnished Memories: The Cromwell Family in Slavery and Segregation, 1692–1972* (Columbia: University of Missouri Press, 2007).

15. John Wesley Cromwell, "The First Negro Churches in the District of Columbia," 7, no. 1 (1922), 101. Documenting the American South, University Library, University of North Carolina at Chapel Hill, 2000, http://docsouth.unc.edu/church/cromwell/cromwell.html.

16. Alexander Crummell to Bishop William Whittingham, June 12, 1872, MDA.

17. St. Mary's to Whittingham, May 22, 1871, 13.

18. Bragg, *Afro-American Church Work*, 3.

19. Petition from St. Mary's to Bishop William Whittingham on behalf of A. A. Roberts, assistant priest, May 1878, 2, MDA.

20. See Melvin R. Williams, *A Blueprint for Change: The Black Community in Washington, DC, 1860–1870, Records of the Columbia Historical Society, Washington, D.C.*, vol. 71/72, the 48th separately bound book (1971/1972), 359–93, https://www.jstor.org/stable/40067781; *Proceedings of the National Convention of the Colored Men of America Held in Washington, D.C. on January 13, 14, 15, and 16, 1869* (Washington, DC: Great Republic Book and Newspaper Printing Establishment, 1869), https://books.google.com/books?id=UMxtAAAAMAAJ&source=gbs_navlinks_s. Cromwell noted he was voted "Treasurer for the District Government" during Reconstruction in Cromwell, *First Negro Churches*.

21. St. Mary's to Whittingham, May 22, 1871, 12, 14.

22. "1874 Convention Journal," 44.

23. "1874 Convention Journal," 146.

24. "Annual Convention Address, 1876," MDA.

25. "1873 Convention Journal, St John's Parish Report," MDA.

26. Alexander Crummell to Bishop Whittingham, January 18, 1874, MDA; Crummell to Whittingham, July 12, 1876; "Convocation of Washington Annual Report, 1879–1880," 113, MDA. Elizabeth Vincent wrote, "Washington, in the early sixties, was a mean and inferior city . . . it was scarcely more than a bare framework, stretching out its empty avenues for miles in every direction from the Capitol; having, on the east, the district called the Navy Yard, and Georgetown on the west, while the southern portion (at that time not a very reputable part of the city) was called 'the Island,' because formerly it had been cut off from the rest of the city by a canal." Elizabeth K. Vincent, *In the Days of Lincoln, Girlhood Recollections and Personal Reminiscences of Life in Washington during the Civil War* (Gardenia: Spanish American Institute Press, 1924), 10.

27. Crummell to Whittingham, January 18, 1874.

28. "Fifth Sunday after Epiphany, February 6th, 1876, P.M. in the Chapel of St. Mary the Virgin," Bishop William Whittingham's Journal from April 21st 1875 to December 28th 1877, 106–7, MDA.

29. Crummell to Pinkney, April 22, 1882, 6.
30. Crummell to Pinkney, April 22, 1882, 2.
31. Crummell to Whittingham, July 12, 1876.
32. Bragg, *Afro-American Church Work*, 1.
33. B. F. DeCosta, *Three Score and Ten: The Story of St. Philip's Church New York City* (New York, 1889), 15.
34. DeCosta, *Three Score and Ten*, 29–30.
35. Crummell to Pinkney, April 22, 1882, 1.
36. Crummell to Pinkney, April 22, 1882, 1, 8; J. W. Cromwell to Bishop Pinkney, April 20, 1882, Alexander Crummell file, MDA. That same year, Cromwell "distinguished himself for his extensive knowledge" in a spelling bee and founded *The People's Advocate* newspaper. He was an attorney, educator, and grocer who "took an active part in politics" serving as one of "four colored men on the jury which convicted several government officials of conspiracy to defraud the United States government" and was "appointed as chief examiner of the division of the money order department," in 1874. Cromwell witnessed a "political murder" on the Richmond & Danville railroad. He was shot at and his schoolhouse subsequently burned to the ground in 1869. For more about Cromwell, see Adelaide M. Cromwell, *Unveiled Voices, Unvarnished Memories: The Cromwell Family in Slavery and Segregation, 1692–1972* (Columbia: University of Missouri Press, 2007); *Simmons, Men of Mark*, 898–907.
37. Crummell to Pinkney, April 22, 1882, 6.
38. Crummell to Pinkney, April 22, 1882, 2.
39. Calbraith Perry to Bishop Whittingham, May 25, 1874, MDA. Perry and Crummell's friendship and respect for one another is a matter of historical record. Perry's letter to the bishop on May 25, 1874, reflects his early liking for Crummell. He wrote to say Crummell "preached a very fine sermon for us last evening" and ended it by asking, "Is he not a remarkable man?"
40. See for instance the February 6, 1876, and March 3, 1877, entries in Bishop Whittingham's Journal.
41. Perry, *Twelve Years*, 32.
42. George U. Rigsby, *Alexander Crummell: Pioneer in Nineteenth-Century Pan-African Thought* (New York; Greenwood Press, 1987), 175.
43. Bishop Whittingham's Journal, March 3, 1877, MDA.
44. Crummell to Pinkney, April 22, 1882, 1.
45. "The Grand Union Concert," *The Washington Post*, February 12, 1878.
46. "Grand Union Concert."
47. *Christian A. Fleetwood Papers, 1797–1945*. Diary, September 11, 1864. Manuscript Division, Library of Congress. https://www.loc.gov/search/?fa=partof:christian+a.+fleetwood+papers.
48. Alice Moore Dunbar-Nelson, ed., *Masterpieces of Negro Eloquence: The Best Speeches Delivered by the Negro from the Days of Slavery to the Present Time* (Robert John Nelson, 1914), 187, https://www.gutenberg.org/cache/epub/22240/pg22240-images.html#Page_187.
49. See, for instance, "The Day of Decoration," *The Washington Post*, May 30, 1881.
50. Fleetwood's diary, Sunday, September 11, 1864.
51. Crummell to Pinkney, April 22, 1882, 1.

52. Fleetwood's diary, Monday, July 25, 1864.

53. "1878 Convention Journal," 79, MDA.

54. "1880 Diocesan Convention of Maryland Report," 56, MDA; *Historical Sketches of the Parishes and Missions in the Diocese of Washington* (Washington, DC: 1928), 85, 88–91, MDA. The resolution changing the congregation's name was officially adopted May 27, 1880, although by the time of their move in November 1879, they were already using the name St. Luke's. The report stated that there were "urgent reasons for the change." Evidently, some members stayed behind at the old church to continue the educational programs under way in the community. In 1880 there were essentially two congregations, necessitating the need for two different names. Most St. Mary's communicants went to the new larger church.

55. Moses, *Alexander Crummell*, 198.

56. "A Rector's First Decade," *The Washington Post*, June 18, 1883.

57. Dreck Spurlock Wilson, ed., *African American Architects: A Biographical Dictionary, 1865–1945* (New York: Routledge, 2004), 81.

58. Arnold van Gennep, *The Rites of Passage*, trans. Monika B. Vizedom and Gabrielle L. Caffee (Chicago: University of Chicago Press, 1960), 187. In 1909, van Gennep defined "rites de passage" as those that accompany "the transition from one stage of life to another, or from one social position to another." By erecting and moving into a new, costly, and beautiful building, St. Mary's congregation experienced what they saw as a change of social position.

59. Eddie S. Glaude Jr., *An Uncommon Faith: A Pragmatic Approach to the Study of African American Religion* (Athens: University of Georgia Press, 2018).

60. Kidada E. Williams, *I Saw Death Coming: A History of Terror and Survival in the War Against Reconstruction* (New York: Bloomsbury, 2023), 53.

61. Turner, *Anthropology of Experience*, 125.

62. Turner, *Ritual Process*, 94–95.

63. Turner, *Ritual Process*, vii.

64. Turner, *Ritual Process*, 167.

65. Crummell to Pinkney, April 22, 1882, 3.

66. Crummell to Pinkney, April 22, 1882, 5.

67. Wilhelm Dilthey, *W. Dilthey: Selected Writings*, trans. and ed. H. P. Rickman (Cambridge: Cambridge University Press, 1976), 210.

68. Turner, *Anthropology of Experience*, 35.

69. Turner, *Anthropology of Experience*, 35.

70. Turner, *Anthropology of Experience*, 35–36.

71. Turner, *Ritual Process*, 167.

72. Turner, *Anthropology of Experience*, 37.

73. Turner, *Anthropology of Experience*, 5–6.

74. Bishop William Pinkney to the Vestry of St. Mary's, December 13, 1879, 1, MDA.

75. Possibly the then twenty-nine-year-old career military man and Medal of Honor recipient Sergeant Henry Johnson at home on leave after the Battle of Milk Creek against the Ute Indians, October 2–5, 1879. Johnson was promoted to sergeant but was demoted for a third time when he "tangled with the bar tender at the Fort Robinson post canteen after the latter cut him off." Johnson likely was married with a family in DC. For more

on Johnson and the relationship between Black soldiers and Native Americans at war, see Frank N Schubert, "Ten Troopers: Buffalo Soldier Medal of Honor Men Who Served at Fort Robinson," *Nebraska History* 78 (1997): 151–57, http://www.nebraskahistory.org/publish/publicat/history/full-text/NH1997TenTroopers.pdf.

76. "1880 Diocese Convention of Maryland Report," 102.

77. Moses, *Alexander Crummell*, 198.

78. Moses, *Alexander Crummell*, 199.

79. Crummell to Pinkney, April 22, 1882, 12.

80. J. William Cole, who was often found at "entertainments" hosted by Major Frederick C. Revells, the only other Black battalion leader besides Fleetwood. Decidedly a singer, as a member of the mysteriously named "Q.C.T.," he sometimes sang at these private events known for their "beautiful ladies and chivalric and gifted men," as well as concerts like the one directed by Fleetwood on December 16, 1874, which according to the *National Republican* was attended by an audience "representing the best circles of our most refined and cultivated fellow-citizens" (Cole received a standing ovation after singing "Coal-Black Wine," a clever play on his name). See *National Republican* December 18, 1874, 4 and *New National Era and Citizen*, January 8, 1874, 3 for examples of Cole's social and musical activities. His presence at a dinner for the Institute for Colored Youth of Pennsylvania suggests he could be the brother of Rebecca J. Cole, the physician (*National Republican*, December 9, 1874, 4). See Ronald D. Cunningham, "'His Influence with the Colored People Is Marked': Christian Fleetwood's Quest for Command in the War with Spain and Its Aftermath," *Army History* no. 51 (2001): 20–28 for more about Frederick C. Revells. Revells, Fleetwood, Solomon Johnson, and Henry Johnson were all vestry members at St. Andrews Church in 1870 (*Daily National Republican*, April 20, 1870). These four appear to have served in the army together.

81. For at least ten years, Jerome Johnson, Solomon Johnson, Walker Lewis, and William Wormley were connected socially and politically through their membership in the First Ward Republican Club. In April 1869, two months after African Americans gained voting rights, under Jerome Johnson's leadership as president and chair, they saw to "getting ready for the campaign," were present at the city hall "every day during the registration," and served as "judges and clerks of election" (*Evening Star*, April 23, 1869, 4). "Sir Solomon Johnson" was officer and "eminent commander" for the Knights Templar order of the Freemasons, later the "worshipful master" at Pythagoras Lodge and first sergeant for "a select military group" known as "the Home Guards." See *Evening Star*, October 17, 1873, 4, October 26, 1875, 4, and December 21, 1875, 4.

82. Crummell to Pinkney, April 22, 1882, 19–24; Crummell gives detailed descriptions of these four vestrymen.

83. Cromwell, *Unveiled Voices, Unvarnished Memories*, 105.

84. Crummell to Pinkney, April 22, 1882, 8.

85. Crummell to Pinkney, April 22, 1882, 7.

86. Crummell to Pinkney, April 22, 1882.

87. Crummell to Pinkney, April 22, 1882, 9.

88. The paper is referring to Gilbert and Sullivan's popular comic operetta "H.M.S. Pinafore," which first came out in 1878. It was staged by an amateur theatrical company. Fleetwood and Mattie Johnson were in the performance together. Mattie Lawrence

became something of a local celebrity. Henry Johnson and others presented her with "a handsome gold watch and chain, accompanied with a beautiful autograph album containing the names of all the donors" at the Jubilee Singers concert on February 16, 1882 (*Evening Star*, February 17, 1882, 4).

89. "St. Luke's Choir Disbanded," *The Washington Post*, March 24, 1880. There is no evidence to support the idea that Crummell wanted a boys' choir.

90. "Dr. Crummell Contradicts," *The Washington Post*, March 26, 1880; "The St. Luke's Church Trouble," *The Washington Post*, March 27, 1880.

91. Crummell to Pinkney, April 22, 1882. The letter from Hopkins is also printed in "Dr. Crummell Contradicts."

92. "St. Luke's Church Trouble."

93. Crummell to Pinkney, April 22, 1882, 12.

94. Turner, *Anthropology of Experience*, 40.

95. Turner, *Ritual Process*, 175.

96. "Fleetwood to James Hall," June 8, 1865. National Park Service, https://www.nps.gov/rich/learn/historyculture/writings3.htm. The original letter is in the Carter G. Woodson collection at the Manuscript Division, Library of Congress.

97. Crummell to Pinkney, April 22, 1882, 13.

98. "A Church's Differences. More Trouble between St. Luke's Rector and His Vestry," *The Washington Post*, October 26, 1880.

99. St. Luke's Vestry to Bishop William Pinkney, October 30, 1880. MDA.

100. Bishop William Pinkney to St. Luke's Vestry, October 30, 1880. MDA.

101. Alexander Crummell to Bishop William Pinkney, October 27, 1880. MDA.

102. Alexander Crummell to Bishop William Pinkney, November 9, 1880. MDA.

103. Rita Lloyd Moroney, *Montgomery Blair, Postmaster General* (Washington, DC: US Government Printing Office, 1963), 8.

104. Crummell to Pinkney, April 22, 1882, 11.

105. "1881 Convention Journal," 86. MDA.

106. St. Luke's Vestry to Bishop William Pinkney, March 28, 1882. MDA.

107. Communicant members of St. Luke's PE Church to Bishop William Pinkney, April 3, 1882. MDA.

108. Crummell to Pinkney, April 22, 1882, 14–15.

109. Two letters survive that were written to the bishop by laymen of St. Luke's on behalf of Crummell. Langston W. Allen told the bishop, "I have no sympathy for these bad men who are fighting Dr. Cr[u]mmell and I am not mean enough to join in with drinking and notorious characters to fight a minister even if they are vestrymen of the church" (Langston W. Allen to Bishop Pinkney, April 19, 1882. Alexander Crummell file MDA). The second letter was written by J. W. Cromwell who informed the bishop that he had been attending St. Luke's "long before some who are now active in the affairs of the Church found it their duty to leave other communions then more thriving and fashionable" and that he found Crummell to be "a most conscientious rector with a hearty support from many." His letter urged the bishop to weigh all the facts before taking any action regarding Crummell (Cromwell to Pinkney, April 20, 1882).

110. Bishop William Pinkney to St. Luke's Church, May 3, 1882, copy, Bishop's Journal, MDA.

111. Crummell to Pinkney, April 22, 1882, 13–14.
112. "1883 Diocese of Maryland Parochial Report," 92–93. MDA.
113. Vestry of St. Luke's to Bishop William Pinkney, February 6, 1883. MDA.
114. "St. Luke's Troubles," *The Washington Post*, March 27, 1883.
115. Richard Henry Nugent and his wife Narcissus George were enslaved then adopted and educated by Quakers in Pennsylvania. After emancipation, Richard was employed as a doorman at the Supreme Court and possibly worked for Chief Justice Edward Douglass White. He was the grandfather of Henry Bruce Nugent, an influential writer and painter during the Harlem Renaissance. See Thomas H. Wirth, ed., *Gay Rebel of the Harlem Renaissance* (Durham: Duke University Press, 2002), 7.
116. Probably Douglas Syphax, one of ten children born to Mariah and Charles Syphax, who lived free on fifteen acres of their own land on the Custis plantation in Arlington, VA, now Arlington House at the Arlington Cemetery. Douglas Syphax relocated to Philadelphia and worked in real estate, hiring Calvin Brent (the architect that designed St. Luke's) to build houses for him. See Wilson, *African American Architects*.
117. Daniel Murray was a librarian at the Library of Congress. See Alex H. Poole, "'The Sage of Negro Bibliography:' Daniel A. P. Murray, the Librarian as Public Intellectual," *Library Quarterly* 90, no. 1 (2020), https://doi.org/10.1086/706306.
118. Langston Allen was then US Minister to Haiti. See John Dirk Fulton, "Langston Mercer Allen, United States Minister to Haiti, 1877–1885" *Student Work*, 1969, https://digitalcommons.unomahoa.edu/studentwork/462; "John Mercer Langston," *Negro History Bulletin* 5, no. 4 (1942): 93–93, http://www.jstor.org/stable/44246678.
119. "St. Luke's Troubles, Two Vestries, a Pressing Debt, and Decreased Revenues," *The Washington Post*, March 27, 1883.
120. "Saved from the Hammer," *The Washington Post*, April 9, 1883.
121. "1884 Convention Journal," 93. MDA.
122. "1885 Convention Journal, Work Among Colored People." MDA.
123. *Shades and the Lights*, 31.
124. "1885 Convention Journal, Work Among Colored People." Printed letter from E. M. Edson, President of the Girl's Friendly Society, May 1880, MDA.
125. "1884 Diocese of Maryland Parochial Report." MDA.
126. Floyd, *Power of Black Music*, 222.
127. Floyd, *Power of Black Music*, 223.
128. *Shades and the Lights*, 24.

AFTERWORD

1. William E. Matthews, *John F. W. Ware and His Work for the Freedmen. An Address in the African Methodist Church, Charles Street, Boston, April 11, 1881. By William E. Matthews of Baltimore. With Introductory Remarks by Hon. John D. Long* (Boston: Press of Geo. H. Ellis, 1881), 6–7. United Methodist Archives, Drew University, Madison, NJ.
2. Glaude, *Black Democracy*, 182.

BIBLIOGRAPHY

PRIMARY SOURCES

Biographies, Memoirs, and Other Narratives

Albert, Octavia V. Rogers. *The House of Bondage, or, Charlotte Brooks and Other Slaves, Original and Life Like, as They Appeared in Their Old Plantation and City Slave Life; Together with Pen-Pictures of the Peculiar Institution, with Sights and Insights into Their New Relations as Freedmen, Freemen, and Citizens*. New York: Hunt & Eaton, 1890. Documenting the American South, University Library, University of North Carolina at Chapel Hill, 2000.

Allen, Richard. *The Life, Experience, and Gospel Labours of the Rt. Rev. Richard Allen. To Which Is Annexed the Rise and Progress of the African Methodist Episcopal Church in the United States of America. Containing a Narrative of the Yellow Fever in the Year of Our Lord 1793: With an Address to the People of Colour in the United States*. Philadelphia: Martin & Boden, 1833. Documenting the American South, University Library, University of North Carolina at Chapel Hill, 2000.

Andrews, William L., ed. *Sisters of the Spirit: Three Black Women's Autobiographies of the Nineteenth Century*. Bloomington: Indiana University Press, 1986.

Baker, T. Lindsay and Julie P. Baker, eds. *The WPA Oklahoma Slave Narratives*. Norman: University of Oklahoma Press, 1996.

Blight, David W., ed. *A Slave No More: Two Men Who Escaped to Freedom, Including Their Own Narratives of Emancipation*. Orlando: Harcourt, 2007.

Born in Slavery: Slave Narratives from the Federal Writer's Project, 1936–1938. Manuscript Division, Library of Congress.

Bragg, George F., Jr. *Afro-American Church Work. Historical Addresses*. Baltimore: G. F. Bragg, 1918.

Bragg, George F., Jr. *The First Negro Priest on Southern Soil*. Baltimore: Church Advocate Print, 1909.

Bragg, George F., Jr. *The First Negro Organization: The Free African Society Established on April 12th, 1787*. Baltimore: G. F. Bragg, 1924.

Bragg, George F., Jr. *Men of Maryland*. Baltimore: Church Advocate Press, 1914. Documenting the American South, University Library, University of North Carolina at Chapel Hill, 2001.

Bremer, Fredrika. *America of the Fifties: Letter of Fredrika Bremer*. Edited by Adolph B. Benson. New York: American-Scandinavian Foundation; London: Humphrey Milford, Oxford University Press, 1924.

Brown, Hallie Q. *Homespun Heroines and Other Women of Distinction*. Xenia: Aldine, 1926. Reprint, New York: Oxford University Press, 1988.

Butt, Israel L. *History of African Methodism in Virginia OR Four Decades in the Old Dominion*. Hampton: Hampton Institute Press, 1908. Documenting the American South, University Library, University of North Carolina at Chapel Hill, 2000.

Christian A. Fleetwood Papers, 1797–1945. Diary, 1864. Manuscript Division, Library of Congress. https://www.loc.gov/search/?fa=partof:christian+a.+fleetwood+papers.

Coker, Daniel. "Sermon Delivered Extempore in the African Bethel Church in the City of Baltimore, on the 21st of January, 1816, to a Numerous Concourse of People, on Account of the Coloured People Gaining Their Church (Bethel) in the Supreme Court of the State of Pennsylvania." In *The Methodist Experience in America: A Sourcebook*. Edited by Russell E. Richey, Kenneth E. Rowe, and Jean Miller Schmidt, 127–30. Nashville: Abingdon Press, 2000.

Cooper, Anna Julia. *A Voice from the South. By a Black Woman from the South*. Xenia, Ohio: Aldine Printing House, 1892. Documenting the American South, University Library, University of North Carolina at Chapel Hill, 2000. https://docsouth.unc.edu/church/cooper/cooper.html.

Cromwell, John Wesley. "The First Negro Churches in the District of Columbia." *The Journal of Negro History* 7, no. 1 (1922): 64–106. February 5, 2001.

DeCosta, B. F. *Three Score and Ten: The Story of the St. Philip's Church, New York City*. New York: 1889.

De Guimps, Roger. *Pestalozzi: His Life and His Work*. Translated by J. Russell. New York: D. Appleton, 1904.

Dickerson, Donna L. *The Reconstruction Era: Primary Documents on Events from 1865 to 1877*. Westport: Greenwood Press, 2003.

Dixon Long, John. *Pictures of Slavery in Church and State; Including Personal Reminiscences, Biographical Sketches, Anecdotes, Etc., Etc., with an Appendix Containing the Views of John Wesley and Richard Watson on Slavery*. Philadelphia, 1857. Documenting the American South, University Library, University of North Carolina at Chapel Hill, 2000.

Douglass, Frederick. *Narrative of the Life of Frederick Douglass, an American Slave, Written by Himself*. Edited by Benjamin Quarles. Cambridge, MA: Belknap Press of Harvard University Press, 1960.

Du Bois, W. E. Burghardt. *Black Reconstruction in America*. New York: Harcourt, Brace, 1935. Reprint, New York: Touchstone, 1995.

Du Bois, W. E. Burghardt. "The Freedmen's Bureau." *Atlantic Monthly* 87, no. 519 (1901). http://www.theatlantic.com/issues/01mar/dubois.htm.

Du Bois, W. E. Burghardt. *The Souls of Black Folks*. Chicago: A. C. McClurg, 1903. Reprint, New York: Penguin Books, 1996.

BIBLIOGRAPHY

Edwards, Paul, ed. *Equiano's Travels: His Autobiography, the Interesting Narrative of the Life of Olaudah Equiano or Gustavus Vassa the African*. Portsmouth, NH: Heinemann, 1969.

Escott, Paul D. *Slavery Remembered: A Record of Twentieth-Century Slave Narratives*. Chapel Hill: University of North Carolina Press, 1979.

Federal Writers' Project: Slave Narrative Project, Vol. 9, Mississippi, Allen-Young. 1936. Library of Congress, Manuscript/Mixed Material. Accessed September 20, 2023. www.loc.gov/item/mesn090/.

Gibbs, Mifflin W. *Shadow and Light: An Autobiography*. Washington, DC: M. W. Gibbs, 1902. Reprint, New York: Arno Press and New York Times, 1968.

Goodwin, Pamela Helen. "Methodist Episcopal Sunday-School, Akron, Ohio." In *The Methodist Experience in America: A Sourcebook*. Edited by Russell E. Richey, Kenneth E. Rowe, and Jean Miller Schmidt, 2:376–78. Nashville: Abingdon Press, 2000.

Handy, James A. *Scraps of African Methodist Episcopal History*. Philadelphia: A.M.E. Book Concern, 1902. Documenting the American South, University Library, University of North Carolina at Chapel Hill, 2000.

Heard, Josephine Delphine Henderson. *Morning Glories*. Philadelphia, 1890. Schomburg Center for Research in Black Culture, the New York Public Library.

Henry, Thomas W. *Autobiography of Rev. Thomas W. Henry, of the A.M.E. Church*. Documenting the American South, University Library, University of North Carolina at Chapel Hill, 2003.

Henry, Thomas W. *From Slavery to Salvation: The Autobiography of Rev. Thomas W. Henry of the A.M.E. Church*. Baltimore, 1872. Reprint, Jackson: University Press of Mississippi, 1994.

Loewenberg, Bert James, and Ruth Bogin, eds. *Black Women in Nineteenth-Century American Life*. University Park: Pennsylvania State University Press, 1988.

Jackson-Coppin, Fanny. *Reminiscences of School Life, and Hints on Teaching*. Philadelphia: A.M.E. Book Concern, 1913. Documenting the American South, University Library, University of North Carolina at Chapel Hill, 1999.

Jacobs, Harriet. *Incidents in the Life of a Slave Girl, Written by Herself*. Boston, 1861. Reprint, Cambridge, MA: Harvard University Press, 1987.

Jeter, Henry N. *Pastor Henry N. Jeter's Twenty-Five Years Experience with the Shiloh Baptist Church and Her History. Corner School and Mary Streets, Newport, R.I.* Providence: Remington Printing, 1901. Documenting the American South, University Library, University of North Carolina at Chapel Hill, 2001.

Johnson, Thomas L. *Twenty-Eight Years a Slave, or the Story of My Life in Three Continents*. Bournemouth: W. Mate & Sons; London: Christian Workers' Depot, 1909. Documenting the American South, University Library, University of North Carolina at Chapel Hill, 1999.

Keckley, Elizabeth. *Behind the Scenes, or Thirty Years a Slave and Four Years in the White House*. New York: G. W. Carleton, 1868. Documenting the American South, University Library, University of North Carolina at Chapel Hill, 1999.

Langston, John Mercer. *The Exodus: The Causes Which Led the Colored People of the South to Leave Their Homes—the Lesson of the Exodus*. Washington, DC: Rufus H. Darby, Book and Job Printer, 1879.

Licorish, Joshua E. *Harry Hosier. African Pioneer Preacher: Including Brief History of African Zoar Methodist Church Founded 1794, Philadelphia, Pennsylvania.* Philadelphia: Afro-Methodist Associates, 1967. "Zoar File," St. George's United Methodist Church Archives, Philadelphia.

Matthews, William E. *John F. W. Ware and His Work for the Freedmen. An Address in the African Methodist Church, Charles Street, Boston, April 11, 1881. By William E. Matthews of Baltimore. With Introductory Remarks by Hon. John D. Long.* Boston: Press of Geo. H. Ellis, 1881. United Methodist Archives, Drew University, Madison, NJ.

Memoir of Old Elizabeth, a Colored Woman and Other Testimonies of Women Slaves. Oxford: Benediction Classics, 2010.

Morgan, Joseph. *Morgan's History of the New Jersey Conference of the A.M.E. Church, from 1872 to 1887, and of the Several Churches, as Far as Possible from Date of Organization, with Biographical Sketches of Members of the Conference.* Camden: S. Chew, Printer, 1887. United Methodist Archives, Drew University, Madison, NJ.

Palmer, Phoebe. *The Way of Holiness, with Notes by the Way; Being a Narrative of Religious Experience Resulting from a Determination to Be a Bible Christian.* New York, 1854.

Payne, Daniel Alexander. *History of the African Methodist Episcopal Church.* Nashville: Publishing House of the A.M.E. Sunday-School Union, 1891. Documenting the American South, University Library, University of North Carolina at Chapel Hill, 2001.

Payne, Daniel Alexander. *Recollections of Seventy Years.* Nashville: Publishing House of the A.M.E. Sunday School Union, 1888. Documenting the American South, University Library, University of North Carolina at Chapel Hill, 2001.

Perry, Calbraith B. *Twelve Years among the Colored People: A Record of the Work of Mount Calvary Chapel of S. Mary the Virgin, Baltimore.* New York: James Pott, 1884.

Raybold, G. A. *Reminiscences of Methodism in West Jersey.* New York: Lane & Scott, 1849. Drew University Library, Madison, NJ.

Robbins, Hollis, and Henry Louis Gates Jr., eds. *The Portable Nineteenth-Century African American Women Writers.* New York: Penguin Books, 2017.

Russell, Henry. *Cheer! Boys, Cheer!: Memories of Men & Music.* London: J. Macqueen, 1895.

Russell, William Howard. *My Diary North and South.* Boston: T. O. H. P. Burnam, 1863.

Simmons, William J. *Men of Mark: Eminent, Progressive, and Rising.* Cleveland: Geo. M. Rewell, 1887. Documenting the American South, University Library, University of North Carolina at Chapel Hill, 2000.

Steward, Theophilus Gould. *Fifty Years in the Gospel Ministry from 1864 to 1914. Twenty-seven Years in the Pastorate; Sixteen Years' Active Service as Chaplain in the U. S. Army; Seven Years Professor in Wilberforce University; Two Trips to Europe; A Trip in Mexico.* Philadelphia: A.M.E. Book Concern, ca. 1921. Documenting the American South, University Library, University of North Carolina at Chapel Hill, 2000.

Still, William. *The Underground Railroad. A Record of Facts, Authentic Narratives, Letters, &C., Narrating the Hardships, Hair-Breadth Escapes and Death Struggles of the Slaves in Their Efforts for Freedom, as Related by Themselves and Others, or Witnessed by the Author; Together with Sketches of Some of the Largest Stockholders, and Most Liberal Aiders and Advisers, of the Road.* Philadelphia: Porter & Coates, 1872.

Trotter, James M. *Music and Some Highly Musical People: Containing Brief Chapters on I. A Description of Music, II. The Music of Nature, III. A Glance at the History of Music, IV. The Power, Beauty, and Uses of Music. Following Which Are Given Sketches of the Lives of Remarkable Musicians of the Colored Race. With Portraits, and an Appendix Containing Copies of Music Composed by Colored Men.* Boston: Lee and Shepard; New York: Charles T. Dillingham, 1881.

Tyerman, Luke. *The Life and Times of the Rev. John Wesley, M.A., Founder of the Methodists*, Vol. 3. London: Hodder and Stoughton, 1871.

Vincent, Elizabeth K. *In the Days of Lincoln: Girlhood Recollections and Personal Reminiscences of Life in Washington During the Civil War.* Gardenia: Spanish American Institute Press, 1924.

Washington, Booker T. *Up from Slavery: An Autobiography.* New York: Doubleday, Page, 1901.

Waters, Andrew, ed. *Prayin' to Be Set Free: Personal Accounts of Slavery in Mississippi.* Winston-Salem: John F. Blair, 2002.

Watkins, James. *Struggles for Freedom; or The Life of James Watkins, Formerly a Slave in Maryland, U.S.; in Which Is Detailed a Graphic Account of His Extraordinary Escape from Slavery, Notices of the Fugitive Slave Law, the Sentiments of American Divines on the Subject of Slavery, etc., etc.*, 19th ed. Manchester: Printed for James Watkins, 1860. Documenting the American South, University Library, University of North Carolina at Chapel Hill, 2000.

Wesley, John. "Minutes of Several Conversations between the Rev. Mr. Wesley and Others; from the Year 1744 to the Year 1789." Vol. 7: *The Works of the Reverend John Wesley, A. M.* Edited by John Emory. New York: T. Mason and G. Lane, 1839.

Willson, Joseph. *The Elite of Our People: Joseph Willson's Sketches of Black Upper-Class Life in Antebellum Philadelphia.* Edited by Julie Winch. Philadelphia: Merrihew and Thompson, printers, 1841. Reprint, University Park: Pennsylvania State University Press, 2000.

Woodson, Carter G. *The History of the Negro Church.* 2nd ed. Washington, DC: Associated Publishers, 1921. http://docsouth.unc.edu/church/woodson/woodson.html#woods185.

Wright, Richard R., Jr. *Centennial Encyclopaedia of the African Methodist Episcopal Church Containing Principally the Biographies of the Men and Women, Both Ministers and Laymen, Whose Labors during a Hundred Years, Helped Make the A.M.E. Church What It Is; Also Short Historical Sketches of Annual Conferences, Educational Institutions, General Departments, Missionary Societies of the A.M.E. Church, and General Information about African Methodism and the Christian Church in General; Being a Literary Contribution to the Celebration of the One Hundredth Anniversary of the Formation of the African Methodist Episcopal Church Denomination by Richard Allen and Others, at Philadelphia, Penna., in 1816.* Philadelphia: Book Concern of the A.M.E. Church, 1916. Documenting the American South, University Library, University of North Carolina at Chapel Hill, 2001.

Church and Conference Records

African Methodist Episcopal Zion Church in America, Annual Conference and the Annual Report of the Mission Board, under the Superintendence of the Rt. Rev. Sampson Talbot. Held in Union Wesley Church, Washington, DC, April 7–18, 1866. Minutes. Washington, DC: Wm. H. Moore, 1866. Schomburg Center for Research in Black Culture, the New York Public Library. Microfilm.

African Methodist Episcopal Zion Church, General Conference, 1864. Minutes. Hartford: S. M. Giles, 1864. Schomburg Center for Research in Black Culture, the New York Public Library. Microfilm.

Alexander Crummell Papers. Maryland Diocesan Archives, Baltimore, MD.

Asbury United Methodist Church Records, 1836–1986. Schomburg Center for Research in Black Culture, the New York Public Library. Microfilm.

Bethel African Methodist Episcopal Church Collection, 1825–1936. Maryland State Archives, Annapolis, MD. Microfilm.

Colored Annual Conference of the Methodist Episcopal Church, Held at Zoar Church, Philadelphia, April 5th, 1857. Philadelphia: Higgins & Perkinpine, 1857. St. George's Methodist Episcopal Church Archives, Philadelphia, PA.

Colored Annual Conference of the Methodist Episcopal Church, Held at Wilmington, August 6, 1863. Minutes. Philadelphia: Collins, 1863. St. George's United Methodist Church Archives, Philadelphia.

Delaware Annual Conference, 1864–1888. Minutes. The Schomburg Center for Research in Black Culture, the New York Public Library. Microfilm.

Ebenezer United Methodist Church Records, 1865–1980. Schomburg Center for Research in Black Culture, the New York Public Library. Microfilm.

New England Annual Conference of the African Methodist Episcopal Church, 1894. Minutes. Boston: African Methodist Episcopal Church, 1894. Hay Rider, Brown University Library.

Plymouth Congregational United Church of Christ Records, 1896–1982. Schomburg Center for Research on Black Culture, the New York Public Library. Microfilm.

Sharp Street Memorial United Methodist Church Records, 1873–1993. Schomburg Center for Research in Black Culture, the New York Public Library. Microfilm.

Shiloh Baptist Church Records, 1863–1992. Schomburg Center for Research in Black Culture, the New York Public Library. Microfilm.

St. John's AME Church Records, including Quarterly Conference Minutes, Virginia Annual Conference Minutes, and articles from *The Christian Recorder*. St. John's AME Church, Norfolk, VA.

St. Luke's Episcopal Church Records, Maryland Diocesan Archives, Baltimore, MD.

St. Mary's Episcopal Church Records, Maryland Diocesan Archives, Baltimore, MD.

Union Congregational Church Collection. Newport Historical Society. Newport, RI.

Union Congregational Church File. Rhode Island Black Heritage Society. Providence, RI.

Zoar United Methodist Church Records, 1841–1984. Schomburg Center for Research in Black Culture, the New York Public Library. Microfilm.

Hymnals and Songbooks

Abbey, A. J., and M. J. Munger. *White Robes for the Sunday-School. A Choice New Collection of Songs Quartets, and Choruses for Sunday-Schools, Devotional Meetings, and the Home Circle*. Boston: Oliver Ditson & Co., 1879. School of Theology Archives, Boston University, Boston.

The African Methodist Episcopal Church Hymn Book: Being a Collection of Hymns Designed to Supersede All Others Hitherto Made Use of in That Church. Selected from Various Authors. Philadelphia: Jas. B. Rogers, Printer, 1872. Methodist Library, Drew University.

Kennaday, J. *The Sunday School Speaker, or Exercises for Anniversaries and Celebrations Consisting of Addresses, Dialogues, Recitations, Bible Class Lessons, Hymns, Etc., Adapted to the Various Subjects to Which Sabbath School Efforts Are Directed*. 11th ed. Philadelphia: Perkinpine & Higgins, 1860.

Lomax, Alan, ed. *Folk Song U.S.A. Collected, Adapted and Arranged by John A. and Alan Lomax*. New York: The New American Library, 1966.

Mason, Lowell. *Manual of the Boston Academy of Music, for the Instruction in the Elements of Vocal Music, on the System of Pestalozzi*. 5th ed. Boston: J.H. Wilkins & R. B. Carter, 1839.

New Hymn and Tune Book of the African Methodist Episcopal Zion Church. Charlotte: A.M.E. Zion Publication House, 1892. Schomburg Center for Research in Black Culture, the New York Public Library.

O'Kane, T. C. *Every Sabbath: A New Collection of Music Adapted to the Wants and Capacities of Sunday-Schools, the Home Circle and Devotional Gatherings*. Cincinnati: John Church & Co., 1874. School of Theology Archives, Boston University, Boston.

Phillips, Philip. *Musical Leaves for Sabbath Schools, Composed of Musical Leaves Nos. 1, 2, 3, and 4, with an Addition of One Hundred Popular Hymns*. Cincinnati: Philip Phillips & Co., 1865. School of Theology Archives, Boston University, Boston.

Pratt, George W., and J. C. Johnson. *Pestalozzian School Song Book*. Boston: Geo. P. Reed & Co., 1855. School of Theology Archives, Boston University, Boston.

Slave Songs of the United States. Edited by William Francis Allen, Charles Pickard Ware and Lucy McKim Garrison. New York: A. Simpson, 1867. Author's personal collection.

Turner, H. M., ed. *The Hymn Book of the African Methodist Episcopal Church: Being a Collection of Hymns, Sacred Songs and Chants Designed to Supersede All Others Hitherto Made Us of in That Church; Selected from Various Authors*, 5th ed. Philadelphia: Publication Division of the A.M.E. Church, 1877), accessed November 1, 2023. https://archive.org/details/bookafricaoori/page/n3/mode/2up.

Turner, H. M., ed. *The Hymn Book of the African Methodist Episcopal Church, Being a Collection of Hymns, Sacred Songs and Chants, Designed to Supersede All Others Hitherto Made Use of in That Church. Selected from Various Authors*. 6th ed. Philadelphia: Publication Department of the A.M.E. Church, 1878, Harris Collection of American Poetry and Plays, Brown University, Providence.

Turner, H. M., ed. *The Hymn Book of the African Methodist Episcopal Church, Being a Collection of Hymns, Sacred Songs and Chants, Designed to Supersede All Others Hitherto Made Use of in That Church. Selected from Various Authors*. 9th ed.

Philadelphia: Publication Department of the A.M.E. Church. United Methodist Archives, Drew University, Madison, NJ.

White, Edward L. & J. Edgar Gould. *The Wreath of School Songs; Consisting of Songs, Hymns and Chants, with Appropriate Music: Designed for the Use of Common Schools, Seminaries, &C. &C. To Which Are Added the Elements of Vocal Music. Arranged According to the Pestalozzian System of Instruction; with Numerous Exercises, Intended to Supersede (in Part) the Necessity of the Black-Board.* Boston: Benjamin B. Mussey & Company 1848, School of Theology Archives, Boston University, Boston.

Constitutions, Records, Reports, and Studies

African Zoar Methodist Episcopal Church Constitution. Philadelphia: Manly, Orr and Lippencott, 1842, Methodist Archives, Drew University, NJ.

Bacon, Benjamin. *Statistics of the Colored People of Philadelphia Taken by Benjamin C. Bacon and Published by Order of the Board of Education Of "The Pennsylvania Society for Promoting the Abolition of Slavery," Etc.* 2nd ed. Philadelphia: Board of Education, 1859.

Brackett, Jeffrey R. *The Negro in Maryland: A Study of the Institution of Slavery.* Baltimore: Johns Hopkins University, 1889. Reprint, Freeport and New York: Books for Libraries Press, 1969.

Brandt, Lillian. "The Make-up of Negro City Groups." *Charities and the Commons* 15, no. 1 (1905): 7–11.

Constitution of the African Zoar Methodist Episcopal Church. Philadelphia: Manly, Orr and Lippencott, 1842. United Methodist Archives, Drew University, Madison, NJ.

Du Bois, W. E. B. *The Negro Church. Report of a Social Study Made under the Direction of Atlanta University; Together with the Proceedings of the Eighth Conference for the Study of the Negro Problems, Held at Atlanta University, May 26th, 1903.* Atlanta: Atlanta University Press, 1903. Documenting the American South, University Library, University of North Carolina at Chapel Hill, 2001.

Du Bois, W. E. B. *The Philadelphia Negro: A Social Study. With a New Introduction by Elijah Anderson, Together with a Special Report on Domestic Service by Isabel Eaton.* Philadelphia: University of Pennsylvania Press, 1899. Reprint, Philadelphia: University of Pennsylvania Press, 1996.

Haynes, George Edmund. "Conditions among Negroes in the Cities." In *Black Communities and Urban Development in America 1720–1990: From Reconstruction to the Great Migration.* Edited by Kenneth L. Kusmer. New York: Garland Publishing, 1991.

"History and Roster of Maryland Volunteers, War of 1861–6, Volume 2," Maryland State Archives, Annapolis, MD. https://msa.maryland.gov/megafile/msa/speccol/sc2900/sc2908/000001/000366/html/am366--252.html.

May, Samuel. *The Fugitive Slave Law and Its' Victims.* New York: The Anti-Slavery Society, 1861.

"Mission Sketches." *Charities and the Commons* 15, no. 1 (1905): 59–63.

Morals and Manners among Negro Americans: Report of a Social Study Made by Atlanta University under the Patronage of the Trustees of the John F. Slater Fund; with the Proceedings of the 18th Annual Conference for the Study of the Negro Problems, Held at Atlanta University, on Monday, May 26, 1913. Atlanta: The Atlanta University Press, 1914, Documenting the American South, University Library, University of North Carolina at Chapel Hill, 2000.

"The Negro in the Cities of the North." *Charities and the Commons* 15, no. 1 (1905): 1–6.

Peddleton, Helen B. "Negro Dependence in Baltimore." *Charities and the Commons* 15, no. 1 (1905): 50–58.

Statement of L.G. Martin, William C. Clay, Joseph Warren, and John H. Murphy, relative to their election as delegates to the Republican national convention from the fourth Congressional district of Maryland. Baltimore, Md. May 15. Baltimore, 1884. Library of Congress, pdf, accessed October 4, 2023. https://www.loc.gov/item/2020778329/.

US Bureau of the Census. *Population of the United States in 1860; Compiled from the Original Returns of the Eighth Census, under the Direction of the Secretary of the Interior, by Joseph C. G. Kennedy, Superintendent of Census*. Washington, DC: Government Printing Office, 1864. http://www.census.gov/.

US Bureau of the Census. *The Statistics of the Population of the United States, Embracing the Tables of Race, Nationality, Sex, Selected Ages, and Occupations to Which Are Added the Statistics of School Attendance and Illiteracy, of Schools, Libraries, News-Papers and Periodicals, Churches, Pauperism and Crime, and of Areas, Families and Dwellings. Compiled from the Original Returns of the Ninth Census, (June 1, 1870,) under the Direction of the Secretary of the Interior, by Francis A. Walker, Superintendent of Census*. Washington, DC: Government Printing Office, 1872. http://www.census.gov/.

US Bureau of the Census. *Statistics of the Population of the United States at the Tenth Census (June 1, 1880,) Embracing Extended Tables of the Population of States, Counties, and Minor Civil Divisions, with Distinction of Race, Sex, Age, Nativity, and Occupations; Together with Summary Tables, Derived from Other Census Reports, Relating to Newspapers and Periodicals; Public Schools and Illiteracy; the Dependent, Defective, and Delinquent Classes, Etc., by Francis A. Walker, Superintendent of the Census*. Washington, DC: Government Printing Office, 1881.

US Bureau of the Census. *Vital Statistics of the District of Columbia and Baltimore Covering a Period of Six Years Ending May 31, 1890, by John S. Billings, M.D., Expert Special Agent*. Washington, DC: Government Printing Office, 1893.

US Bureau of the Census. *Report on Education in the United States at the Eleventh Census: 1890, by James H. Blodgett, Special Agent*. Washington, DC: Government Printing Office, 1893.

US Bureau of the Census. *Vital Statistics of Boston and Philadelphia Covering a Period of Six Years Ending May 31, 1890, by John S. Billings, M.D., Expert Special Agent*. Washington, DC: Government Printing Office, 1895.

US Bureau of the Census. *Report on Population of the United States at the Eleventh Census: 1890, by Robert P. Porter, Superintendent of Census*. Washington, DC: Government Printing Office, 1895.

Waring, J. H. N. "Some Causes of Criminality among Colored People." *Charities and the Commons* 15, no. 1 (1905): 45–49.

Wright, James M. *The Free Negro in Maryland: 1634–1860*. New York: Columbia University, 1921.

Sermons, Speeches, Celebrations, and Souvenirs

African Methodist Episcopal Zion Church. *Centennial Souvenir, 1796–1896*. United Methodist Archives, Drew University, Madison, NJ.

Coker, Daniel. "Sermon Delivered Extempore in the African Bethel Church in the City of Baltimore, on the 21st of January, 1816, to a Numerous Concorse of People, on Account of the Coloured People Gaining Their Church (Bethel) in the Supreme Court of the State of Pennsylvania." In *The Methodist Experience in America: A Sourcebook*. Edited by Russell E. Richey, Kenneth E. Rowe, and Jean Miller Schmidt. Nashville: Abingdon Press, 2000.

Foner, Philip S., and Robert J. Branham, ed. *Lift Every Voice: African American Oratory, 1787–1900*. Tuscaloosa: University of Alabama Press, 1998.

The Journal of Zoar Celebrating the Centennial of the Delaware Annual Conference the Methodist Church, 1864—1964 and the One Hundred and Seventieth Anniversary of Zoar Methodist Church, 1794—1964. "Zoar File." St. George's United Methodist Church Archives, Philadelphia.

M'Kim, J. Miller. *The Freedmen of South Carolina. An Address Delivered by J. Miller M'kim, in Sansom Hall, July 9th, 1862. Together with a Letter from the Same to Stephen Colwell, Esq., Chairman of the Port Royal Relief Committee, to Stephen Colwell, Esq., Chairman of the Port Royal Relief Committee*. Philadelphia: Willis P. Hazard, 1862. Historical Society of Pennsylvania, Philadelphia.

Shades and the Lights of a Fifty Years' Ministry. 1844 to 1894. Jubilate. A Sermon by Alex. Crummell, Rector, and a Presentation Address by Mrs. A.J. Cooper, St. Luke's Church, Washington, DC, December 9th, 1894. Washington, DC: R. L. Pendleton, Printer, 1894, Maryland Diocesan Archives, Baltimore.

Twenty-Eighth Anniversary of the Zoar M. E. Sabbath School, Sunday Afternoon, April 24, 1870 at 2 1/2 O'clock, P.M. In the Church, Brown Street, above Fourth. Philadelphia: Senseman & Son, 1870. The Historical Society of Pennsylvania, Philadelphia.

Newspapers

Afro-American (Baltimore). April 29, 1893—January 3, 1914. Maryland State Archives, https://msa.maryland.gov/megafile/msa/speccol/sc4900/sc4968/html/aanews.html.

The American Citizen (Baltimore). April 19, 1879. *Chronicling America: Historic American Newspapers*. Library of Congress. 2024.

The Baltimore Sun, June 1, 1875—May 8, 1877. Newspaper Archive. Newspaperarchive.com.

The Christian Recorder (Philadelphia). March 6, 1869. *African American Newspapers*. Accessible Archives, 2021.

The Evening Sun (Washington, DC). January 6, 1868—December 26, 1882. *Chronicling America: Historic American* Newspapers. Library of Congress.

The New York Herald. August 11, 1873 and September 7, 1874. Newspaper Archive. Newspaperarchive.com.

The Sun (New York, NY), November 12, 1899. *Chronicling America: Historic American* Newspapers. Library of Congress. 2024.

The Weekly Anglo-African (New York). June 2, 1860. Library of Congress. 2024.

SECONDARY SOURCES

Books

Anderson, Vinton R. "'Under Our Own Vine and Fig Tree:' Sunday Morning Worship in the African American Methodist Episcopal Church." In *The Sunday Service of the Methodists: Twentieth-Century Worship in Worldwide Methodism*. Edited by Karen B. Westerfield Tucker, 157–72. Nashville: Kingswood Books, 1996.

Andrews, Doris. "The African Methodists of Philadelphia, 1794–1802." In *Perspectives on American Methodism: Interpretive Essays*. Edited by Kenneth E. Rowe, Russell E. Richey, and Jean Miller Schmidt, 145–55. Nashville: Kingswood Books, 1993.

Arnesen, Eric. *Black Protest and the Great Migration: A Brief History with Documents*. Boston: Bedford/St. Martin's, 2003.

Bell, Catherine. *Ritual Theory, Ritual Practice*. New York: Oxford University Press, 1992.

Berry, Daina Ramey, and Kali Nicole Gross. *A Black Women's History of the United States*. New York: Beacon Press, 2020.

Best, Wallace D. *Passionately Human, No Less Divine: Religion and Culture in Black Chicago, 1915–1952*. Princeton: Princeton University Press, 2005.

Bilhartz, Terry D. *Urban Religion and the Second Great Awakening: Church and Society in Early National Baltimore*. Cranbury: Associated University Presses, 1986.

Blockson, Charles. *The Underground Railroad in Pennsylvania*. Jacksonville: Flame International, 1981.

Booker, Vaughn A. *Lift Every Voice and Swing: Black Musicians and Religious Culture in the Jazz Century*. New York: New York University Press, 2020.

Bourdieu, Pierre. *Distinction: A Social Critique of the Judgement of Taste*. Translated by Richard Nice. London: Harvard University Press and Routledge, 1984. Reprint, 2010.

Brackett, Marc. *Permission to Feel: The Power of Emotional Intelligence to Achieve Well-Being and Success*. New York: Celadon Books, 2019.

Brooks Higginbotham, Evelyn. *Righteous Discontent: The Women's Movement in the Black Baptist Church, 1880–1920*. Cambridge, MA: Harvard University Press, 2003.

Brown, Courtney. *Politics in Music: Music and Political Transformation from Beethoven to Hip-Hop*. Atlanta: Farsight Press, 2008.

Brown, Frank Burch. *Religious Aesthetics: A Theological Study of Making and Meaning*. Princeton: Princeton University Press, 1989.

Brown, Leslie. *Upbuilding Black Durham: Gender, Class, and Black Community Development in the Jim Crow South*. Chapel Hill: University of North Carolina Press, 2008.

Bushman, Richard L. *The Refinement of America: Persons, Houses, Cities*. New York: Knopf, 1992. Reprint, New York: Vintage Books, 1993.

Butler, Judith, et al. *The Power of Religion in the Public Sphere*. New York: Columbia University Press, 2011.

Caldwell, Hansonia L. *African American Music: A Chronology, 1619–1999*. Los Angeles: Ikoro Communications, 1995.

Cerulo, Massimo, and Adrian Scribano, eds. *The Emotions in the Classics of Sociology: A Study of Social Theory*. New York: Routledge, 2022.

Charters, Samuel. *Songs of Sorrow: Lucy McKim Garrison and "Slave Songs of the United States."* Jackson: University Press of Mississippi, 2015.

Clark-Lewis, Elizabeth. *Living In, Living Out: African American Domestics and the Great Migration.* New York: Kodansha International, 1994.

Collier-Thomas, Bettye. *Jesus, Jobs, and Justice: African American Women and Religion.* New York: Knopf, Borzoi Books, 2010.

Cone, James. *The Spirituals and the Blues, with a New Introduction by Cheryl Townsend Gilkes.* 50th anniversary ed. Maryknoll: Orbis Books, 2022.

Costen, Melva Wilson. *African American Christian Worship.* Nashville: Abingdon Press, 1993.

Cruz, Jon. *Culture on the Margins: The Black Spiritual and the Rise of American Cultural Interpretation.* Princeton: Princeton University Press, 1999.

Curry, Leonard P. *The Free Black in Urban America: The Shadow of the Dream.* Chicago: University of Chicago Press, 1981.

Dailey, Jane, Glenda Elizabeth Gilmore, and Bryant Simon, eds. *Jumpin' Jim Crow: Southern Politics from Civil War to Civil Rights.* Princeton: Princeton University Press, 2000.

Davis, Angela Y. *Blues Legacies and Black Feminism.* New York: Vintage Books, 1999.

Dilthey, Wilhelm. *Selected Writings.* Translated and edited by H. P. Rickman. Cambridge, UK: Cambridge University Press, 1976.

Drake, Jamil W. *To Know the Soul of a People: Religion, Race, and the Making of Southern Folk.* New York: Oxford University Press, 2022.

Dyson, Michael Eric. *Entertaining Race: Performing Blackness in America.* New York: St. Martin's Press, 2021.

Edwards, Laura. *Gendered Strife and Confusion: The Political Culture of Reconstruction.* Champaign: University of Illinois Press, 1997.

Ehrenreich, Barbara. *Dancing in the Streets: A History of Collective Joy.* New York: Holt, 2006.

Fabre, Geneviève. "African-American Commemorative Celebrations in the Nineteenth Century." In *History and Memory in African-American Culture.* Edited by Geneviève Fabre and Robert O'Meally, 72–91. New York: Oxford University Press, 1994.

Floyd, Samuel A., Jr. *The Power of Black Music: Interpreting Its History from Africa to the United States.* New York: Oxford University Press, 1995.

Floyd, Samuel A., Jr., with Melanie L. Zeck and Guthrie Ramsey. *The Transformation of Black Music: The Rhythms, the Songs, and the Ships of the African Diaspora.* New York: Oxford University Press, 2017.

Foner, Eric. *Forever Free: The Story of Reconstruction and Emancipation.* New York: Alfred A. Knopf, 2005.

Frazier, E. Franklin. *Black Bourgeoisie.* New York: Free Press, 1957. Reprint, New York: Free Press Paperbacks, 1997.

Frazier, E. Franklin. *The Negro Church in America.* New York: Schocken Books, 1963.

Fredrickson, George M. *Black Liberation: A Comparative History of Black Ideologies in the United States and South Africa.* New York: Oxford University Press, 1995.

Frey, Sylvia R., and Betty Wood. *Come Shouting to Zion: African American Protestantism in the American South and British Caribbean to 1830.* Chapel Hill: University of North Carolina Press, 1998.

Fuke, Richard Paul. "Land, Lumber and Learning: The Freedmen's Bureau, Education, and the Black Community in Post-Emancipation Maryland." In *The Freedmen's Bureau and Reconstruction: Reconsiderations*. Edited by Paul A. Cimbala and Randall M. Miller, 288–314. New York: Fordham University Press, 1999.

Fulop, Timothy E., and Albert J. Raboteau, eds. *African-American Religion: Interpretive Essays in History and Culture*. New York: Routledge, 1997.

Gac, Scott. *Singing for Freedom: The Hutchinson Family Singers and the Nineteenth-Century Culture of Antebellum Reform*. New Haven: Yale University Press, 2007.

Gaines, Kevin K. *Uplifting the Race: Black Leadership, Politics, and Culture in the Twentieth Century*. Chapel Hill: University of North Carolina Press, 1996.

Gatewood, Willard B. *Aristocrats of Color: The Black Elite, 1880–1920*. Bloomington: Indiana University Press, 1990.

Gellerman, Robert F. *The American Reed Organ and the Harmonium*. Vestal: Vestal Press, 1996.

Genovese, Eugene. "Religious Foundations of the Black Nation." In *African American Religious Thought: An Anthology*. Edited by Cornel West Jr. and Eddie S. Glaude, 301–308. Louisville: Westminster John Knox Press, 2003.

Giggie, John M. *After Redemption: Jim Crow and the Transformation of African American Religion in the Delta, 1875–1915*. New York: Oxford University Press, 2008.

Glaude, Eddie S., Jr. *An Uncommon Faith: A Pragmatic Approach to the Study of African American Religion*. Athens: University of Georgia Press, 2018.

Glaude, Eddie S., Jr. *Exodus! Religion, Race, and Nation in Early Nineteenth-Century Black America*. Chicago: University of Chicago Press, 2000.

Glaude, Eddie S., Jr. "Of the Black Church and the Making of a Black Public." In *African American Religious Thought: An Anthology*. Edited by Cornel West Jr. and Eddie S. Glaude, 338–65. Louisville: Westminster John Knox Press, 2003.

Gomez, Michael. *Exchanging Our Country Marks: The Transformation of African Identities in the Colonial and Antebellum South*. Chapel Hill: University of North Carolina Press, 1998.

Graham, J. H. *Black United Methodists: Retrospect and Prospect*. New York: Vantage Press, 1979.

Gregg, Robert. *Sparks from the Anvil of Oppression: Philadelphia's African Methodists and Southern Migrants, 1890–1940*. Philadelphia: Temple University Press, 1993.

Griffin, Farah Jasmine. *"Who Set You Flowin?" The African-American Migration Narrative*. New York: Oxford University Press, 1995.

Hahn, Steven. *A Nation under Our Feet: Black Political Struggles in the Rural South from Slavery to the Great Migration*. Cambridge: Belknap Press of Harvard University Press, 2003.

Hall, Perry A. *In the Vineyard: Working in African American Studies*. Knoxville: University of Tennessee Press, 1999.

Halpin, Dennis Patrick. *A Brotherhood of Liberty: Black Reconstruction and Its Legacies in Baltimore, 1865–1920*. Philadelphia: University of Pennsylvania Press, 2019.

Harrison, Alfredteen, ed. *Black Exodus: The Great Migration from the American South*. Jackson: University Press of Mississippi, 1991.

Hemphill, Katie M. *Bawdy Houses: Commercial Sex and Regulation in Baltimore, 1790–1915*. Cambridge, UK: Cambridge University Press, 2020.

Hershberg, Theodore. "Free Blacks in Antebellum Philadelphia: A Study of Ex-Slaves, Freeborn, and Socioeconomic Decline." In *African Americans in Pennsylvania: Shifting Historical Perspectives*. Edited by Joe William Trotter Jr. and Eric Ledell Smith, 123–47. Philadelphia: Pennsylvania Historical Museum Commission and Pennsylvania State University Press, 1997.

Herskovits, Melville J. *The New World Negro*. Bloomington: Indiana University Press, 1966.

Hunter, Tera W. *Slave and Free Black Marriage in the Nineteenth Century*. Cambridge: Belknap Press of Harvard, 2017.

Japtok, Martin, and Jerry Rafiki Jenkins, eds., *Authentic Blackness/Real Blackness: Essays on the Meaning of Blackness in Literature and Culture*. New York: Peter Lang, 2011.

Johnson, Mark A. *Rough Tactics: Black Performance in Political Spectacles, 1877–1932*. Jackson: University Press of Mississippi, 2021.

Jones, Charles Edwin. *Black Holiness: A Guide to the Study of Black Participation in Wesleyan Perfectionist and Glossolalic Pentecostal Movements*. Metuchen: Scarecrow Press, 1987.

Jones, Leroi. *Blues People*. New York: W. Morrow, 1963.

Jones, Martha S. *Birthright Citizens: A History of Race and Rights in Antebellum America*. Cambridge, UK: Cambridge University Press, 2018.

Jones, Martha S. *Vanguard: How Black Women Broke Barriers, Won the Vote, and Insisted on Equality for All*. New York: Basic Books, 2020.

Joseph, Peniel. *The Third Reconstruction: America's Struggle for Racial Justice in the Twenty-First Century*. New York: Basic Books, 2022.

Katz, Bernard, ed. *The Social Implications of Early Negro Music in the United States*. New York: Arno Press and New York Times, 1969.

Keck, George R., and Sherrill V. Martin, ed. *Feel the Spirit: Studies in Nineteenth-Century Afro-American Music*. Westport: Greenwood Press, 1988.

Kirby, James E., Russell E. Richey, and Kenneth E. Rowe. *The Methodists*. Westport: Praeger, 1998.

Kramer, Lawrence. *Music as Cultural Practice, 1800–1900*. Berkeley: University of California Press, 1990.

Krehbiel, Henry E. *Afro-American Folksongs: A Study in Racial and National Music*. New York: G. Schirmer, 1914. Reprint, New York: F. Ungar, 1962.

Kusmer, Kenneth L., ed. *From Reconstruction to the Great Migration, 1877–1917*. New York: Garland, 1991.

Langer, Susanne. *Feeling and Form: A Theory of Art Developed from Philosophy in a New Key*. New York: Charles Scribner's Sons, 1953.

Langer, Susanne. *Philosophy in a New Key*. 3rd ed. Cambridge, MA: Harvard University Press, 1957.

Levine, Lawrence W. *Black Culture and Black Consciousness: Afro-American Thought from Slavery to Freedom*. 30th anniversary ed. New York: Oxford University Press, 2007.

Levine, Lawrence W. *High Brow/Low Brow: The Emergence of Cultural Hierarchy in America*. Cambridge: Harvard University Press, 1990.

Lincoln, C. Eric, and Lawrence H. Mamiya. *The Black Church in the African American Experience*. Durham: Duke University Press, 1990.

Locke, Alain. *The Negro and His Music*. Albany: J. B. Lyon Press, 1939. Reprint, New York: Arno Press and New York Times, 1969.

Lott, Eric. *Love & Theft: Blackface Minstrelsy & the American Working Class*. 20th Anniversary ed. New York: Oxford University Press, 2013.

Lyerly, Cynthia. *Methodism and the Southern Mind, 1770–1810*. New York: Oxford University Press, 1998.

Mamiya, Lawrence. "A Social History of the Bethel African Methodist Episcopal Church in Baltimore: The House of God and the Struggle for Freedom." In *American Congregations, Portraits of Twelve Religious Communities*. Edited by James P. Wind and James W. Lewis, 221–92. Chicago: University of Chicago Press, 1994.

Marks, Carole. *Farewell—We're Good and Gone: The Great Black Migration*. Bloomington: Indiana University Press, 1989.

Melton, J. Gordon. *A Will to Choose: The Origins of African American Methodists*. Lanham: Rowman & Littlefield, 2007.

Mitchell, Henry. *Black Church Beginnings: The Long-Hidden Realities of the First Years*. Grand Rapids: W. B. Eerdmans, 2004.

Montgomery, William E. *Under Their Own Vine and Fig Tree: The African-American Church in the South, 1865–1900*. Baton Rouge: Louisiana State University Press, 1993.

Moroney, Rita Lloyd. *Montgomery Blair, Postmaster General*. Washington, DC: US Government Printing Office, 1963.

Moses, Wilson Jeremiah. *Alexander Crummell: A Study of Civilization and Discontent*. Oxford: Oxford University Press, 1989.

Myers Turner, Nicole. *Soul Liberty: The Evolution of Black Religious Politics in Postemancipation Virginia*. Chapel Hill: University of North Carolina Press, 2020.

Pitts, Walter F., Jr. *Old Ship of Zion: The Afro-Baptist Ritual in the African Diaspora*. New York: Oxford University Press, 1993.

Raboteau, Albert J. *Slave Religion: The "Invisible Institution" in the Antebellum South*. Oxford: Oxford University Press, 1980.

Radano, Ronald. *Lying up a Nation: Race and Black Music*. Chicago: University of Chicago Press, 2003.

Ramsey, Guthrie P., Jr. *Who Hears Here? On Black Music, Pasts & Present*. Oakland: University of California Press, 2022.

Reynolds, William J., Milburn Price, and David W. Music. *A Survey of Christian Hymnody*. Carol Stream: Hope, 1999.

Rigsby, George U. *Alexander Crummell: Pioneer in Nineteenth Century Pan-African Thought*. New York: Greenwood Press, 1987.

Rockman, Seth. *Scraping By: Wage Labor, Slavery, and Survival in Early Baltimore*. Baltimore: Johns Hopkins University Press, 2009.

Schenbeck, Lawrence. *Racial Uplift and American Music: 1878–1943*. Jackson: University Press of Mississippi, 2012.

Shelley, Braxton D. *Healing for the Soul: Richard Smallwood, the Vamp, and the Gospel Imagination*. New York: Oxford University Press, 2021.

Sigler, R. Matthew. *Methodist Worship: Mediating the Wesleyan Liturgical Heritage.* New York: Routledge, 2019.
Southern, Eileen. *The Music of Black Americans: A History.* 2nd ed. New York: Norton, 1983.
Spencer, Jon Michael. *Protest & Praise: Sacred Music of Black Religion.* Minneapolis: Fortress Press, 1990.
Spencer, Jon Michael. *Theological Music: Introduction to Theomusicology.* New York: Greenwood Press, 1991.
Spencer, Jon Michael. *Black Hymnody: A Hymnological History of the African-American Church.* Knoxville: University of Tennessee, 1992.
Stuckey, Sterling. *The Ideological Origins of Black Nationalism.* Boston: Beacon Press, 1972.
Stuckey, Sterling. *Slave Culture: Nationalist Theory & the Foundations of Black America.* New York: Oxford University Press, 1987.
Tate, Claudia. *Domestic Allegories of Political Desire.* Oxford: Oxford University Press, 1992.
Townsend Gilkes, Cheryl. "The Roles of Church and Community Mothers: Ambivalent American Sexism or Fragmented African Familyhood?" In *African American Religion: Interpretive Essays in History and Culture.* Edited by Timothy E. Fulop and Albert J. Raboteau, 365–88. New York: Routledge, 1997.
Turner, Richard Brent. *Soundtrack to a Movement: African American Islam, Jazz and Black Internationalism.* New York: New York University Press, 2021.
Turner, Victor. *The Anthropology of Experience.* Urbana: University of Illinois Press, 1986.
van Gennep, Arnold. *The Rites of Passage.* Translated by Monika B. Vizedom and Gabrielle L. Caffee. Chicago: University of Chicago Press, 1960.
Walker, Wyatt T. *Somebody's Calling My Name: Black Sacred Music and Social Change.* Valley Forge: Judson, 1979.
Ward, Andrew. *Dark Midnight When I Rise: The Story of the Jubilee Singers Who Introduced the World to the Music of Black America.* New York: Farrar, Straus, and Giroux, 2000.
Weliver, Phyllis. *Women Musicians in Victorian Fiction, 1860–1900.* Burlington: Ashgate, 2000.
Wells-Oghoghomeh, Alexis. *The Souls of Womenfolk: The Religious Cultures of Enslaved Women in the Lower South.* Chapel Hill: University of North Carolina Press, 2021.
West, Cornel. "Prophetic Religion and the Future of Capitalist Civilization." In Judith Burler et al., *The Power of Religion in the Public Sphere.* New York: Columbia University Press, 2011.
Westerfield Tucker, Karen B. *American Methodist Worship.* Oxford: Oxford University Press, 2001.
White, James F. *Protestant Worship: Traditions in Transition.* Louisville: Westminster/John Knox Press, 1989.
White, Shane, and Graham White. *The Sounds of Slavery: Discovering African American History through Songs, Sermons, and Speech.* Boston: Beacon Press, 2005.
Whyte, James H. *The Uncivil War: Washington during the Reconstruction.* New York: Twayne, 1958.
Williams, Kidada E. *I Saw Death Coming: A History of Terror and Survival in the War against Reconstruction.* New York: Bloomsbury, 2023.

Wilson, Dreck Spurlock, ed. *African American Architects: A Biographical Dictionary, 1865–1945.* New York: Routledge, 2004.

Wilson, Olly. "The Heterogeneous Sound Ideal in African American Music." In *Signifyin(g), Sanctifyin,' & Slam Dunking: A Reader in African American Expressive Culture.* Edited by Gena Dagel Caponi, 157–71. Amherst: University of Massachusetts Press, 1999.

Wright, W. D. *Black Intellectuals, Black Cognition, and a Black Aesthetic.* Westport: Praeger, 1997.

Xygalatas, Dimitris. *Ritual: How Seemingly Senseless Acts Make Life Worth Living.* New York: Little, Brown Spark, 2022.

Journal Articles

Friesen, Michael. "Two Indiana Organbuilders in Baltimore." *The Tracker: Journal of the Organ Historical Society* 54, no. 2 (2010): 20.

Gordon, Sarah Barringer. "The African Supplement: Religion, Race, and Corporate Law in Early National America." *William & Mary Quarterly* 72, no. 3 (2015): 385. https://scholarship.law.upenn.edu/faculty_scholarship/1575.

Jackson, Irene V. "Music among Blacks in the Episcopal Church: Some Preliminary Considerations." *Historical Magazine of the Protestant Episcopal Church* 48 (1979): 21–35.

Lynerd, Benjamin T. "Republican Ideology and the Black Labor Movement, 1869–1872." *Phylon* (1960–) 56, no. 2 (2019): 19–36.

Nzewi, Meki. "Backcloth to Music and Healing in Traditional African Society." *Voices: A World Forum for Music Therapy* 2, no. 2 (2002). https://voices.no/index.php/voices/article/view/1592/1351.

Price, Tanya Y. "Rhythms of Culture: Djembe and African Memory in African-American Cultural Traditions." *Black Music Research Journal* 33, no. 2 (2013): 227–47. https://doi.org/10.5406/blacmusiresej.33.2.0227.

Shoemaker, Sandy M. "'We Shall Overcome Someday:' The Equal Rights Movement in Baltimore, 1935–1942." *Maryland Historical Magazine* 89, no. 3 (1994): 261–73.

Southern, Eileen. "Musical Practices in Black Churches of Philadelphia and New York, ca. 1800–1844." *Journal of the American Musicological Society* 30, no. 2 (1977): 296–312.

Wells, Jeremy Dwight. "Civil War Song in Black and White: Print and the Representation of the Spirituals." *Humanities* 11, no. 6 (2022): 142. https://doi.org/10.3390/h11060142.

Web Sources

Cohen, Francesca. "The Office of John H. Murphy, Sr." *Explore Baltimore Heritage.* Accessed October 11, 2023. https://explore.baltimoreheritage.org/items/show/723.

Digital Tradition Folk Music Database. "Hold the Fort" and "Hold the Fort (2)." History and lyrics. Accessed November 1, 2023. http://sniff.numachi.com/pages/tiHOLDFORT;ttHOLDFORT.html and http://sniff.numachi.com/pages/tiHOLDFRT2;ttHOLDFORT.html.

El Haj, Mohamad, et al., "Self-Defining Memories during Exposure to Music in Alzheimer's Disease." *International Psychogeriatrics* 27, special issue 10: *Psychosocial and Ethical Aspects of Dementia* (2015): 1719–30. https://www.cambridge.org/core/journals/international-psychogeriatrics/article/abs/selfdefining-memories-during-exposure-to-music-in-alzheimers-disease/81C594D467755ECB81A96D1D5C175CDC.

Johnson, Charles. "Fleetwood's Biography." National Park Service. http://www.nps.gov/rich/historyculture/cfbio.htm.

Maryland State Archives. "William Watkins (b. circa 1803–d. circa 1858), Educator and Minister, Baltimore City, Maryland." Biographical Series, MSA SC 5496–002535. Accessed October 3, 2023. https://msa.maryland.gov/megafile/msa/speccol/sc5400/sc5496/002500/002535/html/002535bio.html.

Ross, Alex. "Black Scholars Confront White Supremacy in Classical Music." *The New Yorker,* September 14, 2020. https://www.newyorker.com/magazine/2020/09/21/black-scholars-confront-white-supremacy-in-classical-music.

INDEX

Page numbers in *italics* indicate illustrations.

a cappella, 25, 101
Addison, Thomas, 126
African American religious music, 15–49; aesthetic effect and, 28–29; baptism, marriage, and funeral ceremonies, 23–25; celebrations and special events, 44–47, *45*; choral music, 31–35; church building and dedications, 28–29; community and unity, 19–21; congregational singing, 30–31; described, 15–16; as discourse, 21–23; freedom of expression and, 27–28; hymns and gospel songs, 22–23, 38–41, 88–91; imaginative thinking and, 18–19; liturgical conversations and, 23; minstrelsy and, 26; music specialists, 34–35, 41–44, *42–43*; organ music, 25, 35–37; outdoor religious meetings, 47–49; political music, 17–18; role of, 16–17; singing schools, 37–38; storytelling and, 18; summary, 49. *See also* Black identity
African American women, 7, 9, 39, 43, 54, 72, 94, 106, 132
African Americans, 4–8, 6–7, 136. *See also* enslaved people; free Black people; racism; southern migrants
African Methodist Episcopal (AME) Church, 19, 25, 29–31, 46, 56, 66, 70, 73, 77
African Methodist Episcopal Zion (AMEZ) Church, 17–18, 22, 34, 38, 41, 46

African music and worship, 15–16, 19, 30–31, 36–37, 60, 67
African Union Meeting House (Providence, RI), 37–38
Afro-American (newspaper), 24, 34, 55
agency, 12, 137
"All Hail the Power of Jesus' Name" (hymn), 84
"All the Way My Savior Leads Me" (Crosby), 89–90
Allen, Langston W., 131, 171n109
Allen, Richard, 38–39, 80, 83, 86
Alston, William J., 108–9
Ambush, Joseph, 41
Appo, William, 44, 59
"Are We Yet Alive and See Each Other's Face" (Wesley), 84–85
Asbury, Francis, 84
Asbury Methodist Episcopal Church (Washington, DC), 16, 25, 31–32, 35, 38–39, 41
"Asleep in Jesus, O How Sweet" (hymn), 25
Augusta, A. T., 130

Baltimore, MD, 6–7, 50–51, 61–62
bands, singing and praying, 58–59, 67
Baptist movement, 83
Baraka, Amiri, 23
Barbadoes, F. G., 132
Becker, J. W., 75

Bell, Thomas P., 38
Bethel African Methodist Episcopal Church (Baltimore), 50–77; Black identity and, 51–52, 54, 57, 60–61, 69; bush meetings, 74–75; case study of, 13, 50–51, *51*, 77; choir at, 31, 34; congregation and leadership, 52–56; female identity and resistance at, 72–74; financial control as resistance, 76–77; mission churches, 71–72; music-worship conflict, 67–70; organs and organists, 25, 43, 61, *61*, 63–64, *64*, 157n46; religious freedom exercised at, 70–71; repression and reforms at, 62–67; restriction and resistance at, 30, 56–62; as a worship model, 86
Bethel Church v. Carmack, 57
Beulah, Jeffrey, 84
Biddle, E. George, 17–18
Black Baptists, 30, 40
Black church, 4–5, 7–9, 11–14, 136–38. *See also specific denominations and churches*
Black Democracy (Glaude), 138
Black Episcopalians, 32
Black identity: agency and, 12; AMEZ Church and, 18; ancestral connectedness and, 20; Bethel AME Church and, 51–52, 54, 57, 60–61, 69; Black church music and, 16, 49, 137; Black women and, 72–74; in early Reconstruction, 9; gospel songs and, 88, 90; minstrelsy and, 26; St. Luke's PE Church and, 107, 116, 118–20, 132; Zoar ME Church and, 82, 84, 90–91, 93, 103
Black Methodists, 30, 58, 84, 88
Blackness, 12, 80
Blair, Montgomery, 126
Blake, Peter, 29
Bliss, Philip, 17–18, 89
"Blow, ye, the trumpet blow" (hymn), 24
Booker, Vaughn A., 26
Bourdieu, Pierre, 10
Brackett, Marc, 4
Bradford, Thomas, 60–61
Bremer, Fredrika, 60
Brent, Calvin, 116, 172n116
Broughton, Isaiah, 93

Brown, Courtney, 18
Brown, Frank Birch, 28
Brown, Hallie Q., 7
Brown, S. H., 33
Brumley, Albert E., 137
bush meetings, 49, 74–75, 86
Butt, Israel La Fayette, 53

call-and-response, 19, 30, 60, 65, 71, 100
camp meetings, 47–49, 67
Carmack, Joel, 57
Caruthers, Belle, 38
"Charge to Keep I Have, A" (hymn), 84
Chesley, John, 57
"Children's Hosanna, The" (song), 100–101
choral music, 31–35
Christian Recorder, The (newspaper), 26
Civil War, 17, 61–62
classical music, 9–10, 32, 82, 113
Coker, Daniel, 54, 57–58
Cole, J. William, 122, 131, 170n80
Collection of Spiritual Songs and Hymns, Selected from Various Authors (Allen), 38–39, 83
"Come Sinners to the Gospel Feast" (Wesley), 19
Compromise of 1877, 110, 117
Cone, James, 4, 90
congregational singing, 30–31
Cooper, Annie J., 105–7, 166n1
Coppin, L. J., 33
"Coronation" (hymn), 32
Cox, Joseph, 30
Cromwell, John Wesley, 108–9, 112, 117, 122, 168n36, 171n109
Crosby, Fanny, 89–90
Crummell, Alexander, 105–6, 109–10, *109*, 134. *See also* St. Luke's Protestant Episcopal Church (Washington, DC)

Davage, James, 76
Davidson, Olivia A., 94
Davis, Clara, 74–75
DeCosta, B. F., 112
Delaware Conference (MEC Church), 23, 25, 86–88, 92, 98, 162n30

Dickerson, Annie, 72
Dickerson, W. C., 83, 161n18
Diddy, P., 137
Dilthey, Wilhelm, 119
Dixon, John, 58
Dorsey, Charles H., 70
Douglass, Frederick, 23
Draper, James E., 41
Draper, William, 41
Drewry, Nathaniel, 24
Du Bois, W. E. B., 44, 86, 88, 91–92
Dungee, Charles, 25, 77
Dungee, James, 76
Dungee, John H. B., *43*
Dyson, Michael Eric, 26

Ebenezer African Methodist Episcopal Church (Baltimore), 34
Ebenezer Methodist Episcopal Church (Washington, DC), 33, 41
education, 9–11, 55, 78–79, 88, 91–96
Elaw, Zilpha, 67, 73
Emancipation Proclamation (1863), 40, 45
enslaved people, 23, 27–29
Euston, Eliza, 59
"Evening" (Tanner), 22

"Far beyond This World of Sorrow" (hymn), 101–3
Ferguson, Samuel, 75
Fifteenth Amendment, 116
First Colored American Congregational Church (New York), 28
First Colored Methodist Protestant Church (Baltimore), 57
Fisher, Fannie, 59
Fisher, Ora, 8
Fleet, Hermion, 59
Fleet, James, 59
Fleetwood, Christian Abraham, 112–15, *115*, 117–20, 122–27, 131, 133
Floyd, Samuel A., Jr., 18–19, 40–41, 133
Foote, Julia, 73–75, 159n84
Foundry Methodist Episcopal Church (Washington, DC), 31
free Black people, 6–7, 29

"Freedom's Morn" (Young), 46–47
Frey, Sylvia, 94

Gaines, Causman H., 63, 68
Gellerman, Robert F., 36
Glasgow, Stephen, 69–71
Glaude, Eddie, Jr., 116, 138
"Gloria in Excelsis" (hymn), 112
"God Be with Us Till We Meet Again" (hymn), 84–85
Goodwin, Pamela Helen, 97
gospel songs. *See* hymns and gospel songs
Great Awakening, 83
Green, Robert, 80, 82
Greenfield, Elizabeth Taylor, 59
Grey, James, 68

Habermas, Jürgen, 8
Hahn, Steven, 8
"Hail the Church That Varick Started" (Biddle), 17–18
Hall, Perry, 15
"Hallelujah Chorus" (Handel), 46, 114
Hamar, William B., 33–34
Hammonds, Savage L., 61
Handel, George Frideric, 44, 46
Handy, James, 62, 66, 71–72, 76
Harper, Francis Ellen Watkins, 154n9
Haydn, Franz Joseph, 44, 113–14
Hayes, Rutherford B., 117
Heard, Josephine Henderson: "Music" (poem), 10; "The New Organ" (poem), 36–37
Hemphill, Katie M., 54
Henry, Thomas, 6, 49
Henson, James, 71
Higginbotham, Evelyn Brooks, 9, 146n23
High, James, 31
Highly Musical People (Trotter), 66
Hill, Doritha, 72
hip-hop, 137
History of the African Methodist Episcopal Church (Payne), 61, 154n122
"History of Zoar Methodist Episcopal Church. No. 7" (Dickerson), 83
"Hold the Fort" (Bliss), 17–18, 89

"Hold the Fort" (Knights of Labor), 17
Holiness movement, 73–74
Hooper, Lula, 24
Hoosier, Harry, 84
Hopkins, Jerome, 124
"How Firm a Foundation" (hymn), 12–13, 84
Howard, Martha Elizabeth, 55
hymns and gospel songs, 13, 22–23, 30, 38–41, 88–91

"I'll Be Missing You" (Diddy), 137
"I'll Fly Away" (Brumley), 137
Invisible Institution, 58, 73, 133

Jackson, Charles E., 16, 32
James, Mary, 92
Jeter, Henry N., and family, 44, 45
Jim Crow era, 108, 117
Johnson, Elymus, 30
Johnson, Francis, 44
Johnson, Henry, 120, 122, 124, 131, 169n75
Johnson, J. H., 93
Johnson, Jerome A., 110, 122, 131, 170n81
Johnson, John Thomas, 109–10
Johnson, Linus, 31
Johnson, Professor, and the Monumental Band, 16, 46
Johnson, Solomon, 122, 131, 170n81
Johnson, Thomas L., 92
Jones, Absalom, 80
Jones, LeRoi, 23
Jones, Robert C., 44
Josephus, William H., 108
Jubilee Singers, 15–16, 27

Keckley, Elizabeth, 6–7
Kennaday, J., 96
Knights of Labor, 17
Kramer, C. W., 78

Langer, Susanne, 18–19, 99
Lankford, W. S., 65–71, 74
Lawrence, Mattie, 123, 170n88
legato fingering, 36

Levine, Lawrence, 14
Lewis, Walker, 122, 131, 170n81
Lindsay, John S., 126
lining out, 30, 111–12
literacy, 92
"Lord, Is It I?" (hymn), 100
Lott, Eric, 47
Lowell, Henry, 30

"Magnificat" (Millard), 122
Mansfield, Reverend, 125
Mason, Lowell, 39–40, 94–95
Matthews, William, 135–36
McCoy, Benjamin, 41
Mead, Hannah W., 78
Methodism, 63, 69, 74, 82–83
Meyers, Isaac, 55
migrants. *See* southern migrants
Millard, Harrison, 122
Miller, Lewis, 96
Mills, Amelia E., 78
minstrelsy, 26, 47
Moody, Dwight, 40, 88
Moore, Lillie E., 24
Morgan, H. C., 20–21
Moses, Wilson, 121
Mozart, Wolfgang Amadeus, 32, 44
Mt. Olivet African Baptist Church (New York City), 23–24
Murphy, John H., 55, 156n19
Murray, Charles, 131
Murray, Daniel, 131
Murray, Spencer, Jr., 122, 131
music, as art, 4
"Music" (Heard), 10
Musical Gazette (journal), 15–16
musical performance, 9, 47
"My Country 'Tis of Thee" (song), 46
Myers, Isaac, 55, 62, 155n18

"Nearer, My God to Thee" (hymn), 32
"New Organ, The" (Heard), 36–37
New York Herald, The (newspaper), 47–48
New York Sun, The (newspaper), 24

Nineteenth Street Baptist Church (Washington, DC), 44
Nugent, Richard Henry, 131, 172n115

"O for a Closer Walk with God" (hymn), 65
"O We Are Volunteers" (hymn), 100
Ockermy, Joseph, 66
"Oh! For a Heart to Praise My God" (hymn), 84
"Old Elizabeth" (preacher), 72
organs, organists, and organ music, 3, 9, 25, 35–37, 43, 61, *61*, 63–64, *64*, 85–86, 112
"Our Mission Song" (hymn), 100

Palmer, Phoebe, 73
Payne, Daniel, 22, 31, 33, 52–53, 56–61, 65, 67, 75, 82, 86–87, 154n122, 159n84, 163n37
Payne, James H., 32
Payne, Rebecca, 32
Peck, E. W. S., 35
Peck, Nathaniel, 57–58
Peken, Gilbert, 57
People's Advocate, The (newspaper), 108, 122
Perry, Calbraith, 28, 112–13, 168n39
Pestalozzi, Johann Heinrich, 94–95
Philadelphia, PA, 6–7, 82, 85
Philadelphia Negro, The (Du Bois), 91–92
Philips, Deacon, 48
Pickney, Henry, 25
Pinkney, William, 106, 116, 120–21, 127
"Pisgah's Mountain" (hymn), 99
Pitts, Walter F., Jr., 40
Plymouth Congregational United Church (Washington, DC), 43
Pomplitz & Co. (organ builders), 61, *64*
"Praise God, from whom all blessings flow" (hymn), 17
Price, John E., 22–23
Protestant Episcopal (PE) Church, 32, 112, 117
Prout, Mary Ann, 72

Raboteau, Albert, 103
racial uplift ideology, 11–12, 62, 79, 82, 88, 91–92, 147n26

racism, 10–11, 32, 62, 79, 85, 103
Ramsey, Guthrie, 40
Randall, Jas. F., 34
Ransom, Emma, 41–42
Ransom, Reverdy C., 41
Reconstruction era, 3–4, 8–9, 11, 62, 116, 136
Revels, W. R., 68
Richfield, Serina, 56
ring shouts, 29, 71, 87
Rivers, Prince, 4
Roberts, Bradbury, 50, 69
"Rock of Ages" (hymn), 24
Rockefeller, John D., 96
Ross, Alex, 10
Russell, Henrietta, 53

Sankey, Ira, 40, 88
Schenbeck, Lawrence, 147n26
"Semi-Centennial Hymn" (Morgan), 20–21
Sharp Street Methodist Episcopal Church (Baltimore), 35, 46, 53
Shelley, Braxton, 60
Sheppard, Ella, 27
Shiloh Baptist Church (Newport, RI), 29
Shiloh Baptist Church (Washington, DC), 8, 32, 36
Shiloh Presbyterian Church (New York), 39
Simpson, G. T., 44
slavery, 92, 103
Smith, C. S., 33
Smith, Emma, 114
Smith, J. C., 84
Smith, James, 80–81
"Songs of Freedom" (Young), 22
Southern, Eileen, 30–31
southern migrants, 3, 5, 6–7, 31, 50, 82, 86–87, 93, 103, 112
St. George's Methodist Episcopal Church (Philadelphia), 80
St. James Protestant Episcopal Church (Baltimore), 35, 61
St. Luke's Protestant Episcopal Church (Washington, DC), 105–34; beginnings of, 108–11; Black identity and, 107, 116,

118, 120, 132; case study of, 13, 105–8, *106*, 132–34; conflict resolution, 130–32; crisis moment at, 127–30, *128*; rector-vestry conflict, 121–27; St. Mary's and, 108, 111–16, 132; transition to St. Luke's, 116–21, 169n54, 169n58
St. Mary the Virgin Protestant Episcopal Church (Baltimore), 112–13
St. Paul's Protestant Episcopal Church (Wilmington, NC), 37
St. Philip's Episcopal Church (New York City), 112
Staten, Anna, 54–55
Stevens, Newton, 42
Steward, Susan S. McKinney, 43
Steward, T. G., 29
Stokes, Darius, 49, 56–57, 60, 154n122
Stone, Marie, 27
Stowe, Harriet Beecher, 15
Sunday school movement, 94, 96
Sunday School Speaker, The (Kennaday), 96
Syphax, D., 131, 172n116

Tanner, Benjamin, 22, 33
Taylor, Ernest, 24
Taylor, Nora Fields, 22
Taylor, William, 66
"There Is a Fountain" (hymn), 32
Thomas, Jacob, 48
Thomas, William H., 96
Trinity African Methodist Episcopal Church (Baltimore), 33–34
Trotter, James, 59, 66
"Try Us O God" (hymn), 65
tuning up, 60
Turner, Henry McNeal, 48–49, 53, 66
Turner, Nicole Myers, 27
Turner, Victor, societal models of, 107–8, 117–19, 124–25, 133

"Uncle John," 12–13, 75
Underground Railroad, 82
uplift ideology. *See* racial uplift ideology
Upshur, Frances, 124

Varick, James, 17–18
Vincent, Elizabeth K., 167n26
Vincent, John Heyl, 94–96
violence, 85

Walker, Wyatt, 91
Wanamaker, John, 96
Washington, Booker T., 3, 9, 94
Washington, DC, 6–7, 16, 108, 167n26
Washington, William, 131
Washington Post, The, 113–14, 123, 125, 130–31
"Watchman! Tell Us of the Night" (Mason), 39–40
Watkins, George T., 50–51, 53–55, 61–65, 67–70, 75
Watkins, James, 26
Watkins, William, Jr., 53–54
Watkins, William, Sr., 53
Watson, John Fanning, 83–84
Way of Holiness, The (Palmer), 73
Wayman, A. W., 62
"We come, we come, we come . . ." (song), 99
"We Shall Overcome" (gospel song), 136
"We Three Kings of Orient Are" (song), 100
Weekly Anglo-African, The (newspaper), 28, 39
Weliver, Phyllis, 9–10
Wells-Oghoghomeh, Alexis, 54
Wesley, Charles: "Are We Yet Alive and See Each Other's Face," 84–85; "Come Sinners to the Gospel Feast," 19
Wesley, John, 30–31, 87, 163n37
West, Cornel, 5
Westcott, Nimrod, 76
"When the Roll Is Called Again" (Price), 22–23
White, Caroline, 54
white church, 12, 15, 31, 87, 91
white Methodists, 30, 83
White Robes (song book), 33
white supremacy, 16, 26, 132, 143
Whittingham, Bishop, 110–11, 113
"Why do we mourn for dying friends" (hymn), 25

Williams, Jas. M., 28
Williams, Kidada E., 117
Wilson, Olly, 16
Wood, Betty, 94
Wormley, James, 59, 117
Wormley, William, 170n81
Wormley Compromise. *See* Compromise of 1877
Wright, W. D., 32

Young, Howard E., 33
Young, W. H., 22, 46–47

Zeck, Melanie, 40
Zion Colored Methodist Episcopal Church (New York), 48
Zoar Methodist Episcopal Church (Philadelphia), 78–104; beginnings of, 80–83, *81*, 160n3; Black identity and, 82, 84, 90–91, 93, 103; case study of, 13–14, 78–80, *79*, 103–4; celebration program at, 78, *97–98*, 98–103; gospel songs and, 88–91; music and worship culture at, 83–88; Sabbath school, 78–79, 91–98, 103
Zundel, John, 43

ABOUT THE AUTHOR

Photo by Lori Brystan

Carolynne Hitter Brown is a pianist and singer. She teaches Christian history at Gordon-Conwell Seminary. Hitter Brown earned her doctor of theology from Boston University School of Theology, and her work has appeared in the *Journal of Pan-African Pentecostalism*, *Three-Fifths Magazine*, and other publications.

Printed in the United States
by Baker & Taylor Publisher Services